T0180867

IFIP Advances in Information and Communication Technology

645

Editor-in-Chief

IFIP – The International Federation for Information Processing

IFIP was founded in 1960 under the auspices of UNESCO, following the first World Computer Congress held in Paris the previous year. A federation for societies working in information processing, IFIP's aim is two-fold: to support information processing in the countries of its members and to encourage technology transfer to developing nations. As its mission statement clearly states:

IFIP is the global non-profit federation of societies of ICT professionals that aims at achieving a worldwide professional and socially responsible development and application of information and communication technologies.

IFIP is a non-profit-making organization, run almost solely by 2500 volunteers. It operates through a number of technical committees and working groups, which organize events and publications. IFIP's events range from large international open conferences to working conferences and local seminars.

The flagship event is the IFIP World Computer Congress, at which both invited and contributed papers are presented. Contributed papers are rigorously refereed and the rejection rate is high.

As with the Congress, participation in the open conferences is open to all and papers may be invited or submitted. Again, submitted papers are stringently refereed.

The working conferences are structured differently. They are usually run by a working group and attendance is generally smaller and occasionally by invitation only. Their purpose is to create an atmosphere conducive to innovation and development. Refereeing is also rigorous and papers are subjected to extensive group discussion.

Publications arising from IFIP events vary. The papers presented at the IFIP World Computer Congress and at open conferences are published as conference proceedings, while the results of the working conferences are often published as collections of selected and edited papers.

IFIP distinguishes three types of institutional membership: Country Representative Members, Members at Large, and Associate Members. The type of organization that can apply for membership is a wide variety and includes national or international societies of individual computer scientists/ICT professionals, associations or federations of such societies, government institutions/government related organizations, national or international research institutes or consortia, universities, academies of sciences, companies, national or international associations or federations of companies.

More information about this series at https://link.springer.com/bookseries/6102

José Abdelnour-Nocera ·
Elisha Ondieki Makori ·
Jose Antonio Robles-Flores ·
Constance Bitso (Eds.)

Innovation Practices for Digital Transformation in the Global South

IFIP WG 13.8, 9.4, Invited Selection

 Springer

Editors
José Abdelnour-Nocera 🆔
University of West London
London, UK

Elisha Ondieki Makori 🆔
University of Nairobi
Nairobi, Kenya

Jose Antonio Robles-Flores 🆔
Esan University
Lima, Peru

Constance Bitso 🆔
University of Fort Hare
Alice, South Africa

ISSN 1868-4238   ISSN 1868-422X (electronic)
IFIP Advances in Information and Communication Technology
ISBN 978-3-031-12827-1   ISBN 978-3-031-12825-7 (eBook)
https://doi.org/10.1007/978-3-031-12825-7

This Springer imprint is published by the registered company Springer Nature Switzerland AG
The registered company address is: Gewerbestrasse 11, 6330 Cham, Switzerland

Preface

This collection of chapters is an initiative from the IFIP Working Groups 13.8 and 9.4 from Technical Committees 13 and 9, respectively. The book presents experiences and research on the topic of digital transformation and innovation practices in the global south. The works presented are anchored on digital transformation initiatives for novel innovative technological developments, practices, and applications relating to marginalized people in the global south. These chapters provide real cases of digital transformation for people whose human experiences and life perspectives emphasize the value of new technologies and skills. The IFIP Working Groups 13.8 and 9.4 also document challenges that face low-income communities outside the global south. While addressing the concerns and arguments that systematically prohibit society from leveraging the conceptions of the digital era in underdeveloped and developing countries, creative lessons in innovation are critical and fundamental in sustaining social and economic development.

Chapter one discusses the digital transformation of indigenous communities in the global south founded on a community-based codesign approach. The innovation practice used a drone and embraced local practices and epistemologies. Chapter two is framed on the digital transformation of Mandhwane, a rural community in South Africa, by fostering a community network with local internet access and innovative new digital services. Chapter three explicates the sociotechnical dimension of trucking sector operations in India using digitalization in a bottom-up fashion. Chapters four and five highlight self-healthcare monitoring mobile applications used to continuously educate and sensitize people about the need to adopt healthy lifestyles to prevent non-communicable diseases. There is evidence that mobile applications with educational content on healthy lifestyle and self-healthcare monitoring contribute to the adoption of healthy lifestyles.

Chapter six covers the digital discovery of a marginalized community engaged in science, technology, engineering, arts, and mathematics (STEAM) activities, and exposes the challenges that many low-income communities face. Sociocultural factors, capital knowledge, and creative lessons in innovation were noted from this community in the northeastern region of Mexico. Chapter seven highlights a machine-readable passport project concerning the automation of the passport transaction process involving multiple organizations in Bangladesh. Despite being successful, complex power dynamics, sociocultural factors, and the political environment were noted as challenges. Chapter eight shows that digital platforms have made entrepreneurial processes less bounded, where products and services keep on evolving long after being endorsed by the end user. Digital entrepreneurship has enhanced innovation, competences, control, financing, institutions, and ecosystems for social and economic development.

Chapter nine examines critical and fundamental arguments that systematically prohibit society from leveraging the conceptions of the digital era in underdeveloped and developing countries. Digital transformation is critical to achieving social and epistemic justice, more so in the increasingly dynamic virtual spaces in education. Finally, chapter ten details the change and application of digital transformation within the context of the Latin American theater. Based on the innovative process employed at The Experimental Theater of Cali, the transition from analogue tradition to digital economy produced two different infrastructure approaches – relationship infrastructure guiding spectators and actors during staging and theater infrastructure as an agent of change. Here, digital transformation is about social, economic, and political protagonism.

The digital economy, also called the Internet economy or the Internet of Things economy, has transformed economies and societies in this knowledge society. With the digital discovery environment, digital platforms have expanded business enterprises with immense opportunities and prospects in rural settings. Digital platforms have enhanced and achieved innovations and competences in various sectors of the economy. With new digital innovations, and ideas and insights being witnessed across the globe in this free and open economy, there is a need for participation and collaboration from industry, academia, the public sector, and other stakeholders in order to achieve and sustain the gains in human transformation and societal development. We believe this book is a useful mouthpiece for the communities from the global south to be part of the digital transformation for sustainable development.

June 2022

José Abdelnour-Nocera
Elisha Ondieki Makori
Constance Bitso
Jose Antonio Robles-Flores

Organization

Established in 1989, the International Federation for Information Processing Technical Committee on Human–Computer Interaction (IFIP TC 13) is an international committee of 35 member national societies and 10 Working Groups, representing specialists of the various disciplines contributing to the field of human-computer interaction. This includes (among others) human factors, ergonomics, cognitive science, computer science, and design. INTERACT is the flagship conference of IFIP TC 13, staged biennially in different countries around the world. The first INTERACT conference was held in 1984, running triennially before it became a biennial event in 1993.

IFIP TC 13 aims to develop the science, technology, and societal aspects of human–computer interaction (HCI) by encouraging empirical research; promoting the use of knowledge and methods from the human sciences in design and evaluation of computer systems; promoting better understanding of the relation between formal design methods and system usability and acceptability; developing guidelines, models, and methods by which designers may provide better human-oriented computer systems; and cooperating with other groups, inside and outside IFIP, to promote user-orientation and humanization in system design. Thus, TC 13 seeks to improve interactions between people and computers, to encourage the growth of HCI research and its practice in industry, and to disseminate these benefits worldwide.

The main orientation is to place the users at the center of the development process. Areas of study include the problems people face when interacting with computers; the impact of technology deployment on people in individual and organizational contexts; the determinants of utility, usability, acceptability, and user experience; the appropriate allocation of tasks between computers and users especially in the case of automation; modeling the user, their tasks, and the interactive system to aid better system design; and harmonizing the computer to user characteristics and needs.

While the scope is thus set wide, with a tendency toward general principles rather than particular systems, it is recognized that progress will only be achieved through both general studies to advance theoretical understanding and specific studies on practical issues (e.g., interface design standards, software system resilience, documentation, training material, appropriateness of alternative interaction technologies, guidelines, the problems of integrating multimedia systems to match system needs and organizational practices, etc.).

The IFIP Technical Committee 9 (TC 9) on ICT and Society focuses on understanding how ICT innovation is associated with change in society, and on issues of ethics and professionalism. TC 9 comprises ten working groups (WGs) and representatives of the national computer societies of IFIP.

The main work of TC 9 is conducted through its working groups, which organize workshops, conferences, and events regularly. Additionally, TC 9 organizes collectively the series of conferences on Human Choice and Computers (HCC). This is a well established forum for the study of ICT and society – the first HCC conference took place in Vienna in 1974, while the last one was due to take place in Tokyo in 2020 – alas cancelled due to COVID-19. The next HCC will take place in Tokyo in 2022.

The main aim of TC 9 is to develop understanding of how ICT innovation is associated with change in society, and to influence the shaping of socially responsible and ethical policies and professional practices. TC 9 fosters multidisciplinary discourse into the role of ICT in the change of particular domains of human activity, including work; the home and private life; and governance. It is also interested in the ethical, political, economic, and cultural dimensions of ICT innovation.

José Abdelnour-Nocera
Elisha Ondieki Makori
Constance Bitso
Jose Antonio Robles-Flores

Contents

Digital Inequities and Societal Context: Digital Transformation as a Conduit to Achieve Social and Epistemic Justice

Siyabonga Mhlongo[1]([✉]) [iD] and Reuben Dlamini[2] [iD]

[1] Department of Applied Information Systems, University of Johannesburg, Johannesburg, South Africa
siyabongam@uj.ac.za
[2] Educational Information and Engineering Technology, University of the Witwatersrand, Johannesburg, South Africa
reuben.dlamini@wits.ac.za

Abstract. In society, digital technology has often been viewed as a solution to systemic inequalities. However, approaching digital technologies from a utility perspective places these tools at crossroads with broader social and contextual issues. This results in epistemological tensions rather than achieving the intended goal of institutional equity. South Africa is confronted with an unprecedented unequal access to quality education, particularly in rural and under-resourced communities. With this backdrop, the authors offer a theoretical critique of epistemological and ontological paradigms on the problematic complexities of digital transformation. They posit that digital transformation is critical to achieving social and epistemic justice, more so in the increasingly dynamic virtual spaces in education. Hence, this chapter offers constructive suggestions to further a paradigm shift on the myopic epistemic that imposes dichotomy in the higher education sector, thereby encumbering quality learning and development. Framing justice as equity and access allows for education to be viewed as a public good, hence the importance of creating commonplaces for knowledge development through constructivist-oriented practices. These commonplaces afford students unprecedented connections to widen their context of learning so to expand their perspectives, bypass gatekeepers to knowledge acquisition and create reciprocal relationships with their educators.

Keywords: Digital transformation · Digital inequity · Social justice · Epistemic justice · Digital divide · Digital capital · Digital economy

1 Introduction

The practicability of achieving institutional equity in the South African context poses a number of challenges given the uneven distribution of resources. Efforts have been made by the government through legislative instruments to ensure

J. Abdelnour-Nocera et al. (Eds.): *Innovation Practices for Digital Transformation in the Global South*, IFIP AICT 645, pp. 1–15, 2022.
https://doi.org/10.1007/978-3-031-12825-7_1

that all nine provinces are developed, however, the one-size-fits-all and vertical governance model has diminished the role of civil society. In an unequal society and culturally complex South Africa, a differentiated approach to development is crucial. Hence, the importance of understanding the interplay between conceptions of the digital era and societal context to build and support community-based initiatives. These conceptions, as solutions to systemic inequalities, are viewed through a set of ontological and epistemological assumptions, looking at the nature (context) of the world and about the knowability of this world [27]. Any effort made without societal context is flawed, hence the importance of understanding the entire economic development ecosystem. The value of digital transformation in an unequal society can only be realized once a complex mapping exercise of all variables has been achieved. Social justice can only be achieved once everyone has the opportunity to access resources, regardless of their social position, thus eliminating any disadvantage that could stand in the way of achieving their potential. This chapter views epistemic justice to be achievable when everyone, regardless of their social standing, can access information resources without being dominated in order to function at their optimal level.

Perhaps what is known from research is that the relevance of social, economic, political, and cultural power structures is important in achieving equity [7,20,30]. The timely adoption of cutting-edge digital technologies and equitable distribution of digital resources must be achieved to prevent the loss of significant opportunities. However, socio-economic challenges are a reality, especially in under-resourced communities, and these were made visible during the COVID-19 pandemic [20]. Importantly, this requires considerable expenditure of scarce resources to first develop and then support these under-resourced communities in developing economies. Thus, digital resources, such as information and communication technologies (ICTs), are considered contributing factors to social and economic disparities [3,14]. Conversely, insufficient investment in digital infrastructure and tools has the potential to stifle economic activities and make it difficult for local people to participate in the global economy [7]. Exacerbating the slow pace in South Africa is the vertical governance model which results in a one-size-fits-all approach, where there are defects in all the structures of governance. Various sectors in South Africa, particularly the education and small businesses sectors, have not kept apace with the advances (however significant) of ICTs. For this reason, there have been stand-alone ICT innovations constraining country-wide digital transformation.

The journey towards inclusive and equitable growth is complex. It is therefore important that any development must be relevant to all community levels so that the journey is not futile. To leapfrog the economy and accelerate growth, South Africa should take advantage of digital technologies and a viable public–private partnership (PPP)[1] framework must be developed to attract private sector par-

---

[1] In line with the view of the World Bank, a PPP is a commercial legal phrase used to harness private sector investment in public assets and services. Some countries have crafted laws and regulations that guide the implementation of PPP endeavours.

ticipation in an effort to cultivate digital capital. Beyond financial investment in public assets and services, the collaboration ought to be built around capacity and expertise. Digital technologies, especially the internet, have become significant for social and economic development in South Africa and globally. With limited government resources in developing economies, especially in the global south, adopting a PPP approach is essential. Although the shift towards digital technologies has always been on the to-do list for businesses and education institutions, the COVID-19 pandemic accelerated this transition within these and various other sectors. This transition was not smooth as there were systemic deficits creating systemic inequalities that affected individuals and businesses [8]. This meant that despite all the affordances of adopting digital technologies, only a fraction of individuals and businesses with access to digital resources gained real competitive advantage. Therefore, it is with little doubt that the COVID-19 pandemic served as a catalyst for digital change, and more specifically, for the adoption of digital technologies. However this created a dichotomous scenario of the 'have' and the 'have nots.'

At the core of this social and economic development is digital equity, which is instrumental in transitioning to a digital economy and in the provisioning of education. Resta and Laferrière identified the following five components of digital equity: (a) hardware; (b) software; (c) internet connectivity; (d) high-quality digital content; and (e) digital fluency [23]. Coincidentally, these are the essential basic components, the absence (or more appropriately, the unjust distribution) of which has perpetuated the notion of the digital divide as we have come to know it. Central to digital equity is digital capital, where users have access to digital technologies with the ability to use them for professional and personal purposes [31, p. 1]. Digital capital is inclusive of digital equipment, connectivity, and digital fluency [21]. Interestingly, Marolla underscores that "countries performing well on ICT do equally well on the [United Nations General Assembly's] SDGs [Sustainable Development Goals], while those underperforming on ICT are also lagging on SDG achievement" [17, p. xiii], which is one of the key findings emanating from the *2017 Huawei ICT Sustainable Development Goals Benchmark*.

Yes, the potential benefits of adopting ICT at both community and individual levels have been well theorised, demonstrated, and are indeed innumerable [2,20]. Thus, what can South Africa and other countries of similar stature do to achieve digital equity, proliferate digital capital, and digitally transform their status quo? True digital transformation lies not just in the documented technological innovation it promises, but in deploying digital infrastructure, addressing challenges with internet connectivity, ensuring widespread access to computing devices, and building human capital and skills. Equitable provisioning of digital infrastructure is a necessary condition for sustainable economic growth, but for the internet to be an enabler, it must be accessible and affordable. The absence of massive and directed investments on digital infrastructure and skills has the

---

See for instance the policy developed by India: https://ppp.worldbank.org/public-private-partnership/library/india-national-public-private-partnership-policy/.

potential to perpetuate different forms of exclusion [16]. Any form of exclusion has far-reaching impact on the digital ecosystem and on economic development. Figure 1 illustrates a recent view of global internet access grouped by geographical region. This view shows the percentage of the total (national, regional, or world) population that uses the internet.

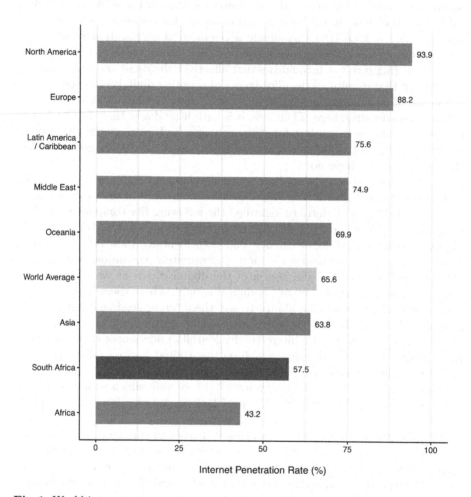

Fig. 1. World internet penetration rates by geographic region, including South Africa and the world average, adopted from Internet World Stats accessible at https://www.internetworldstats.com/stats.htm and based on estimates as at 31 Mar 2021.

From this illustration, it is clear that the African region faces a steep challenge if it is to catch up with the rest of the world in reaping the provisions of the conceptions of the digital era. Although the South African average of 57.5% is almost 15% higher than its regional average, it still falls short of the world average, implying that it is not exempt from these regional challenges. This has dire consequences in the setting up of robust digital operations and the development of innovative products and services. While emphasis has been placed on huge investments in digital infrastructure across the country, the need to measure the impact on development is the missing link.

2   Ontological and Epistemological Assumptions

Equity and opportunity are intimately linked, and they exist in the context of human beings. In an unequal society, there exists different levels of access depending on the position an individual (or a classification of individuals) holds in that society's hierarchical setup [10,26]. Those with strong social networks are more likely to be at the top of the hierarchy, and thus, have uncontested preference when it comes to accessing opportunities [10,26]. In order to balance the scales towards achieving social and epistemic justice, this chapter argues that effective inequality monitoring systems are essential. Adopting digital technologies has the potential to improve transparency and accountability, more especially in underdeveloped (or developing) countries or global regions suffering from inequalities and multiple injustices.

Against this backdrop, ontological and epistemological paradigms afforded the authors the opportunity to carefully think about the South African context, especially in the context of education. Ontologically, the authors reflected on the nature of reality and the different variables leading to an unequal society [25]. Beyond understanding the contextual reality, the authors undertook an epistemological reflection on social justice and the fundamental principles of inclusion [12].

According to Hage, Ring, and Lantz, social justice is underpinned by fundamental principles, which include "values of inclusion, collaboration, cooperation, equal access, and equal opportunity" [12, p. 2795]. To this end, the authors explored the complex nature of digital transformation and the type of intellectual and financial resources required in order to realise these fundamental principles in the context of education, especially during a challenging pandemic period overwhelmed by uncertainty. Dlamini and Dewa argued about the importance of social and cultural capital in accessing various resources and development opportunities [9]. On the one hand, social capital is said to include "resources embedded in one's social networks, resources that can be accessed or mobilized through ties in the networks" [15, p. 51]. In other words, "resources accrued by virtue of membership in a group" [5, p. 1042]. On the other hand, cultural capital is said to incorporate "scarce symbolic goods, skills, and titles" [5, p. 1042]. Arguably, the inequalities that exist around digital access and transformation are due to an imbalance in information society and cultural capital.

Cultural capital is considered a source of social inequality [4]. Therefore, the need for a systematic approach instead of a one-size-fits-all approach to adopting digital technologies is inevitable. The implementation of digital infrastructure must be accompanied by digital skills training and development opportunities that address all forms of inequalities, but most prominently access and adoption. In South Africa, the unequal distribution of digital skills is problematic at best. For instance, this is evident with: blue collar workers, who hold a negative perception of technology and are convinced that they will lose their jobs to it [13,18]; or teachers, who perceive technology as disruptive and time consuming [1,19]. Thus, it is important to help those low-level workers understand the role of technology and digital transformation in their various professions.

The argument that this chapter brings forth is embedded on the assumption that there is a correlation between digital fluency and innovation, which in turn would drive entrepreneurial activities.

3   Conceptions of the Digital Era

Notable research efforts in the mid to late 1990 s and early 2000 s were focused on unravelling issues surrounding the then so-called *digital divide*. Scholars adopted a multitude of theoretical viewpoints (including social, economical, political, and cultural) in order to understand this phenomenon. This granted researchers and relevant authorities the ability to draw cross-cutting commonalities, and provided a basis from which theory and practice could benefit. The digital divide was primarily conceptualised as the apparent gap between those (individuals, communities, or nations) that have and those that do not have access to computing devices and the internet, prominently so in the underdeveloped (or developing) than in developed countries.

Thus, it goes without saying that digital (in)equity, digital capital, and all the other conceptions of the hitherto digital era—chief of which are: (a) digitisation[2]; (b) digitalisation (see footnote 2); and (c) digital transformation;—are all tightly-bound functions of the digital divide. This implies that in order for digital transformation to be realised, the concept and implementation of digitalisation must be fully mature, and for that to be the case, the notion of digitisation must reach the same level of maturity. Of course, realising digitisation implies an intentional and practical reconfiguration of the elementary components of digital (in)equity as contemplated by Resta and Laferrière [23].

At its core, digital transformation encompasses not only the adoption of cutting-edge digital technologies to unlock previously untapped potential and value, but also the scope within which, as well as the unprecedented scale and speed at which this adoption happens [32]. This has expanded the appeal of this phenomenon well beyond the business realm into other societal spheres, such as governmental and educational institutions, primarily concerned with serving a public good. The use of digital technologies in these and similar institutions is nothing new. What is new is the reimagined use of these cutting-edge digital technologies (primarily brought about by innovative advances in technology and

---

[2] For the definitions of *digitisation* and *digitalisation*, this chapter leans on the Oxford English Dictionary definition of the two terms. It defines digitisation as "[t]he action or process of digitizing; the conversion of analogue data [...] into digital form" and defines digitalisation as "[t]he adoption or increase in use of digital or computer technology by an organization, industry, country, etc." (available by subscription at https://www.oed.com/).

the upskilling or reskilling of the people who interface with these technologies), coupled with their versatility and transformative power to catapult society into its ideal future.

With such prospects, digital transformation is well-poised as a redress tool through which social and epistemic justice can be realised. In the context of South Africa and other African countries however, although not impossible, the task at hand gets challenged by a systematically complex environment. That which is characterised by inequity, inequality, marginalisation, segregation, ruralism, and other unjust constructs inherited from colonial governments of yesteryear. Figure 2 provides some insights into just one facet of systematic complexity in the South African environment as reported by Statistics South Africa in the latest (2019) compilation of the *General Household Survey*.

Statistics South Africa further indicates that the proportion of households[3] who have access to the internet anywhere is at an average of 63.3% nationally. This is an indication that in about two in three South African households, at least one member of the household has access to the internet, albeit in different places. Zooming in to only those households in which at least one member thereof has access to the internet at home, this figure drops drastically to an average of one in eleven (9.1%) South African households [28]. This is as shocking as it is significant, as it highlights the plight of access disparities in a country attempting to make formidable effort to institutionalise digital transformation.

Another critical question thus becomes: in spite of these systematic complexities (as corroborated by views depicted in Figs. 1 and 2), how can society leverage the prospects of digital transformation towards attaining institutional equity?

4   Theoretical Perspectives

In attempting to answer the preceding critical question, it becomes necessary to adopt a multi-faceted approach. There is no one fitting theoretical lens through which to fully explore and comprehend the utility of digital transformation as a conduit through which institutional equity can be achieved. More so under the contextual complexities that have so far been highlighted. However, framing institutional equity as a continual realisation of social and epistemic justice, paves a way for inquiry into this contextual juncture from an educational point of view. Thus, this chapter grounds its approach on, and draws its perspectives from: (a) the syntheses and theoretical perspectives put forth by Hage, Ring, and Lantz [12], Cazden [6], and Sutherland [29] on social justice in education settings; (b) the ideology of Walzer's spheres of justice as interpreted and developed further by Resh and Sabbagh [22,24]; and (c) Fuller's conceptualisation of epistemic justice [11].

---

[3] The *General Household Survey* reports that "the mean household size was estimated at 3.31 persons per household for the country, the estimate ranges from 3.11 in urban areas to 3.73 in rural areas." [28, p. 8].

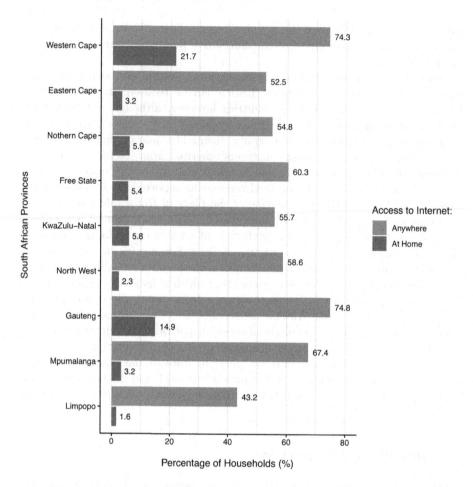

Fig. 2. Percentage of households with internet access in South Africa, adopted from Statistics South Africa [28, p. 51].

4.1   Social Justice and Education

Hage, Ring, and Lantz advance a general definition of social justice, stating that it concerns the "fair and equitable distribution of power, resources, and obligations in society to all people" [12, p. 2795]. They further state that this definition is underpinned by fundamental principles, which include "values of inclusion, collaboration, cooperation, equal access, and equal opportunity" [12, p. 2795]. The distributive nature of social justice is also emphasised by Cazden as one dimension of social justice, alluding that intellectual and monetary resources require equitable distribution in educational settings [6]. Another important dimension that she unpacks encompasses access to an "intellectually rich curriculum for all students" across and within all educational institutions and "not just in the rhetoric of policy and plans" [6, p. 182]. Clearly, a pathway leading to social justice—particularly in educational environments—entails just distribution of key resources and requires further inquiry.

In his seminal work of *Spheres of Justice*, Walzer recognises the need to consider education (a critical social good[4]) as a distinct distributive *sphere of justice* [33]. He emphasises the importance of just distribution of social goods, in such a manner as not to incubate domination or foster an exclusionary society. Resh and Sabbagh build on this work by conceptualising five sub-spheres of justice within the education sphere, each of which is centred on the distribution of educational resources [22,24]. These sub-spheres are: (a) the right to education; (b) educational places; (c); pedagogy; (d) grading; and (e) teacher–student relations. The subsections below delve into each of these sub-spheres, highlighting the rationale and importance of each as contemplated by Resh and Sabbagh.

The Right to Education. From a global perspective, the right to education has been recognised as a fundamental basic human right, advocated through and by reputable international organisation bodies (such as the United Nations General Assembly through its adoption of The International Bill of Human Rights as well as through its formulation of the SDGs—specifically SDG 4). It is also enshrined in the constitution of many countries, often with provisions, assurances, and protections from the state. This sub-sphere relates to the distribution of education goods, emphasising the provision of access to educational institutions, and includes the allocation of all the requisite resources necessary to realise this right.

Education Places. This sub-sphere pertains the allocation of learning spaces to students. This allocation is often an autonomous exercise taking place within educational institutions at the discretion of the institutions' leadership bodies and teachers. This sub-sphere also relates to the distribution of learning opportunities available to students once they have been allocated to various learning spaces. Resh and Sabbagh argue that it is this allocation that regulates the distribution of these learning opportunities, including the access to knowledge, and it is often acknowledged as a fundamentally meritocratic and competitive process owing to the limited and divisible number of learning spaces available for allocation.

Pedagogy. This sub-sphere relates to the pedagogical practices which teachers adopt in the teaching and learning processes. At their core, these include the philosophical and methodological approaches to teaching and learning, and at the very least, encompass the way teachers operationalise classroom discourse, the way in which they encourage learning, and the manner in which they promote knowledge acquisition. The need for just distribution of pedagogical practices cannot be overstated as they have a direct influence on learning opportunities

---

[4] A *social good* is not universally defined but rather it is a contextual intrinsic function (or construct) of the sphere within which it is located or it is the actual sphere itself.

from which students can learn and develop to ultimately become successful contributors to society.

Grading. Grading is an evaluative process which is central in the teaching and learning processes. It allows for teachers to keep abreast with student performance, while also serving as a gatekeeping mechanism for various other subsequent stages in the life of a student all the way up to determining employment opportunities. Much has been written about the psychological effects of grading on students. This sub-sphere is concerned about the just distribution of grades in classrooms, especially considering the differential and meritocratic rules that apply to the allocation thereof.

Teacher–student Relations. Resh and Sabbagh highlight several relational goods in need of just distribution when it comes to teacher–student interactions in educational institutions. Included in these are help (in various forms as would be needed by students from time to time), attention, encouragement, respect, affection, and discipline. This sub-sphere relates to the distribution of these relational goods, particularity because any perceived injustice in their distribution may invariably lead to attitudinal and behavioural consequences on the part of students.

4.2   Epistemic Justice

Epistemic justice is often interpreted and interrogated in terms of its inverse, epistemic injustice. This simplistic, two-dimensional approach not only dwarfs the intellectual importance of epistemic justice, but also undermines the efforts of those scholars who are at the forefront of epistemic justice inquiry. Arguably, attempting to advance research on matters pertaining knowledge and power is a huge and daunting undertaking, however, not tackling it head-on is an epistemic injustice in itself.

In a formidable attempt, Fuller simplifies the notion of epistemic justice, asserting that it "concerns the optimal distribution of knowledge and power in society" [11, p. 24]. He dissects the much familiar aphorism *knowledge is power*, illustrating the dynamism central to the knowledge–power reciprocal relationship. He goes on to suggest that there are essentially two approaches through which epistemic justice can be achieved. The first, he suggests, is to "inhibit the power effects of new knowledge by distributing it as widely as possible" [11, p. 25]. This implies that the inability to effectively distribute knowledge renders those that possess this knowledge undesirably powerful. The second approach, Fuller suggests, is to "define a piece of knowledge in terms of the functions it serves" [11, p. 25], an approach that would potentially spur individuals on to founding alternative approaches to serving those functions. This approach cultivates innovation and encourages epistemic diversification, which are the essence of epistemic justice.

The reality of the knowledge–power dynamic is that it is accumulative and compounds over time. This has allowed for certain sectors of society to accumulate specific forms of knowledge over long historical periods of time, resulting in pockets of powerful societal clusters. This is particularly evident in countries which have recently emerged from the clutches of colonialism, or those deemed to be underdeveloped (or developing), or both. Fuller argues that it thus becomes the function of the state to "regularly redistribute the advantage that these forms of knowledge have accumulated over time" [11, p. 26] through ingeniously institutionalising epistemic justice in educational institutions at the very least, but with the aim of achieving much grander scales of institutionalisation.

4.3 Pursuing Institutional Equity

The catalyst in the pursuit of institutional equity through adopting a social and epistemic justice approach is knowledge, and the acquisition of this knowledge must happen in commonplaces attuned to this process. These commonplaces must be characterised by fair distribution practices of social goods within each sub-sphere of justice in order to be socially just, and must encourage innovation, collaboration, and epistemic diversification. Through broad digital transformation efforts, these commonplaces can manifest as digital learning platforms, however it remains imperative to further probe:

1. In what ways are digital learning platforms creating environments of knowledge acquisition and widening the context of learning to cultivate equity? Or put differently, in what ways *can* digital learning platforms create environments of knowledge acquisition and widen the context of learning to cultivate equity?
2. What are the perceptions that advance or inhibit educators' transition to constructivist-oriented practices in digital learning platforms to achieve instructional equity?

The scope of these digital learning platforms ought to extend beyond the ideology of learning management systems and massive open online course platforms. They ought to be context-relevant entities—favouring virtual learning communities or virtual communities of practice—ripe with opportunities for members to learn through and from each other, collaborate on ideas, and encourage a culture of social entrepreneurship and innovation. These are key constructivist-oriented practices which if attainable, will serve as a societal bedrock in the transitioning to a digital economy.

5 Discussion and Implications

Digital technologies, as the hallmark of civilisation, need to be widespread across the country otherwise digital transformation, together with all its prospects, will remain a pipe dream. Marolla attests that digital dividends have the potential to help countries achieve higher-quality economic growth and alleviate social and economic disparities [17]. Therefore, the South African *National Development Plan 2030*, which sets out a long term vision of the country, must be operationalised through context-relevant community-based initiatives. This will go a long way towards avoiding a one-size-fits-all approach and will instead create responsive ICT-driven socio-economic development policy and rollout plan to empower strategic groups at various levels in both rural and urban areas.

This policy and rollout plan ought to be accompanied by measurable deliverables aimed at attacking inequality in its various manifestations, while making significant strides towards a knowledge-based information society. This attack on inequality must be strategic and coordinated through meaningful investments to improve digital infrastructure access, develop and harness appropriate digital skills, and improve the quality of education. Importantly, it must aim to build the digital capacity of the state through community-based programmes to overcome the current structural defects and revolutionise the digital space. Digital transformation has the potential to foster social inclusion and expand participation in economic activities. However, it must be institutionalised to improve coordination and PPPs. This is to ensure that digital infrastructure and fluency is fairly distributed to promote greater digital transformation inclusion.

The theoretical grounding of this chapter is that social and epistemic justice breed equity. Thus, engaging with and understanding the theoretical underpinnings of both social justice and epistemic justice is necessary in order to inform inquiry into how digital technologies can assist towards attaining institutional equity. Notwithstanding, Sutherland warns that "digital technologies can exacerbate inequalities and so a much more critical approach has to be taken with respect to the relationship between digital technologies and social justice" [29, p. 24]. Therefore, it is important to maintain an objective outlook as we navigate the pursuit of justice (and thus, equity) in and through education.

6   Conclusion

This chapter has presented a critical argument on: (a) a foundational lack that systematically prohibits society from leveraging the conceptions of the digital era (digitisation, digitalisation, and digital transformation); in order to fulfil (b) the urgent need to address matters pertaining digital equity and digital capital; through (c) harnessing the power and utility of these conceptions of the digital era, under favourable conditions, for achieving institutional equity and transitioning to a digital economy. It has further argued for: (d) the need for context-relevant digital learning platforms that will create environments for knowledge acquisition, through constructivist-oriented practices, in order to achieve institutional equity; functioning under (e) a viable PPP framework. The thread that holds all of this together is just access to both digital devices and the internet, which remains a jarring issue faced by underdeveloped (or developing) countries or global regions as Figs. 1 and 2 depict.

Attending to each of these five arguments put forth requires extensive pragmatic and empirical inquiry efforts. If South Africa and other African countries are to pull themselves out of this depicted situation, such inquiry efforts must be self-driven and must invite equal participation across all sectors, least of which must be the state, academia, and private organisations.

References

1. Bilwani, A., Zehra, R.: Perceptions of teachers regarding technology integration in classrooms: a comparative analysis of elite and mediocre schools. J. Educ. Educ. Dev. **3**(1), 1–29 (2016)
2. Birisci, S., Kul, E.: Predictors of technology integration self-efficacy beliefs of pre-service teachers. Contemp. Educ. Technol. **10**(1), 75–93 (2019). https://doi.org/10.30935/cet.512537
3. Booyens, I.: Creative industries, inequality and social development: developments, impacts and challenges in Cape Town. Urban Forum **23**(1), 43–60 (2012). https://doi.org/10.1007/s12132-012-9140-6
4. Bourdieu, P.: Erving Goffman, discoverer of the infinitely small. Theor. Cult. Soc. **2**(1), 112–113 (1983). https://doi.org/10.1177/0263276483002001012
5. Brock, A., Kvasny, L., Hales, K.: Cultural appropriations of technical capital: black women, weblogs, and the digital divide. Inf. Commun. Soc. **13**(7), 1040–1059 (2010). https://doi.org/10.1080/1369118x.2010.498897
6. Cazden, C.B.: A framework for social justice in education. Int. J. Educ. Psychol. **1**(3), 178–198 (2012). https://doi.org/10.4471/ijep.2012.11
7. Choi, Y.C.: Prioritizing Korean ICT ODA project areas and project types for Africa. Psychol. Educ. J. **57**(9), 6897–6906 (2020)
8. Dlamini, R., Ndzinisa, N.: Universities trailing behind: unquestioned epistemological foundations constraining the transition to online instructional delivery and learning. S. Afr. J. High. Educ. **34**(6), 52–64 (2020). https://doi.org/10.20853/34-6-4073
9. Dlamini, R., Dewa, A.: Beyond optimistic rhetoric: social and cultural capital as focal deterrents to ICT integration in schools. Int. J. Educ. Dev. Inf. Commun. Technol. **17**(3), 19–37 (2021)
10. Dubois, D., Ordabayeva, N.: Social hierarchy, social status, and status consumption. In: Norton, M.I., Rucker, D.D., Lamberton, C. (eds.) The Cambridge Handbook of Consumer Psychology, pp. 332–367. Cambridge University Press, Cambridge, United Kingdom, October 2015. https://doi.org/10.1017/cbo9781107706552.013
11. Fuller, S.: The Knowledge Book: Key Concepts in Philosophy, Science, and Culture. Routledge, Abingdon (2007)
12. Hage, S.M., Ring, E.E., Lantz, M.M.: Social justice theory. In: Levesque, R.J.R. (ed.) Encyclopedia of Adolescence, pp. 2794–2801. Springer, New York, August 2011. https://doi.org/10.1007/978-1-4419-1695-2_62
13. Hampel, N., Sassenberg, K., Scholl, A., Reichenbach, M.: Introducing digital technologies in the factory: determinants of blue-collar workers' attitudes towards new robotic tools. Behav. Inf. Technol. 1–15 (2021). https://doi.org/10.1080/0144929x.2021.1967448
14. Kwapong, O.A.T.F.: Equitable Access: information and Communication Technology for Open and Distance Learning. iUniverse Inc, Bloomington, IN (2010)
15. Lin, N.: A network theory of social capital. In: Castiglione, D., van Deth, J.W., Wolleb, G. (eds.) The Handbook of Social Capital, pp. 50–69. Oxford University Press, Oxford (2008)

16. Macupe, B.: 'Covid-19 to deepen inequalities in education' – report. June 2020. https://mg.co.za/education/2020-06-24-covid-19-to-deepen-inequalities-in-education-report/. Accessed 14 Jan 2022
17. Marolla, C.: Information and Communication Technology for Sustainable Development. CRC Press, Boca Raton (2018)
18. Millington, A.K.: How changes in technology and automation will affect the labour market in Africa. K4D Helpdesk Report, Institute of Development Studies, Brighton, United Kingdom, Febuary 2017. https://opendocs.ids.ac.uk/opendocs/handle/20.500.12413/13054
19. Mokoena, M., Simelane-Mnisi, S., Mji, A.: Teachers' perceptions towards the pedagogical use of interactive whiteboard in South African high schools. In: Chova, L.G., Martínez, A.L., Torres, I.C. (eds.) EDULEARN20 Proceedings, pp. 7825–7833. IATED, July 2020. https://doi.org/10.21125/edulearn.2020.1974
20. Ndzinisa, N., Dlamini, R.: Responsiveness vs. accessibility: pandemic-driven shift to remote teaching and online learning. High. Educ. Res. Dev. 1–16 (2022). https://doi.org/10.1080/07294360.2021.2019199
21. Ragnedda, M., Ruiu, M.L., Addeo, F.: Measuring digital capital: An empirical investigation. New Media Soc. 22(5), 793–816 (2019). https://doi.org/10.1177/1461444819869604
22. Resh, N., Sabbagh, C.: Justice and education. In: Sabbagh, C., Schmitt, M. (eds.) Handbook of Social Justice Theory and Research, pp. 349–367. Springer, New York (2016). https://doi.org/10.1007/978-1-4939-3216-0_19
23. Resta, P., Laferrière, T.: Issues and challenges related to digital equity. In: Voogt, J., Knezek, G. (eds.) International Handbook of Information Technology in Primary and Secondary Education, vol. 20, pp. 765–778. Springer, US, Boston, MA (2008). https://doi.org/10.1007/978-0-387-73315-9_44
24. Sabbagh, C., Resh, N.: Unfolding justice research in the realm of education. Soc. Justice Res. 29(1), 1–13 (2016). https://doi.org/10.1007/s11211-016-0262-1
25. Schwandt, T.A.: Dictionary of Qualitative Inquiry, 2nd edn. SAGE Publications Inc, Thousand Oaks (2001)
26. Sidanius, J., Pratto, F.: Social Dominance: An Intergroup Theory of Social Hierarchy and Oppression. Cambridge University Press, Cambridge, United Kingdom, July 1999. https://doi.org/10.1017/cbo9781139175043
27. Sommer Harrits, G.: More than method?: a discussion of paradigm differences within mixed methods research. J. Mixed Methods Res. 5(2), 150–166 (2011). https://doi.org/10.1177/1558689811402506
28. Statistics South Africa: General household survey, 2019 (Statistical Release P0318). December 2020. http://www.statssa.gov.za/publications/P0318/P03182019.pdf. Accessed 25 Sep 2021
29. Sutherland, R.: Education and Social Justice in a Digital Age. Policy Press, Bristol, United Kingdom, January 2014. https://doi.org/10.2307/j.ctt9qgszm
30. Thapa, D., Sæbø, Ø.: Exploring the link between ICT and development in the context of developing countries: a literature review. Electron. J. Inf. Syst. Dev. Countries 64(1), 1–15 (2014). https://doi.org/10.1002/j.1681-4835.2014.tb00454.x
31. Vartanova, E.L., Gladkova, A.A.: Cifrovoj kapital v kontekste koncepcii nematerial'nyh kapitalov [Digital capital within the context of the intangible capitals concept]. Mediaskop (1) (May 2020). https://doi.org/10.30547/mediascope.1.2020.8

32. Vial, G.: Understanding digital transformation: a review and a research agenda. J. Strateg. Inf. Syst. **28**(2), 118–144 (2019). https://doi.org/10.1016/j.jsis.2019.01.003
33. Walzer, M.: Spheres of Justice: A Defense of Pluralism and Equality. Basic Books Inc, New York (1983)

Complexities and Challenges of Multi-stakeholder Involvement in Digital Transformation in the Global South: The Machine-Readable Passport Project in Bangladesh

Ahmed Imran(⊠) [iD] and Safiya Okai-Ugbaje [iD]

School of Information Technology and Systems, University of Canberra, Canberra, Australia
ahmed.imran@canberra.edu.au

Abstract. Digital transformation initiatives must meet specific demands, mainly to improve existing processes or provide a more efficient way to address a problem or situation. When such interventions are required for large projects in the public sector, the involvement of multiple stakeholder groups becomes inevitable. The literature indicates that this often leads to complex stakeholder interrelations and conflicting interests because of diverse perspectives and power dynamics. This paper presents the case of a machine-readable passport project whose purpose was to automate the passport transaction process in Bangladesh; that involved multiple organisations with diverse portfolios from the public and private sectors. Although considerable success was achieved, it was not without challenges because of the complex power dynamics and the sociocultural and political environments of the various stakeholder groups involved. Using the salience model, this study examined stakeholder relations, interests, and power plays and provides rich insight into the complexities and challenges of the stakeholder relationships. Data were collected from a series of interviews, focus group discussion, and observations of participants during the early stage of the project. The findings suggest that information and communications technology innovation, implementation, and organisational change in developing countries is deeply rooted in sociocultural and organisational norms, vested interests, and power politics at multiple levels. In addition to contributing to new knowledge in digital transformation interventions in developing countries, the study has policy implications and practical lessons for designers and implementers working in developing countries.

Keywords: Complex ICT projects · Digital transformation · ICT for development · Public sector · Salience model · Stakeholder management · Digital inequality

© IFIP International Federation for Information Processing 2022
Published by Springer Nature Switzerland AG 2022
J. Abdelnour-Nocera et al. (Eds.): *Innovation Practices for Digital Transformation in the Global South*, IFIP AICT 645, pp. 16–33, 2022.
https://doi.org/10.1007/978-3-031-12825-7_2

1 Introduction

Despite some variations in the definition of a stakeholder, it is predominantly anchored in Freeman's definition [1] of stakeholders as "any group or individual who can affect or is affected by the achievement of the organization's objectives" (p. 46). Over time, this definition has evolved beyond referring to organisational settings to include a variety of contexts and disciplines, including project management. Hence, it is generally agreed that a stakeholder is anyone who can affect or is affected by the process of a project, its outcome, or both [2, 3]. Due to their growing demands and complexities, most large IT interventions require diverse stakeholder groups. As a result, it becomes necessary to consider the interests of those groups and their effects on the project [4, 5]. This promotes transparency, inclusive decision-making, and actions necessary to ensure that the final product meets specifications and achieves the intended objectives; however, it also presents many challenges [6, 7].

The involvement of a diverse range of stakeholders triggers uncertainties and controversies because of complex stakeholder interrelations, power dynamics, and conflicting interests [4, 8, 9]. Stakeholder analysis is a valuable tool in understanding and managing such multi-stakeholder influence and power imbalance [10, 11]. Hence, there is a growing body of literature on stakeholder identification, engagement, and mapping. However, studies that bring together these relevant aspects while considering complex stakeholder interrelations from the context of a developing country such as Bangladesh are scarce. Therefore, the goal of this study was to provide such a perspective by analysing the roles of various stakeholder groups involved in an extensive IT intervention, the machine-readable project (MRP).

The MRP was a large multistakeholder initiative to automate the passport transaction process in Bangladesh. As in many other developing countries, Bangladesh's business entities and government agencies lacked the high proficiency required to deal with paperless transactions such as those in the MRP. The project involved several contextual and noncontractual parties and entities from eight distinct and diverse groups. They comprised Bangladesh military task force's project management office (PMO), ministry of foreign affairs (MOFA), department of immigration and passports (DIP), the special branch (SB) of the police, external vendors (local and multinational), the Sonali Bank (a commercial bank), the prime minister's (PM's) office, and the general public (citizens who apply for passports). Although the project has been rolled out, and still evolving with multiple iterations and phases including a complete biometric e-passport, this paper focuses on the stakeholder interrelations in the course of the project and the challenges encountered, particularly during the initial phases. In addition to technological inadequacies that threaten the success of IT projects in developing countries, the MRP also faced several challenges because of complex stakeholder interrelations and power dynamics and the socio-political influences in Bangladesh, which were exacerbated by a history of unscrupulous and inefficient business practices typical of many such developing countries [12]. These problems often override technological challenges, and thus become crucial to reduce for the ultimate success of IT interventions in developing countries [13, 14]. It is, therefore, imperative that they are effectively managed.

First, this paper contributes to the body of knowledge of complex stakeholder relations in the unique sociocultural context of a developing country. Spangenberg et al.

[15] and Ginige, Amaratunga, and Haigh [16] argued that the increasingly interconnected nature of the diverse portfolios of stakeholders, which is necessary to address societal challenges in the Global South, require stakeholder analysis to identify, assess, and map stakeholder views and interests, along with their power and influence on project execution. Hence, the second contribution of this paper is its examination of how one of the stakeholder analysis tools, the salience model, enables the categorisation and analysis of stakeholders in a complex web where politics and power dynamics are at play. In view of this, Sect. 1.1 describes the theoretical framework adopted by this study. This is followed by the data collection and analysis techniques in Sect. 2 and the findings in Sect. 3. The paper concludes with some reflections and discussions on what the findings mean in terms of the theoretical framework, prior literature, and further research directions.

1.1 Theoretical Framework

Stakeholder analysis provides a strategic pathway to understand, assess, and manage the interests and needs of a diverse range of stakeholders [17, 18], while strategically identifying the roles and responsibilities of each stakeholder and their influence on the project [2, 19]. Accordingly, an array of stakeholder analysis tools and techniques exist. Most of them centre on power versus interest grids [20, 21], providing a basis for prioritising stakeholders based on power and interest while aligning their influence and corresponding effects on project outcomes [20, 22]. Other useful tools include the onion model and 9Cs stakeholder analysis framework for identifying and classifying critical stakeholders [23]; stakeholder categorisation based on descriptive accuracy, instrumental power and normative validity [24]; and the triangle framework to understand stakeholders' expectations and fears [25]. Although these tools and techniques provide valuable strategies to manage stakeholder influence and improve project outcomes, the salience stakeholder model in addition to assessing power, uniquely recognises and emphasises stakeholders' legitimacy and urgency. This enables stakeholder classification based on a recognition of their attributes [26]. This characteristic of the salience model made it an optimal tool for analysing the stakeholders involved in the MRP because of the diverse portfolios of each stakeholder group. Moreover, the salience model has been widely used in information systems research to identify, classify, and prioritise stakeholders based on their possession of one or more attributes and to examine their influence on project outcomes (see, for example, [27, 28], and in the context of developing countries [14, 23, 29]). The findings of these studies suggested that the salience model is an appropriate tool for the MRP project.

1.2 The Salience Model

The salience stakeholder model developed by Mitchell, Agle, and Wood [30] is based on three key attributes: power, legitimacy, and urgency. The framework conceptualizes *power* as the measure of authority a stakeholder has to influence the execution of the project; *legitimacy* as the measure of how much right a stakeholder has to make a request; and *urgency* as the measure of how much immediate action, attention, or response a stakeholder can demand. Based on these, Mitchell, Agle, and Wood [30] defined salience as the degree of priority given to stakeholders based on their possession of at least one of the three attributes. Building on these, the authors developed a typology that categories stakeholders according to their possession of one, two, or all three attributes. A brief account of different kinds of stakeholders according to Mitchell, Agle, and Wood [30] and their corresponding typology and attributes is given below, followed by a summary (Table 1).

Latent: Stakeholders in this category have only one of the three attributes; hence, they have low salience and are less likely to substantially affect decisions that might affect the project. Latent stakeholders with *power* are in the dormant category; they can impose their demands but have no legitimacy or authority to demand urgency. A stakeholder with only *legitimacy* is considered discretionary; they have the right to make requests but no power to influence the project or demand urgent actions. Finally, stakeholders with only *urgency* can make urgent claims but lack the power or legitimacy to move their claims. However, any latent stakeholder can acquire additional attributes and become more salient.

Expectant: Stakeholders in this category have two of the three attributes. They have moderate salience and a higher probability of influencing the project. Those with *power* and *legitimacy* are called dominant stakeholders due to their influence on vital decision-making processes because they have the legitimacy to make requests and the power to enforce their will. Stakeholders with *urgency* and *legitimacy* are called dependent stakeholders because although they have the right to make claims and demand urgency, they have no power to enforce their will. Finally, there are the dangerous stakeholders, who possess *power* and *urgency* but lack legitimacy. Dangerous stakeholders might be coercive. They must be watched closely and managed cautiously.

Definitive: Stakeholders in this category have all three attributes and therefore have high salience. They have the legitimacy to make requests, the power to enforce change, and the authority to demand urgency.

Table 1. Stakeholder categorisation in accordance with the salience model (based on Mitchell, Agle, and Wood [30]

Stakeholder class and salience degree	Attributes	Typology
Latent stakeholders (low salience)	Power	Dormant
	Legitimacy	Discretionary
	Urgency	Demanding
Expectant stakeholders (moderate salience)	Power and legitimacy	Dominant
	Urgency and legitimacy	Dependent
	Power and urgency	Dangerous
Definitive stakeholders (high salience)	Power, legitimacy, and urgency	Definitive

The uniqueness of the salience model in analysing stakeholders according to their influence, as determined by the attribute(s), made it a useful tool to categories and analyse stakeholders involved in the MRP. Accordingly, the research questions this study aimed to answer were:

- What attributes of the salience model are possessed by stakeholders in the MRP project?
- What complexities and challenges, if any, arise from the diverse stakeholder groups involved the MRP project?

2 Methods

Given its exploratory nature, this research employed a qualitative interpretative case study approach to gather and analyse the study's data [31]. Interpretive research helps understand human action in social and organisational contexts and provides deep insights into information systems phenomena [32]. The objective was to generate a variety of disciplinary and stakeholder perspectives that could provide clear understandings and potentially uncover major underlying problems in the MRP project.

2.1 Data Gathering

Data were collected through a series of face-to-face interviews, one focus group discussion (FGD), and on-the-ground observations from September to October 2012. Fifteen semi-structured interviews were done with the relevant and major project stakeholder categories, each lasting 1 to 1½ h. The chosen strategy was to interview a sample of staff members directly involved in the MRP project development who could provide rich insight into the entire project and its associated problems. Although, the project had eight stakeholder groups, data for this study were collected from the four major stakeholders who were responsible for executing the project. The top-level distribution of the interviewees is shown in Table 2.

Table 2. Description of study participants

Major stakeholder group	Typology	No. of participants	Code used in analysis
Department of immigration and passports (DIP)	Dependent	3 (top- and mid-level)	DIP 1 to 3
Project management office (PMO)	Dominant	7 (top-, mid-, and front-level)	PMO 1 to 7
Special branch of police (SB)	Dormant	2 (mid-level)	SB 1 and 2
Vendor groups	Dependent	3 (top- and mid-level)	V 1 to 3

Supplementary and follow-up questions were used to encourage further elaboration or to check the meaning that interviewees associated with certain words they used. However, the aim at all times was to provide opportunities for the interviewees to reveal their experience of the phenomena as fully as possible, without the interviewer introducing any new aspects not previously mentioned by the interviewee.

Next, an FGD involved at least two representatives from the four major stakeholder groups: PMO, DIP, SB, and vendors. The FGD participants were chosen based on their ability to provide different perspectives on the challenges. As such, the FGD provided a commentary and rich insight in addition to the individual face-to-face interviews, and provided an additional platform to exchange and clarify each stakeholder's viewpoints, concerns, and interests. The FGD protocol included the application of a 'nominal group technique' (NGT) to identify and prioritise challenges from each group in a more structured way than discussion alone [33, 34]. The NGT method allowed each person to spend several minutes in silence individually brainstorming all possible challenges without consulting each other and then write the challenges on yellow Post-it notes, one per page. Those were posted on a flip chart visible to the entire group for further grouping and discussion. That process facilitated the analysis of the theme, and formed categories based on clarifications and discussions among participants.

Ethical clearance was obtained following the UNSW's ethical clearance process. All interviews and the FGD were tape recorded, and the recordings were transcribed with the interviewee's permission. However, participant names and clear designations were not revealed, to maintain confidentiality as per the ethical clearance.

2.2 Data Analysis

The qualitative data analysis tool NVivo (version 10.0) was used to store, code and analyse all the qualitative data including the FGD, interviews, and field notes. Analysis followed a grounded, bottom up approach incorporating these steps:

1. English versions of the full interview and FGD transcripts were used as source documents for analysis using NVivo 10.
2. Initial coding schemes were prepared following three coding procedures—selective, axial, and open/emerging codes (from the data based on some transcripts).
3. Coding, memoing, and concept mapping were done using NVivo, and new/emerging codes were added during the process.
4. Node-wise reports were produced after all transcripts were coded, which offered some scope to reorganise the data by changing, merging, and adding codes and categories through a second level of analysis, as shown in Figs. 2 and 3.

Further, an iterative process was followed that involved repeated readings of the transcripts in search of the underlying themes and intentions expressed in them, comparing transcripts for similarities and differences, and looking for key structural relations among the key constructs. As more meaningful key themes and dimensions started to emerge (as shown in Table 3), the analysis shifted to confirmation, contradiction, modification, and filtering of emerging themes following the double hermeneutic circle principle of case study development [31]. That continued until a consistent set of categories emerged, as shown in Table 3. Direct quotes were used to validate and paint a clear picture of corresponding categories and themes or both.

3 Findings

3.1 Stakeholders

There were eight distinct stakeholder groups who had varying and sometimes conflicting roles.

Department of Immigration and Passports. Under the Bangladesh ministry of home affairs, the DIP is the sole authority to issue, refuse, revoke, withhold, recover, and monitor the use of passports and visas for Bangladesh. The department was responsible for overseeing the entire project because it was directly within its jurisdiction. The DIP headquarters has data centres, passport printing sectors, a disaster recovery site, and 34 regional passport offices across the country. Out of 58 Bangladesh embassies, 28 now also issue MRP visas.

Project Management Office (PMO). A military project management and implementation team headed by a brigadier general was placed under the home ministry on deputation to implement the MRP project, initially for a duration of 2 years. The team included officers with electrical and mechanical engineering backgrounds from the corps of electronics and mechanical engineers, signals, artillery, and other branches, including navy and air force representatives.

Special Branch of Police. The SB is involved in passport issues in two ways: for verification and background checks and for immigration control at all border posts. According to the manual of rules and orders for the working of the district special branch in Bangladesh (1919), the SB is responsible for verifying passport applications. Special branch offices must wait until they receive a hard-copy application. Despite the intricacies of receiving a hard copy from MRP offices, verifying, and reporting back to the MRP offices, the process takes an average of only 8–10 days.

Vendor Groups. The project vendor group was part of a consortium. The original tender bid was won by Irish JV, which comprised Irish Corporation Malaysia as the solution provider, Data Edge limited Bangladesh as the hardware provider, and Polish Security Printing Works as the passport book provider. Irish JV also subcontracted iPeople to provide operational support by ensuring an adequate number of personnel, which Irish JV did not have. To run the day-to-day operation, Irish JV required 700 people but had only 100; they were sourced by iPeople.

Ministry of Foreign Affairs. MOFA staff were involved as stakeholders to ensure execution of the project in line with the ministry's mandate and international best practices. The MOFA controlled not only the issuing of red diplomatic passports, but also issued, managed, and provided manpower for consular services to all missions.

Sonali Bank. This was the only bank designated and authorised to collect and disburse all revenue related to the project, including accepting passport fees from citizens.

Prime Minister. The PM of Bangladesh had the supreme authority and final say about the major decisions, choices, and directions of the project, which might have superseded any activities and arrangements.

Citizens. The citizens of Bangladesh were the primary users and recipients of MRP services.

The eight distinct stakeholder groups had varying and sometimes conflicting roles. As indicated, the DIP was initially responsible for overseeing the entire project because it was directly within its jurisdiction. However, the DIP was sluggish in executing the project. Consequently, the office of the PM, based on the Bangladesh army's previous involvement and success in a very low cost national ID card project (with one-third of the total budget, a rare feat to prepare a voter database for 80 million people within 18 months), decided to give the project implementation responsibility to the Bangladesh armed forces PMO in collaboration with relevant stakeholders. With the appointment of the PMO, the project gained momentum, albeit amid some feelings of lost control and dissatisfaction among the DIP and other stakeholders.

3.2 Stakeholder Salience

Data analysis showed that all eight stakeholder groups had at least one attribute of the salience model indicated in Table 1. Stakeholders such as the PMO, SB, MOFA, and DIP had some degree of each of the three attributes based on their fundamental responsibilities and how those roles affected the project directly and indirectly. However, within the purview of the MRP project, only the most prominent attributes with a direct effect on the project implementation and outcome were considered, as shown in Fig. 1.

The Sonali Bank, by virtue of its role in the project, was a discretionary stakeholder. It had the legitimacy to request changes or suggest a more efficient way of processing payments but had no authority to demand that its requests be acted upon urgently or power to impose its will.

The vendors were dependent stakeholders because they had the legitimacy to make requests and were in the position to demand that their requests be acted upon urgently when deemed necessary for the expected project outcome; however, they had no power to enforce their demands.

The SB, on the other hand, seemed to move between various stakeholder categories. By virtue of their fundamental roles in maintaining and enforcing law and order, they had the power to impose their will to instate security requirements and the authority to demand urgency in meeting such requests. This made them dangerous stakeholders. However, in the absence of such threats, they were dormant stakeholders, with only power and no legitimate relation and authority to demand urgency.

The MOFA, by ensuring the execution of the project in line with the ministry's mandate and international best practices, had the power to demand changes and the right to request that their demands be acted upon urgently; hence they were dangerous stakeholders.

The DIP at the inception of the project was the definitive stakeholder because they had the mandate to oversee the project and ensure compliance with global MRPs. However, changes mandated by the PM's office led the DIP to lose the power attribute, which made them dependent stakeholders for the purpose of the MRP project.

The PMO, on the other hand, acquired power in addition to their legitimacy and hence became dominant stakeholders who influenced vital decision-making processes that led to a positive turnaround in the project implementation and outcome.

The PM was the definitive stakeholder, having all three attributes. Our understanding of the salience model suggested that citizens who apply for the MRP fell into the demanding category because they might make claims and demand that their claims be met urgently. However, in the context of that project, they lacked the power and legitimacy to enforce and move their claims. Figure 1 shows where each identified stakeholder group sat within the salience model.

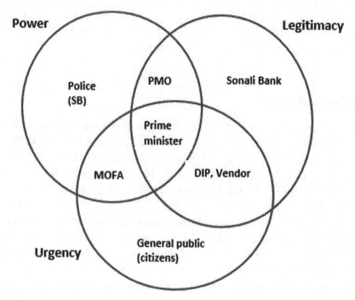

Fig. 1. Stakeholders position on the salience model (adapted from Mitchell, Agle and Wood 1997)

3.3 Complexities and Challenges

In determining how the above classification affected stakeholder interrelations, many challenges were revealed in our findings. Complexities arose mainly from a lack of stakeholder analysis, absence of project management methodologies, lack of planning and change management, different work cultures, and power dynamics. The findings also indicated that most stakeholders did not clearly understand their and other people's roles in the project. This was caused by an ad hoc arrangement with confusion at various levels in the absence of a project document specifying clear roles. Even seeking clarification on those ambiguities appeared risky because they were highly contentious and sensitive issues for different players and groups with varying and unclear power structures. As a result, various stakeholders other than the project director adopted a dormant, wait-and-see behaviour. The communication gap between the PM's message and the understanding among important stakeholders was evident. Thus, the MRP project took approximately eight months to make a start. Figures 2 and 3 show some of the themes and categories that emerged from the analysis with NVivo.

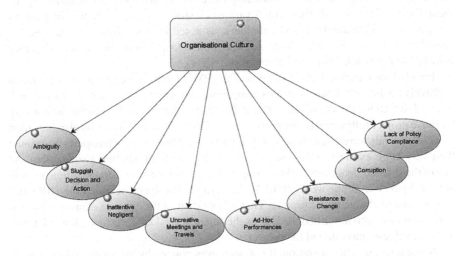

Fig. 2. Project challenges resulting from organisational culture

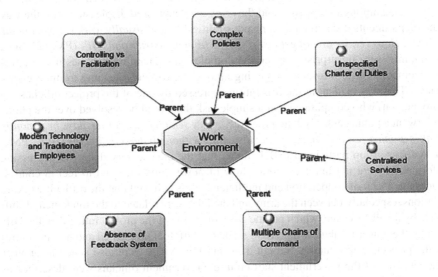

Fig. 3. Challenges from the project work environment

The data trail leading to these categories from interviewee responses were unpacked as follows:

The lack of clarity of each stakeholder's role led to difficult working relations and a sense that vested interests and gains were often prioritised over project goals and outcomes. For example, one respondent (V 2) noted that '*A big number of inefficient government people are enjoying the project but do nothing… the government people have different personal interests (like promotion, appreciation, international trips, etcetera.)*'. An unclear reporting structure, lack of transparency in the business process, and compartmentalised information sharing within various clusters generated a culture of mistrust and power struggle among the stakeholders, as noted by one of the respondents: '*… people were not transparent, they did not want others to access the information that they hold because this would not give them power*' (V 1).

For obvious reasons, the introduction of the PMO run by armed forces was not taken positively by the DIP: It was seen as a demeaning response to their inefficiency and lack of capability to handle the project, where they had to hand over the control of that very lucrative project following the instruction of the PM's office. A perception also prevailed that DIP officials were resistant to change because the automation of passports threatened their very large extra income from the existing paper-based passport issue system. As one of the stakeholders from the DIP said, '*If outsiders get into our organisation, we will not have freedom at our work*' (DIP 3). The army's involvement ended the DIP's full power to be in charge of the project. That was evident in the concern expressed by one of the vendors, who described the DIP as the 'main actors' of the project, felt sidelined, and seemed less interested in the project.

Some form of noncooperation, if not open, was noticed by external vendors as well: '*… now the situation is like that they* [DIP people] *are happy if something goes wrong in the project, although they do not express them verbally*' (V 2). Stakeholders seemed to be bickering among themselves, and the army also expressed displeasure with the way other departments discharged their responsibilities: '*… we usually work very fast in the military. However, we do not get fast response from ministries and DIP*' (PMO 2). Such complaints were unsurprising given the complex bureaucratic processes that seemed to accompany basic information sharing among departments, leading to unnecessary delays. That was evident in the frustration expressed by one of the project officials (an army person) who complained that a simple task that could be resolved over the phone underwent an unnecessarily long process '*… they send letter after ten days or a month. It takes another few days to reply, and they reply without understanding the issue*' (PMO 1). A focus group participant (SB 1) noted that the unnecessary delays in processing information were not unrelated to a 'show of power' and the need to feel in control, leading to a lack of cooperation and inefficiency. It is believed that the difficult working relations, especially between the army and the DIP, were related to the fundamental shift made by the PM's office, which put the army in charge of the project rather than the DIP. Losing the power attribute would have made the DIP feel threatened and less in control of the project. Unproductive foreign trips and field visits were also stated as another characteristic of the government staff culture. Government officials were described as 'tourists' who went on foreign and local trips without producing reports that could aid institutional learning '*… because they do not have the technical capacity to supervise or understand the issue*' (PMO 5). A more detailed account of the associated challenges resulting from the identified complexities and their corresponding quotes is shown in Table 3.

Table 3. Complexities and associated challenges in the machine-readable passport project

Complexity	Associated challenges	Corresponding quotes and responses
Lack of stakeholder analysis and project management methodologies	Limited understanding of one's own and other people's roles	*'I did not have any prescribed job description. We were not sure if we were under the DIP. Head of DIP and chief of army did not have same understanding on the roles of army when the project started'.* (PMO 3)
	Multiple chains of command	*'I have two bosses who need to be briefed regularly, in addition to a senior government official who is interested in the project. All of these meetings were not guided by any documentary procedures or formal documentation, and I had to rely on the memory of other people at these meetings as evidence of meeting discussions'.* (PMO 3)
	Absence of a defined feedback loop or system	*'The government system does not have a feedback system either from general people or junior staff members... email accounts created are not being used, and there is no clear process to get feedback from people if they would like to report something... no internal feedback system'.* (PMO 7)
	Unspecified or undocumented duties and tasks	*'We were providing service based on verbal understanding, due to bureaucracy... they* [government officials] *have not been able to make decisions even at this critical time'.* (V 2) *'... neither the project document nor any of the consultations provided clear directions of the scope of work'.* (PMO 4)
Absence of performance and value measurements and metrics	Unproductive meetings and travel	*Inter-ministerial meetings were 'fruitless' because they did not have open discussions. Usually, the meetings would end without any fundamental decision.* (PMO 6) *'... having some cups of tea and biscuits and returning back without any conclusive decision have been our reality'.* (PMO 6) *'They made numerous foreign trips to different embassies and countries without bringing any constructive inputs to the project'.* (V 3)
	Absence of defined obligations and rules	*There is nothing called weekly meeting, project management, daily meetings, no one's work is defined, when any problem occurs everybody is pinning their heads* (PMO 7)

(continued)

Table 3. (*continued*)

Complexity	Associated challenges	Corresponding quotes and responses
Different work cultures	Complex bureaucratic processes resulting in sluggish decision-making and actions	*As a private organisation, we do not have bureaucratic decision making… we complete planned activities on time with the agreed quality* (V 1) *Government mechanism is slow to make and implement decisions* (DIP 2)
	Different perspectives, work values, and goals	*The army has a chain of command, and they follow the order of their bosses without any further delay. However, civil service has complex bureaucratic processes together with some attitudinal issues* (PMO 3)
	Nepotism and favouritism rather than due process	'*You must take actions if there is a mistake either by your friend or ally. However, they favour some and do not take any action even if the mistake is serious*'. (V 1) They do their personal jobs which benefit their family, relatives, friends, in-laws, or neighbours (V 1)
	Strong resistance to change	'*The government people although they have exposure and training, would like to maintain status quo and do not like to accommodate the change to their work*' (V 2) In the policy, they have a word '*ittadi*' (similar to 'etc.') which enables an individual to use his/her discretion. Due to this ambiguity, they request for unnecessary documents. This also creates problem to develop an automated system (PMO 1) … they portrayed the automation process as 'heavy and nonfunctional' by making the software seem useless in an effort to continue manual system and corruption efforts to get transfer to lucrative places where they can get bribes (PMO 5)
Gratification and reward	Vested interest	The government people had different personal interests (like promotion, appreciation, international trips, etc.) from the project and did not listen to the recommendations offered by different private companys about the technical and time problems of the project during development of project document (V 2)
	Power dynamics	… because of 'amlatantric jotilota' (red tapism) nobody would like to delegate and share the power that they have been enjoying (SB 2)

4   Discussion and Conclusion

This study used the salience model as a theoretical lens to analyse and understand the influence of the various stakeholder groups involved in the MRP and their effect on the project implementation and outcome. The salience model uniquely classifies stakeholders based on their attributes and considers changes that might arise due to the loss or possession of additional attributes, as well as the diverse interests and (potential) conflicts of stakeholders [35]. Based on this model, this study first identified the attributes possessed by each stakeholder group in the MRP project and their degree of salience, and second, determined the effect of this analysis in managing multiple stakeholders with competing and conflicting interests.

Surprisingly, our findings indicated that despite of the apparent importance of stakeholder analysis to aid successful project implementation [14, 18, 25], no formal analysis was undertaken at the inception of or at any point in the course of the project. Indeed, Şener, Varoğlu, and Karapolatgil [36] noted that the concept of stakeholder analysis is still in its infancy in developing countries. It is believed that the absence of such an analysis was the root cause of the complexities and challenges encountered in the project, given that multi-stakeholder interrelation in itself is a source of project complexity [18]. Conducting a critical stakeholder analysis where the degree of engagement of each stakeholder is considered, along with a detailed engagement guideline and communication plan provides the basis for managing complex stakeholder interrelations [19]. This parallels the findings of Nguyen et al. [18] who argue that 'involvement' and 'participation' are two key elements for successful stakeholder engagement in complex multi-stakeholder projects. Both elements encourage openness, dialogue, and active engagement in accordance with stakeholder classifications and attributes, mostly amongst stakeholders with power and legitimacy [18].

According to the salience model, stakeholders who have legitimacy have much weight because their influence is based upon their possession of virtues perceived to be desirable, proper, or appropriate [30, p. 869]. Hence, based on its professional portfolio, the bank was an important stakeholder in the MRP project. However, its lack of power or urgency meant it had no right or voice to empower its claims. The PMO, however, gained authority because they acquired power. At the inception of the project, the PMO had only legitimacy. However, a mandate by the definitive stakeholder, the PM's office, requested that the PMO be given additional responsibility based on their evident success in a previous project and demanded that the request be acted upon urgently. That led the DIP to lose an attribute and the PMO to gain one. The additional responsibility given to the PMO required that they take control of key responsibilities in the passport automation process, which gave them the authority to impose their will on how they believed things should be done. The acquisition of power gave PMO a higher degree of salience, and by becoming dominant stakeholders were more active and empowered to advance their interest for desired outcomes [28, 35]. It is not uncommon for stakeholders to move within different categories [26]. This was evident in the case of the police, whose movements between the dangerous and dormant stakeholder categories were dependent on circumstances. Furthermore, dependent stakeholders, in this case vendors, maintained the same degree of salience throughout the project. The DIP, on the other hand, seemed to feel threatened because they had lost the power to impose their will.

It is fundamentally assumed that all stakeholder groups and individuals engaged in a project have the same overarching goal of achieving the project objectives despite different notions of how this may be achieved [37]. However, dividing stakeholders into supply and demand stakeholders provides clear and distinct stakeholder categories early on in the project [29]. In this instance, the demand category are stakeholders for whom the project is undertaken, that is, the beneficiaries of the project outcome while the supply category are stakeholders responsible for undertaking the project through funding, design, or implementation [37]. Such categorization provides a concise distinction of stakeholders according to their perceived importance and influence on the project, their salience attributes, and how best to manage stakeholder interrelations. Further categorisation according to degree of salience will help determine a clear chain of command and reporting structure. This is especially important in a situation like the MRP project where stakeholders are directly and indirectly known to each other, either from working together or a perceived understanding of each other's fundamental duties. Although, the project did have a project director, even he seemed unsure of his actual responsibilities within the project during inception period. The current structure and organogram of the public sector organizations in many developing countries, such as Bangladesh, are not adapted to accommodate and manage digital transformation initiatives in the public sector organizations [38]. As a result, the lack of clarity of how the primary responsibilities of stakeholders based on their known portfolios translated into definite duties within the project contributed to the difficult working relations and power struggles in an apparently rigid civil service system inherited from the colonial era.

Nevertheless, the works of De' [37] and Thapa and Sæbø [29] provide evidence of how such categorization of stakeholders in IT projects in developing countries led to transparency, reduced corruption, better management of conflicts, the counteracting of other difficult circumstances such as power struggles, and it essentially clarified what was expected of each stakeholder in the supply category. This would also help to curb accusations of people not doing 'anything' as reported by one of the vendors, and unnecessary delays. Everyone knowing what is expected of the other within the project would make people, even if for the sake of saving face, put the overarching project goals and objectives over personal gains where those are clearly articulated. Overall, the study adds to our understanding of the complexities and hidden problems surrounding digital transformation in developing countries, the solution of which often becomes critical to success [39].

5   Limitations and Further Research Directions

The findings of this study offer practical and theoretical contributions for future projects requiring multi-stakeholder involvements in Bangladesh. This study has highlighted the need for stakeholder analysis at the project's inception. Because the degree of saliency; that is, the number of attributes possessed by each stakeholder, might shift back and forth from the initial analysis as stakeholders lose or acquire attributes [30], stakeholder analysis must be ongoing as the project progresses to ensure the continued balance of stakeholders' influence at different stages of the project implementation [40].

Although the salience model provides a strong basis and useful framework for classifying stakeholders based on their possession of one or more attributes, we agree with the position of Neville, Bell, and Whitwell [41] who argue that recognizing stakeholders based on the presence or absence of attributes is not sufficient. A broader classification should entail determining how much of an attribute a stakeholder possesses. For example, determining the degree of power possessed by stakeholders with that attribute provides a second layer of classification, and by extension a more precise understanding of each stakeholder's influence and their associated impact on the project. Likewise, determining the individual degrees of legitimacy and urgency possessed by each stakeholder may help determine whose claims and requests should be given priority. Hence, this study advocates that future studies should go beyond only recognising the presence or absence of attributes to determining the degree of possession before categorising stakeholders as latent, expectant, or definitive. In addition to these, future studies may consider using a complexity measurement model for a deeper categorisation of complexities resulting from multistakeholder interrelations.

References

1. Freeman, R.E.: Strategic Management: A Stakeholder Approach. Pitman, Boston (1984)
2. Huong, F.T.N.: Stakeholder salience and strategy in event tourism (2017). http://hdl.handle.net/20.500.11937/17396
3. Joos, H.C., zu Knyphausen-Aufseß, D., Pidun, U.: Project stakeholder management as the integration of stakeholder salience, public participation, and nonmarket strategies. Schmalenbach Bus. Rev. **72**(3), 447–477 (2020). https://doi.org/10.1007/s41464-020-00092-0
4. Mukherjee, S.: How stakeholder engagement affects IT projects. Int. J. Innov. Res. Sci. Eng. Technol. **8**, 3516–3518 (2019). https://doi.org/10.2139/ssrn.3415959
5. Todorow, L.: Understanding multi-stakeholder dialogues: the emerging concept of community of practice within a case study involving the UN Global Compact and the UN Principles for Responsible Investment. Bus. Peace Sustain. Dev. **2016**, 8–31 (2017)
6. Ayala-Orozco, B., et al.: Challenges and strategies in place-based multi-stakeholder collaboration for sustainability: learning from experiences in the Global South. Sustain. **10** (2018). https://doi.org/10.3390/su10093217
7. San Cristóbal, J.R., Carral, L., Diaz, E., Fraguela, J.A., Iglesias, G.: Complexity and project management: a general overview. Complexity **2018** (2018). https://doi.org/10.1155/2018/4891286
8. Pade-Khene, C., et al.: Complexity of stakeholder interaction in applied research. Ecol. Soc. **18** (2013). https://doi.org/10.5751/ES-05405-180213
9. Metar, U.: Stakeholder engagement in mega projects. https://www.linkedin.com/pulse/stakeholder-engagement-mega-projects-umesh-metar-pmp-pmi-rmp/?trk=public_profile_article_view. Accessed 30 Oct 2021
10. Heravi, A., Coffey, V., Trigunarsyah, B.: Evaluating the level of stakeholder involvement during the project planning processes of building projects. Int. J. Proj. Manag. **33**, 985–997 (2015)
11. Kowalska, O., Haniff, A.P.: Stakeholder complexity and the impact on the perceptions of project success. In: 25th International EurOMA Conference, pp. 1–10 (2018)
12. Ovi, I.H.: Bureaucratic lethargy making doing business difficult. https://www.dhakatribune.com/business/economy/2020/12/18/bureaucratic-lethargy-making-doing-business-difficult. Accessed 8 Dec 2021

13. Adnan, T.M.: Stakeholder management in complex projects: an empirical case study (2018). http://jultika.oulu.fi/files/nbnfioulu-201808312685.pdf
14. Chigona, W., Roode, D., Nazeer, N., Pinnock, B.: Investigating the impact of stakeholder management on the implementation of a public access project: the case of Smart Cape. South African J. Bus. Manag. **41**, 39–50 (2010). https://doi.org/10.4102/sajbm.v41i2.517
15. Spangenberg, J.H., et al.: Doing what with whom? Stakeholder analysis in a large transdisciplinary research project in South-East Asia. Paddy Water Environ. **16**(2), 321–337 (2018). https://doi.org/10.1007/s10333-018-0634-2
16. Ginige, K., Amaratunga, D., Haigh, R.: Mapping stakeholders associated with societal challenges: a methodological framework. Procedia Eng. **212** (2018)
17. Van Niekerk, M.: The applicability and usefulness of the stakeholder strategy matrix for festival management. Event Manag. **20**, 165–179 (2016). https://doi.org/10.3727/152599516 X14610017108666
18. Nguyen, T.S., Mohamed, S., Panuwatwanich, K.: Stakeholder management in complex project: review of contemporary literature. J. Eng. Proj. Prod. Manag. **8**, 75–89 (2018). https://doi.org/10.32738/jeppm.201807.0003
19. Allen, W., Kilvington, M.: Stakeholder analysis. In: Frame, B., Gordon, R., Mortimer, C. (eds.) Hatched: The Capacity for Sustainable Development, pp. 249–253 (2010)
20. Bryson, J.M., Patton, M.Q., Bowman, R.A.: Working with evaluation stakeholders: a rationale, step-wise approach and toolkit. Eval. Program Plann. **34**, 1–12 (2011). https://doi.org/10.1016/j.evalprogplan.2010.07.001
21. Puranik, S., Bremdal, B.A.: Smart system of renewable energy storage based on INtegrated EVs and bAtteries to empower mobile, Distributed and centralised Energy storage in the distribution grid (2017)
22. Slabá, M.: Stakeholder power-interest matrix and stakeholder-responsibility matrix in corporate social responsibility. In: The 8th International Days of Statistics and Economics, pp. 1366–1374 (2014)
23. Kapiriri, L., Donya Razavi, S.: Salient stakeholders: using the salience stakeholder model to assess stakeholders' influence in healthcare priority setting. Heal. Policy OPEN. **2**, 100048 (2021). https://doi.org/10.1016/j.hpopen.2021.100048
24. Donaldson, T., Preston, L.E.: The stakeholder theory of the corporation: concepts, evidence, and implications. Acad. Manag. Rev. **20**, 65–91 (1995)
25. Ilinova, A., Cherepovitsyn, A., Evseeva, O.: Stakeholder management: an approach in CCS projects. Resources **7**, 1–16 (2018). https://doi.org/10.3390/resources7040083
26. Powell, P., Walsh, A.: Whose curriculum is it anyway? Stakeholder salience in the context of degree apprenticeships. High. Educ. Q. **72**, 90–106 (2018)
27. Ortega, C.P., Hernandez, M.J., Martí, E.G., Vallejo-Martos, M.: The stakeholder salience model revisited: evidence from Agri-Food cooperatives in Spain. Sustainability **11**, 1–14 (2019). https://doi.org/10.3390/su11030574
28. Jonsson, N., Yacobucci, I.: A more sustainable society through stakeholder salience: furthering stakeholder theory by exploring identification and prioritization processes with a focus on intraorganizational perceptions in an SME (2019)
29. Thapa, D., Sæbø, Ø.: How to scale ICT4D projects: a salience stakeholder perspective. In: Proceedings of the 12th International Conference on Social Implications of Computers in Developing Countries, Ocho Rios, Jamaica, pp. 741–752 (2012)
30. Mitchell, R.K., Agle, B.R., Wood, D.J.: Toward a theory of stakeholder identification and salience: defining the principle of who and what really counts. Acad. Manag. Rev. **22**, 853–886 (1997). https://doi.org/10.5465/AMR.1997.9711022105
31. Klein, H.K., Myers, M.D.: A set of principles for conducting and evaluating interpretive field studies in information systems. MIS Q. **23**, 67–93 (1999)

32. Walsham, G.: Doing interpretive research. Eur. J. Inf. Syst. **15**, 320–330 (2006)
33. Varga-Atkins, T., Bunyan, N., McIsaac, J., Fewtrell, J.: The nominal group technique: a practical guide for facilitators (2011)
34. Søndergaard, E., Ertmann, R.K., Reventlow, S., Lykke, K.: Using a modified nominal group technique to develop general practice. BMC Fam. Pract. **19**, 1–9 (2018). https://doi.org/10.1186/s12875-018-0811-9
35. Park, H.S., Lee, Y.H.: Exploring a process model for stakeholder management. Public Relat. J. **9**, 1–17 (2015)
36. Şener, İ, Varoğlu, A., Karapolatgil, A.A.: Sustainability reports disclosures: who are the most salient stakeholders? Procedia Soc. Behav. Sci. **235**, 84–92 (2016). https://doi.org/10.1016/j.sbspro.2016.11.028
37. De', R.: E-government systems in developing countries: stakeholders and conflict. In: Wimmer, M.A., Traunmüller, R., Grönlund, Å., Andersen, K.V. (eds.) EGOV 2005. LNCS, vol. 3591, pp. 26–37. Springer, Heidelberg (2005). https://doi.org/10.1007/11545156_3
38. Hussain, B., Imran, A., Turner, T.: Key challenges for establishing CIO position in the public sector of LDCs: a case of Bangladesh. Paper presented at the 27th Australasian Conference on Information Systems, Wollongong, 5–7 December 2016
39. Imran, A., Gregor, S.: Uncovering the hidden issues in e-government adoption in a least developed country: the case of Bangladesh. J. Glob. Inf. Manag. **18**, 30–56 (2010)
40. Axelsson, K., Melin, U., Lindgren, I.: Stakeholder salience changes in an e-government implementation project. In: Wimmer, M.A., Janssen, M., Scholl, H.J. (eds.) International Federation for Information Processing, pp. 237–249 (2013)
41. Neville, B.A., Bell, S.J., Whitwell, G.J.: Stakeholder salience revisited: refining, redefining, and refueling an underdeveloped conceptual tool. J. Bus. Ethics. **102**, 357–378 (2011). https://doi.org/10.1007/s10551-011-0818-9

From Digital Divide to Digital Discovery: Re-thinking Online Learning and Interactions in Marginalized Communities

Lay-Wah Carolina Ching-Chiang[1,3]([⊠]) [iD], Juan Manuel Fernández-Cárdenas[1,3] [iD],
Nicole Lotz[2,3] [iD], Noé Abraham González-Nieto[2,3] [iD], Mark Gaved[2,3] [iD],
Derek Jones[1,3] [iD], Alejandra Díaz de León[1,3] [iD], and Rafael Machado[4,3]

[1] Tecnologico de Monterrey, Monterrey, México
Lay.ching@tec.mx
[2] The Open University, Milton Keynes, UK
[3] Universidad Autónoma Metropolitana, Mexico City,, México
[4] Insitu, Monterrey, México

Abstract. The digital divide presented between the Global South and North has been exacerbated due to the Covid-19 pandemic causing unequal access to technologies in education, public services, and healthcare. Through an exploratory study in the northeastern region of Mexico, a marginalized community used a hyperlocal network to engage in creative Science, Technology, Engineering, Arts and Mathematics (STEAM) activities. The study uses a qualitative methodology with a reflective approach, informed by sociocultural and dialogic concepts. Data collection primarily involved semi-structured interviews, observations, focus groups, and collection of artifacts. The findings present a rich framework of sociocultural factors and capital knowledge from the community. From the study emerged participants' meanings in three categories: i) the use of offline mobile learning, ii) the educational practices in the non-formal context, and iii) the dialogic opportunities created among participants. From this non-formal context of education experience emerged creative lessons in innovation, agency from the learners, and genuine involvement from the participants.

Keywords: Digital divide · Marginalized communities · Dialogic learning

1 Introduction

The Covid-19 pandemic has caused a lockdown of the entire world, resulting in a global scramble to learn and master new forms of interactions at work and school, within families, across communities, and beyond national boundaries. In the field of education, learning opportunities have been reduced by the pandemic because moving education to a predominantly online modality implies reliable and affordable access to the Internet and electronic devices. Despite the assumption that the world could have been ready for

Published by Springer Nature Switzerland AG 2022
J. Abdelnour-Nocera et al. (Eds.): *Innovation Practices for Digital Transformation in the Global South*, IFIP AICT 645, pp. 34–58, 2022.
https://doi.org/10.1007/978-3-031-12825-7_3

distance and online interactions thanks to widespread usage of information and communication technologies (ICTs), the reality is that the pandemic made visible the challenges that many low-income communities face, in terms of education, public services and healthcare, that were broadened due to unequal access to ICT. These challenges demonstrated a clear divide between the Global North and Global South [1], greatly impacting educational systems and opportunities, especially for traditionally marginalized communities in the South. Furthermore, individuals have not yet developed the digital and future competencies to develop their own identities in a digitally connected world [2, 3] because access to digital technologies is not the only condition for contributing to distance learning, but also the ability to use and appropriate them [4].

In the specific case of Mexico, official data provided from the National Institute of Statistics and Geography [5] in the most recent National Survey on Availability and Use of Information Technologies in Households (ENDUTIH) highlighted the disparity in access to ICT: 55.7% of Mexican households do not have computers and of these, 55.3% attributed this to the lack of economic resources. Moreover, only 56.4% of the households reported a connection to the Internet. Unequal access to ICT has impacted the continuity of education during the pandemic. In marginalized areas, very few students have a permanent Internet connection and devices to attend online classes. During the pandemic confinement, students in marginalized areas are faced with (1) complete drop out of schooling, or (2) having poorer quality education in a formal learning setting. The government's distance education strategy has been to implement a television program series called "Aprende en casa" ["Learning at home"] for primary and secondary schools, which has been a strategy that aimed to cover the majority of the Mexican population, as 92.5% of the population reported having at least one television [5]. In these educational procedures, "teachers assign homework and other learning activities and receive evidence of activities conducted at home" [6] aided using digital and established technologies, such as Internet connections (Learning Management Systems, Email, text messaging, Videoconference, etc.) or phone calls. Nevertheless, 30% of the teachers have reported not having additional contact with their students [7].

Joining an online class has meant that students need to complete their homework in physical notebooks and use their limited Internet access to send schoolwork through applications like Facebook or WhatsApp. The lack of access to technology has widened educational disparities and hindered development opportunities for people in marginalized communities [8]. It is under these circumstances that the Hyperlocal Learning Network La Campana-Altamira was born. The leading research question is: How informal learning opportunities in social settings and using offline networked and mobile ICT engage a marginalized community in authentic educational practices during the pandemic?

'Hyperlocal La Campana-Altamira' has used Raspberry Pis, credit card sized computers that run on open-source software and can create neighborhood digital networks independent of the global Internet, as hubs for local community networking and learning during the Covid-19 pandemic. The project, based on a social justice agenda, aimed to create more equitable access to informal STEAM learning through creative making activities facilitated by low-cost offline ICT. In a prior project, the co-creation of a community FabLab in a local high school[1], a plurality of pathways to learn through informal opportunities had been established and lessons were learned by all participants from the community and from the higher education institutions involved [3, 9]. The development of relevant skills and the motivation to learn needed to be maintained during the pandemic when the FabLab community was closed in March 2020. In the long term, a series of interventions took place aiming at narrowing the digital divide gap and providing quality education and socio-economic development opportunities in the community. Using hyperlocal learning networks and hands-on creative making kits in a marginalized community setting in Monterrey, a northeastern city of Mexico, was a reaction to the further marginalization during the pandemic, but it also aimed to test the potential for alternative ways of constructing inclusive and creative learning environments for the future.

2 Introduction

2.1 STEAM Education

STEAM stands for Science, Technology, Engineering, Arts, and Mathematics. Its pedagogic approaches support the creative integration of skills and knowledge from those disciplines in project-based inquiry, often, at least in face-to-face settings, through social dialogic engagement with others. STEAM education is a concept that derives from the global North and hence needs critical consideration. STEAM education is influenced by a complex interplay of local and global forces [10]. The global economy is still held up by some as a panacea for inequality but is simultaneously shown to be propagating as many inequalities as it is solving. STEAM education might be similarly contradictory, being seen as a universal driving force for international development, but also accentuating social and cultural inequalities. In other words, even if education is a powerful tool to restructure the existing social order, this is only true if educational practices develop a critical consciousness in students by inviting them to bring their personal understandings of their own learning experiences [11]. In this respect, project-based STEAM activities may allow learners to incorporate and critically evaluate scientific and artistic knowledge in everyday life through the lens of local skills derived from their lived experiences [12]. We also suggest that this approach is a 'constructive alliance' between epistemologies of the Global North and Global South, aiming for a decolonised education [13].

---

[1] The fabrication laboratory (FabLab) was installed in 2019 in Monterrey, Mexico, to promote the 'maker' culture involving an agenda of cognitive and social justice through the implementation of a "platform for the democratization of educational practices through the inclusion of participants from different settings, countries and ages, collaborating in the achievement of common goals, while stimulating creative thinking, and strengthening the bonding with participants and their needs" (González-Nieto, et al., 2020, p. 1535).

In several countries, the engagement with STEAM subjects in schools and other non-formal settings has led to its integration into educational policies [14, 15]. Huge emphasis has been placed on the development of STEAM skills for their significance in economic growth and has thus encouraged the development of research in this area in the last decade, particularly focusing on the development of human capital. In North-Eastern Mexico, where Monterrey is located, major social and economic issues are related to, and underpinned by, low engagement with STEAM education. Expanding engagement and emphasis on STEAM would be critical if we are to see improvements in the quality of work for marginalized groups and communities. Consequently, the longer-term benefits of this project aim to generate open spaces for educational innovation to improve social conditions in vulnerable communities.

Monterrey is the largest city of the state of Nuevo León in the North of Mexico and the second largest city in the country. The metropolitan area of Monterrey holds 93% of the population of the entire region (around 5 million people) with 97 men per 100 women. Despite industrial development, Monterrey presents a high number of people in conditions of poverty (19%) and extreme poverty (1.3%). Mexico's rates of daily pay are low; both Mexico and Nuevo León present low gross salaries for the population, averaging a weekly pay of only £70. These are the reasons why we are looking at this intervention in Monterrey through a lens of social justice and decoloniality in the *Global South*.

2.2 Global South

The term *Global South* has been employed by policy makers and academics who have used it to embed multiple meanings and evoke different ideologies. While authors like Dados and Connell [16] consider the *Global South,* a transnational space encompassing Africa, Asia, Latin America, and Oceania, other authors like Esler [17] have used the term interchangeably with *Third World.* Both conceptions have shown limitations. The *Global South* as a geographic space assumes the entire south of the globe as a single region. However, the cases of China, Russia, India, Brazil and Mexico give us lights that counterfeit those assumptions. We cannot assume that the global south is a single region. In the second interpretation of the *Global South,* as interchangeable with the term *Third World*, the limitation is that it portrays racial, religious, political, economic and historical views. In a genealogy construction, the Latin American historian Palomino [18] points out that the terms suggest two different ideas: one being a political affirmation and the other as an expert assessment of a problem.

Thus, a proposal for the term *Global South* in Latin America requires consideration of its colonial history, neo-imperialism, social change and economic development. In that regard, Mahler [19] points to the use of the *Global South* to address spaces and people negatively impacted by capitalist globalization. This broader conception responds to the limitations of *geographic space* and *third world* interpretations for Latin America. Here, the *Global South* term emphasizes the geo-political marker of inequality as well as the impact of globalization in the community. The research in this paper makes use of this conception of the *Global South* to point out precisely the impact of capitalist globalization for a marginalized community in Monterrey in which the study was carried out. Before the pandemic, this community was already characterized by inequality and difficulties in accessing quality science and technological education and related resources.

2.3 Sociocultural Perspective

The concept of the *Global South* term calls for the study to consider a sociocultural perspective in which a dialogic and decolonial approach are fundamental to make the study *for and from* the Latin American context. The empirical work carried out through the Hyperlocal Learning Network La Campana-Altamira - which we refer to in the text by its abbreviated form, 'Hyperlocal', is informed by a **sociocultural perspective** in which the construction of knowledge is mediated by cultural factors which are appropriated and mastered by participants in communities of practice [20–23]. Cultural artifacts, language, and social institutions are tools that can produce cognitive change [24] and transformative learning [25]. In that sense, following a sociocultural perspective, this study emphasizes the understanding of how participants engaged in the design and making of activities. It is the experience and interactions with sociocultural tools provided which became the focus for learning.

Moreover, in this sociocultural perspective, **the dialogic approach** [26–29] becomes fundamental for participants to examine their circumstances of oppression, and relationships among them and with technology. Under this dialogic perspective it is relevant to give a voice to the participants to understand how they are building knowledge, rather than just assimilating instructions and information. Hyperlocal aimed to provide an opportunity to use technology as a catalyst for participants to reflect on their lived history through dialogic and creative scenarios that bloomed with the development of STEAM activities. Similar studies [3, 30] in informal contexts of education have supported the impact of dialogic learning through such enrichment programs, which offer opportunities to explore and study arts and sciences coupled with occasions for emotional development and historization. Freire [26] proposes that the individual becomes conscious of their world and is positioned to have a critical view of their own circumstances, thanks to their relationship with others. Learners become inquirers and builders of their own knowledge and become able to liberate themselves from oppressive 'banking' educational systems, and as a result they redesign and transform the tools according to their circumstances. Very importantly, learners also realize that they become more capable and creative than they originally considered.

Similarly, under the umbrella of a **decolonial perspective** in technology and education, the historization process provided by the dialogic perspective frames this study. Decoloniality and decolonial thinking highlights the pluriverse of systems of knowledge and thought beyond the colonial framework [31]. In that sense, decolonial thinking implies engaging in educational and technological practices that think outside of the categories, hierarchies, and antagonist binary categories of coloniality (individual vs. community, society vs. nature, immanence vs. transcendence) to think more relationally. De Sousa Santos [32] proposes the concept of 'epistemologies of the South' to understand the transformation occurring in our societies, realizing that theories have been based and developed on the experiences from only the side of the North. Therefore, in the knowledge frameworks of education and technology, the study invites participants to challenge themselves to think about who gets to use a tool or service, and to which extent. Moreover, De Sousa Santos [1] claims that this pandemic era can be used as an opportunity to deconstruct the oppression of socioeconomic ways of living linked to capitalism, colonialism, and patriarchy, thus becoming more appreciative of the plurality of lifestyles that can be more relational, sustainable, and caring of others and that are already a way of living in rural, marginalized, and indigenous communities in the *Global South*. De Sousa Santos invites all of us to realize that it is possible to live a different life, and for that, a starting point is to appreciate diversity and multiculturalism, and to be creative in proposing new socioeconomic activities that can be more respectful of each other.

Similarly, the sociocultural and dialogic perspectives offered through the experience of STEAM activities opens the floor to a dialogic space, which can also be an opportunity to realize the potential and capacities one has as a person, as a member of a community, and of a living world with a nature to protect and care. Therefore, the dialogic engagement in which participants, the project team, and community partners were involved, incorporates aspects of reality into the shared sense of identity [33]. Thus, we were aiming to understand dialogic spaces to identify the value participants have for transforming their own circumstances together.

3 Methodology

3.1 Context and Participants

La Campana-Altamira are two neighbouring hills in Monterrey, Mexico, and have traditionally been an urban marginalized area. The first projects to populate the hills aimed at creating housing for public teachers, but corruption cases hindered development, and semi-constructed buildings were left unfinished. As a result of the abandonment of the houses, the hills were later populated mainly by internal migrants from San Luis Potosí, Oaxaca, and Chiapas, who were looking for economic opportunities in Monterrey. The resulting settlements lack urbanization planning, which negatively impacts the socioeconomic opportunities of their inhabitants, for example due to difficult access up and down the steep inclines.

Since 2013, Tecnologico de Monterrey, a higher education institution neighbouring the La Campana-Altamira district, has implemented social program initiatives in the area through Distrito Tec, an urban regeneration initiative promoted by this university. Distrito Tec leads the Campana-Altamira Initiative which looks to engage the community in six lines of action: Social Security and Peace, Social Inclusion, Urban Inclusion, Economic Inclusion, Education, Housing, and Health. Distrito Tec incorporates private and public institutions including CEMEX, Monterrey municipality, and Nuevo Leon state government to implement the Campana-Altamira initiative.

In the line of Education, Distrito Tec supported the creation of the 'Fab Lab Campana-Altamira' [3, 9] because it fit the overall strategy of creating opportunities to provide access to quality STEAM education to the community. This was led by researchers who are now part of the Hyperlocal project. For Distrito Tec, these projects are seeds that support the overall initiative. In that line, the Hyperlocal project accomplished two purposes for them. First, with the pandemic, it was challenging to maintain projects and ways to reach out to community members due to the lockdown regulations and lack of access to ICT devices. It was also difficult for the community to reconnect with fellow learners and to maintain a sense of shared learning from the safety of their homes, especially because the community's priority was the need for basic sustenance. Second, this opened a relationship with the people at the top of the hill. These participants are usually left out of projects because of the difficulty of access. The topology of the district meant that the people at the top of the hill were the most forgotten during the pandemic. The idea of education continuity attracted participants who lacked access to resources from the bottom of the hill.

Hyperlocal was proposed by an international intervention team, including three researchers from the Open University (UK), three from Tecnologico de Monterrey, one from UAM Cuajimalpa, one from In Situ, and supported by one researcher from La Campana Altamira Initiative from Distrito Tec, our implementation partner. Distrito Tec helped us contact the community at the top of the hills by accompanying us to visit and talk to them about the project of STEAM activities from their homes. Their experience with social design projects guided us, and they emphasized the importance of avoiding an interventionist approach but rather, the value of taking a more participatory approach, ensuring we listened to the community and recognised the capital and knowledge resources they could bring to the project.

Thus, ideas from and for them emerged from their side during the project. For example, it was the community participants who decided where we could hold the meetings, and who organized the catering for the end of project celebratory event.

The overarching aim was to continue to engage La Campana Altamira community members in informal, creative, maker-based learning in a social setting during the pandemic to continue developing relevant skills and sustain the motivation to learn and change. We also wanted to test an 'offline' (not connected to the internet) networked social and mobile learning approach with the community. This approach was corroborated by the community leaders we consulted with and supported by informal feedback and observations from other interventions with the community, as well as during the planning of this intervention. The academic and social initiative teams also intended to test the scope of bringing maker education into family homes, rather than the families' coming into a community makerspace, with the aim to reach a broader audience.

Eleven families participated in the Hyperlocal project. Table 1 lists the anonymized names of the adults and children (aged 5–15) who expressed their desire and consented formally to their participation in the project. Later, during the interview process, the research team realized that there were more family members who had become engaged with the project, such as husbands, cousins, and friends. For research ethics reasons, we did not engage directly with these additional 'peripheral participants' but gathered insights into their perspectives through participants who had formally given their consent.

Table 1. Participants from the Hyperlocal project

Family ID	Adults	Children (age)
F1	Martha	Yolanda (12), Pepe (10)
F2	Ivanna	Noah (15), Francesca (6)
F3	Lucía	Aracely (11), Edgar (10)
F4	Isolda	Josefina (11), Ari (7)
F5	Noelle	Lola (12), Marco (9), Miriam (6)
F6	Katy	Amanda (11)
F7	Lily	Brad (5)
F8	Victoria	Juan (9)
F9	Salomé	Gloria (13), Yarezi (12), Emilia (6)
F10	Lime	Alondra (13)
F11	Danuska	Irene (11)

The project was also carried out with the participation of a project team consisting of 8 researchers and 12 undergraduate students from Tecnologico de Monterrey who supported the design, implementation, and celebration phases of the project.

3.2 Tools

To trial the planned approach of using STEAM to engage families during lockdown, the research team designed a craft kit with the materials to engage in established STEAM learning activities. The kit, to be issued to each family, contained materials such as fabric, markers, sewing kits, tape, ruler, papers, glycerin, molds, scented essential oil, among others as seen in Fig. 1. As a result of the successful prior interventions with engagement of some of the community members in creative maker-based learning in a community FabLab, the academic team members proposed four creative activities (Decoder, Draw-bot, Soap making and face mask) that could be carried out at the families' homes to re-engage them in informal learning during the pandemic. All these creative making activities were previously used successfully in the community FabLab and were known to create fun and dialogic engagement and social learning opportunities suitable across different age ranges. In a design education setting, creative making activities develop a sense of agency over what is made and encourage reflection on the purpose of the making and the maker [34–36] particularly when such activity is authentic in, or to, some context [37]. Furthermore, creative learning at a distance benefit from social comparison and collaboration amongst the learners [38]. The Open University provided the funding to purchase the necessary materials and technologies to enable the participants to engage in such learning opportunities, while respecting pandemic lockdown and social distancing regulations.

Fig. 1. Craft Kit for the families

To enable sharing of family activities and to encourage sharing locally, Hyperlocal sought to test the viability of hyperlocal digital networks operating independently of the internet. The project employed a digital platform, MAZI [www.MAZIzone.eu], an open-source software toolset running on Wi-Fi capable small low-cost computers, Raspberry Pis. The MAZI networking software facilitates sharing in community settings, enabling devices such as smartphones, tablets, and laptops to access a common hub and share resources with each other, via Wi-Fi. This hyperlocal network supports dialogic learning approaches by building a networked learning space. Participants can contribute to and receive information from the network furthering opportunities of peer learning. Peer learning is underpinned by dialogic opportunities that arise from interaction around artifacts created and shared online [38]. The hyperlocal network tools enable the community to share their own knowledge and learning locally without a reliance on external network connectivity (internet access). The advantage of this 'offline networked learning' approach [39] is the decoupling of access to knowledge from the socio-technical and economic conditions of the participants.

The MAZI digital platform is available with a set of standard configurations, and the research team customized these to offer Hyperlocal participants three components: *Aprende, Comparte, and Comparte más* (Learn, Share and Share More) as seen in Fig. 2. In the *Aprende* section, families could access preloaded educational videos and guides, in *Comparte* the functionality allowed them to upload pictures and make comments, and in the last section they were able to upload videos and other types of files. Conceptually, the research team wanted to offer (a) the opportunity to access guidance, (b) to start conversations with each around their activity outputs and (c) to engage in extended sharing activities, including videos. The conversational tool (the open-source program "Guestbook" had been designed for the exchange of images and short messages), so to enable video sharing within the limitations of this pilot, the team activated a file sharing program (NextCloud) as *Comparte más*. Each hub offered instructions for four initial creative learning activities for the entire family at their homes. The videos and guides supported making a message decoding device; face masks; soap and a drawing robot.

Fig. 2. MAZI Platform as seen by participants

3.3 Phases of the Intervention

The intervention with the families consisted of three phases: planning, implementation, and celebration.

The *planning phase* with the families started with a series of conversations about the project proposal, and how to implement it within the community. This involved the calling and selection of participants who were willing to be part of the project, and for this action, the Distrito Tec insider knowledge of the community was particularly important. A technical test was carried out to find out the most appropriate homes to place the Raspberry Pis, trialing various locations that would give the best hyperlocal network coverage, considering the short Wi-Fi range (approximately 20 m) of the Pis, and the topography of the hills. After the testing, the team decided to deploy five Pis, seen in Fig. 3. By proximity, at least two families were able to access one Raspberry Pi. However, other members of the nearby hubs could visit and comment on families' contributions and upload their own responses.

Fig. 3. Approximate location of participants. The blue dots represent the participants, and the red dots represent the Raspberry Pis locations. (Color figure online)

For the *implementation phase*, the research team visited the families to give them a craft kit and the smartphone for the project. Each family was given a craft kit with the materials to engage in established STEAM learning activities. Families were also given a smartphone and sim card to access and engage with the hyperlocal network through the Raspberry Pis running the MAZI digital platform. Families were supported during the intervention with a team of academics leading the study and undergraduate students who were doing their community service program. The academics leading the team made weekly visits in which they presented the craft kits, deployed the Pis, and solved technical issues that could not be solved remotely. The undergraduate students' roles included contacting the families by phone calls weekly as a follow-up to understand the progress of activities, and to channel technical difficulties.

For example, during the first week of this phase, families reported that they could not upload pictures to the MAZI platform. As a result, the team designed a step-by-step procedure on how to upload the pictures that were handed to participants. The second week, the families reported the same issue, so a team was deployed. In that technical visit the team realized that there was an issue with software configuration: the maximum file size to be uploaded was set to a small default size. This had become a limitation because the phones were taking pictures with a larger default size. The team tried to decrease the quality resolution in the smartphone camera, but it did not work. During the third week, the team was able to change the setting in the Raspberry Pis.

The *celebration phase* consisted of the team and the families planning a day to share the results of the four activities the families had engaged with and sharing a meal together. The Hyperlocal team printed photos of the project for displaying during the celebration. The families took charge of getting tables, chairs and supplying the food. During this celebration day, the children presented their projects and were given a diploma for participating. Each child had a picture taken with the diploma and then a group picture (See Fig. 4). After that, a focus group interview was carried out with the mothers. Then, the mothers served food they had cooked: tacos, three colour jelly and fruits.

Fig. 4. Celebration day

3.4 Reflective Approach

As outlined before, reflection is an important component for the Hyperlocal project, the contextualization of this reflection is as important as the content of the reflections. In particular, the application of the theoretical lenses of horizontal dialogic spaces [3] were integral to our reflection process. These reflections were informed by the data collected from the participants' engagements during the Hyperlocal intervention. We used a critical stance informed by Freire and contemporary dialogic theory revised above these lines.

Data collection came from semi structured interviews, field notes, a focus group and the MAZI Platform as detailed in Table 2.

Table 2. Data collected

Instrument	Amount	Description
Semi structured interviews - Set 1	11	Done at the beginning of the project to create rapport with participants
Semi structured interviews - Set 2	26	Done during the project to do a follow up about the four activities that the participants were making
Focus group	1	Done at the end of the project for the participants to share their experience with the activities, the raspberry Pi and issues they face with the project
Fieldnotes	6	Done from the first visit to share about the project with participants until the celebratory event at the end of the project
Raspberry Pis (MAZI platform)	5	The information (photos, videos and comments) that was collected from the 5 Raspberry Pis

Using a qualitative approach [40, 41] the data was coded inductively, and grouped to form categories which help to provide an answer to the research question of this paper: *How can informal learning opportunities in social settings and using offline networked and mobile ICT reflectively engage a marginalized community in authentic educational practices during the pandemic, and what change processes can be observed in this community?*

This research question was answered following an emic perspective. Pike [42] proposed a distinction between phonemic and phonetics, which has been taken up by social scientists interested in highlighting the personal and situated adjustments and interpretations that an agent makes of culture. This is a contemporary approach in anthropology [43, 44] which privileges an *emic* perspective where participants interpret social interactions and practices in their own terms versus a more normalized and imposed view of culture (an *etic* perspective).

The international research team held weekly reflective online discussions between 2020 and 2021, initially to plan the design of the study and later to discuss the categorization of the data for evaluation of the intervention. Notes were taken and this resulted in a collaborative 86-page record. Through these reflections we attempted to uncover any processes of social change in the participants who engaged in the Hyperlocal network, including the intervention team.

4 Findings

Three main themes emerged inductively from the data analysis: i) the use of offline networked mobile learning, ii) the educational practices in the non-formal context, and iii) the dialogic opportunities. Within these themes the participants' emic perspective was documented in categories and is presented below.

4.1 The Use of Offline Networked Mobile Learning

The first theme, the use of offline networked mobile learning, is related to how participants used the Raspberry Pis, MAZI platform, and smartphone to engage in the learning activities. The use of offline networked mobile learning as described in Tables 3 and 4 offers a general view of the participants' interactions with the technology.

Table 3. Data in the Raspberry Pis

Raspberry Pi	Families	Photos	Comments	Videos
R1	F1-F2	1	0	1
R2	F9-F10-F11	1	0	0
R3	F5-F6	0	0	0
R4	F7-F8	10	0	4
R5	F3-F4	31	4	4

Table 3 summarizes the data that the families uploaded into the *Comparte and Comparte más* sections of the MAZI organized by Raspberry Pi. The table shows which families accessed each Raspberry Pi and the number of photos, comments, and videos they uploaded. The Raspberry with the most content was number 5 from families 3 and 4. The content with less uploads was "comments", and the one with the most was "photos".

Table 4 has sample content uploaded by participants to the MAZI. From the 43 photos uploaded, only in one of them do adults appear, but in the background. Of the four comments, one is a greeting and the other three are related to creative activities (soap making).

Category 1: Engagement with Technology. Participants found the use of offline networked mobile learning easy, which propelled the thinking of the future uses of technology. The use of the Raspberry Pi to access information allowed participants to explore possibilities that transcended their own prior experiences with technology and offered wider perspectives of how it might be used in the future. The use of this offline network in

Table 4. Samples of content uploaded to the MAZI

Photos	Comments	Videos

Hyperlocal triggered their thinking about the possibilities of this technology for formal education. Transcript 1 is a conversation between a researcher, and two participants, a mother, and her daughter, about the use of the Raspberry Pi.

Transcript 1. The use of the offline network mobile learning for formal education

Luna: What did you learn from the use of technology in your life? Did it leave you any experience having used the Raspberry or the cell phone? How was your experience watching the videos from the Raspberry?

Josefina: From the Raspberry it was quite easy to use and connect.

Luna: What will be easier to watch the videos from the Raspberry or from YouTube?

Josefina: With the device, it is more direct and nothing more.

Salomé: Well, it was fast, you go in and see the video that you wanted to see.

Luna: If your teacher brought you the class videos in the Raspberry, would you use it?

Salomé: Definitely, it will be easier. In that way, it is all there easier to access and watch.

In this transcript, the participants reflect on the ease of accessing videos from the offline network (Raspberry Pi and MAZI) compared to the online networks (cellphone, internet) they may already use. Salomé mentions how the device was fast and helped in the development of the activities. Here it is important to consider that the topography of the participants at the top of the hill was problematic, and limited access to fast and reliable global Internet connections, making the use of an offline device a faster alternative. Moreover, when Luna questioned Salomé about the use of the Raspberry for a formal education, Salomé answered that she would use it and that it would be easier.

Category 2: Catalyst for Reconnecting. The use of offline networked mobile learning was a tool to propel sharing. Participants encountered a limitation with the use of the Raspberry Pi to share information in the *Comparte and Comparte más section* because the photo sharing tool was initially set to only allow 2 Mb photos, which was the default setting. This became problematic because the default size of an image taken by the mobile phone provided was bigger than 2 Mb. However, instead of not sharing their making activities with others, participants pursued workarounds to satisfy their desire to socially share the result of making with their neighbors and relatives using ICTs. Isolda told the team *"My daughter sent it [a photo of the decoder creation] to her cousin through WhatsApp, so they were sharing ideas on how to improve the model"* and Lily said *"Before the pandemic I used to meet with Lucía outside and talk while washing clothes. During Hyperlocal, I met her to talk about the project and share what we were doing and how to solve the technology issues" (Field Note 3)*. In both examples, we can see that technology served as a catalyst to reconnect with other participants as it served as a new (local) platform that was available to people of this community. Therefore, they found a new place in which they can share not only their results but also the process they established to complete the making activities.

4.2 The Educational Practices in the Non-formal Context During the Pandemic

Hyperlocal was developed in the framework of a non-formal educational context during the juncture of the Covid-19 pandemic. During the implementation of the project, families had been confined for 13 months and the children had only had intermittent opportunities to access quality formal education. Hyperlocal was a non-formal opportunity to engage families in educational opportunities. The dynamics of that framework are expressed in the following categories:

Category 3: Motivations. Participants had different motivations to join the program, such as: mothers or grandmothers looking for an educational experience for children; upgrading knowledge; and spending time together. For instance, during an observation, Lucía (a mother) shared that she wanted her children to be part of Hyperlocal because she had previous experiences with opportunities offered by Tecnológico de Monterrey and Distrito Tec such as sports and painting programs. So, she expected Hyperlocal to also help her children in their educational experience. Similarly, For Ivanna, a grandmother, there is a willingness that her granddaughter *"could improve her knowledge with what she is currently learning in school" (Interview-Initial)*. Finally, Katty, another mother, mentioned *"My neighbor told me. My girl likes to do arts & crafts and she says is friends with the other girl. I wanted her to get along with my girl more because sometimes she is really withdrawn, and I'd like to have more time with her (Field Note 4)"*.

In these three cases, adults are willing that their offspring are part of this project as a way to deepen their learning. They are motivated by seeking to achieve more opportunities within and beyond the community, and by learning about technology, making activities, and gaining competencies that are going to be useful for their everyday lives in the present and future stages.

Category 4: Taking Roles. Families had to agree which specific roles each member would take to complete the activities. From the interviews inquiring about who did what in the process, it was seen that roles were decided based on abilities, safety issues, and knowledge. For instance, in an interview with Victoria and her son Juan (see Transcript 2), she described how those factors became relevant to decide who took charge of which part of the process.

Transcript 2. Step by step making of the activities

Luna: Good. Let's start the interview with Victoria and Juan. Well, first, thank you again for allowing me to do this interview. Could you explain to me how you did each of the activities?

Victoria: I think with the face mask we started by cutting the fabric. We made some types of patterns with some leaves and from there we were guided ourselves to cut them. We cut them and sew them. It was there where I taught Juan how to sew. He was very enthusiastic to learn how to do it. He wanted to learn. With the soaps, it was almost all done by Juan. I hardly helped him. I only helped him to melt the soap in the oven because it was hot for him to carry. He emptied them in the mold and put the figurines. He also took care of the rest, the colors, the scents and everything. Next, was the decoder. In that one I helped him because of the scissors. It was more dangerous because you were supposed to cut the cardboard. So, I cut the circles and the messages. He just put it all together. Finally, with the robot, he did it all by himself. But I just helped him glue the battery holder and the motor.

Similarly, the actual abilities and previous knowledge of family members were relevant to the making process of the activities. Even though the fathers did not sign up for Hyperlocal, they participated. When interviewing the families, 6 of them mentioned that dads helped in the drawbot project. Their role was fundamental in helping the families understand how the drawbot works; this can be linked to the fact that 6 families mentioned that the husband works in construction jobs. Additionally, age also became a factor to decide who would take care of the technology. In most families, children took the leading role in using the phone and accessing the MAZI platform. However, in the case of Lily, she took control of the use of the phone because Brad was five years old, and he was rather actively involved and engaged in the making process of the activities.

Category 5: Creativity. The project had four activities with tutorial videos made by the undergraduate students. In Table 5, the first line shows figures of the proposed products from the activities, and in the second one a sample of the products that the families produced, as well as the total quantity created. The products show a lot of personalization and additions to make them look different from what the tutorial videos suggested, showing the families' likes, and innovative ways to execute the activities. The decoder was in most cases coloured and had drawings on it. The face mask was personalized by adding characters or jewels. For example, Juan added Spiderman cuts from an old sock he had, while Aracely used jewels to write "Tik Tok" on her facemask. The soaps had stickers and rings among other objects and colours. Josefina said that she used rings thinking that at the end of the use of the soaps, her sisters could have a prize for washing their hands. The drawbots were decorated and personalized, and the cables were put inside the cups, so they did not show on the outside.

Table 5. Activities proposed vs actual results

	Decoder	Face Mask	Soap	Drawbot
Pro-po-sed				
Ac-tual re-sult s				
	11	45	100	11

Lily commented that she hopes that her child learns to do things by himself. Martha's family mentioned the positivity that comes with engaging in creative activities: *"it opens our heads more, we play, we entertain ourselves as a family. We get a little distracted and we are not thinking negative things (Field Note 5)"*.

As evidenced with the photographs and testimonies, families made an appropriation of the activities by adding novel items and materials that were available in the local community. Furthermore, the creativity shown in this category enhanced the agency and decision-making process of the community to promote a meaningful learning experience through the collaboration with others.

Category 6: Capable of Doing More. Families' members realized that they were more capable of doing things that they believed they could previously do. In Transcript 3, Victoria was amazed by what her son, Juan, did. She could not believe that Juan had used the motor of the drawbot to move to his toys: a car and an airplane.

Transcript 3. Capable of doing more

Victoria: He really liked the soaps, and the robot was what he really liked the most.

Luna: Great!

Victoria: In fact, with the robot's little motor he was putting it in an airplane and a car so that it can move.

Luna: And did it turn?

Victoria: Yes, they moved. I told him to take them off because he did that before the celebration event. I told him to take them off because he was going to show the robot.

People from the community felt comfortable by adding materials or changing some of the original instructions of the activities. They knew that their own knowledge, experience, and materials could enhance the making process to produce a better result that was more relevant for their local conditions and possibilities. With these ideas in mind, people solved problems and felt that they could participate with a more active role by doing more. This category shows how this sense of agency was built through the development of the project in a communitarian and collaborative context.

4.3 The Dialogic Opportunities Created Among Participants

Families created dialogic opportunities through the making of the decoder, mask, soap, and robot, the use of the Raspberry Pi, and their decision-making process.

Category 7: Facing Hardship Together. Historicity focuses on the reflection process in which participants and the project team are able to name their world and verbalize their circumstances. The historization of participants' circumstances was shown through generative themes, topics that were relevant for them. Lucía's historization, as seen in Transcript 4, of socio-economic hardship allows her to point to what really matters - education of her children - and through this she makes connections to future possibilities:

Transcript 4. Historicizing the importance of education

As my father used to say, the only inheritance I can leave to my children is education. In addition, it is very didactic for them, they learn a lot. They were most excited about the soap, but not when they saw those dinosaur molds because they did not like it for a girl. Imagine, if I want to sell it but only for boys. So, I told my daughter that if we see the same ones downtown [molds], we will buy them.

In Transcript 5 (Interview Lucía, Pos 150–153) the dialogue reveals generative themes for Lucía as she continues historization of how she came to live where she is and how she figured out building and equipping her house through 'tandas'[2].

Transcript 5. Generative themes

Lucía: My house is about a block and a half away. I used to live with my mother. When I was pregnant, I didn't want to be with him. While my whole pregnancy lasted, I was with my mom. He sent money and everything he could. After our son

---

[2] This word refers to an informal saving method in which people provide money to a common pool with friends or colleagues. This pool, then, is rotated among the members of the "tanda" to receive the entire money given by all the members of the group. Tandas also serve as a short-term loan, as people can receive big amounts of money in a short period of time (Fundary, 2018, retrieved from https://medium.com/@fundary/tandas-and-the-informal-economy-of-mexico-4f3c80c1c7ce).

was two months old, I moved in with him. I have been living here for 5 years. Here is my room and that's it, we built it upstairs.

Luna: *How was that entire process?*

Lucía: *Well, I told you about the pregnancy: I spent it there with my mom and after our son was two months I came. The truth is that when I came here, well, I had nothing. He didn't have a bedroom' door. We had a bed, but as I told you: I was regretting having left my mom's house, to having said yes. Little by little. I started buying the stove, the fridge and having to cook myself apart. We already built up and down, I have the kitchen here and upstairs we use it for the room. We struggled for what he worked for, but then the good thing is that in challenging times the tandas helped us. We use tandas because there are no loans for us and I don't like them, I feel like I'm going to pay more. So, among all of us, my mom does tandas of 500 or 300 pesos and with my siblings join them; I have one sister and two brothers, my dad, my brother-in-law, one, my sister-in-law. We put the numbers together and raffle the numbers. When the tanda is done, it is no longer necessary to ask for a loan.*

In this transcript the generative themes are tightly related to things that matter to Lucía in daily life: relationships, housing and finance. She reflects about how her pregnancy somehow led her to live with her husband. However, economic difficulties have been presented to build and equip the house. For that reason, they have used 'tandas' which are a way to finance themselves. All the participants in a tanda give a specific amount of money each month and one get all the pot in the month depending on the number they got. So, if the "tanda" was 100 pesos per month with 5 people, each month the tanda would be 500 pesos. If Lucía got the number one, she would get the 500 pesos for the first month, the next month she has to pay 100 pesos. The concern about economic sources generated that later in the interview, she mentioned the possibility of selling the soaps that she learned to make in Hyperlocal. Other generative themes that appeared in the findings were schooling, women violence, abilities, gangs, and the Covid-19 pandemic.

Category 8: Projection of Future Possibilities. After the intervention, the families had the opportunity to make reflections about their future and possibilities. As part of that opportunity the families expressed their previous desires for the future before and after the intervention. Their previous desires for the future revolved around their ambitions for their children to have opportunities for a different job profession than what their parents currently have. Transcript 6 (Interview Salomé, Pos 269–286) is a conversation with a mom and her two daughters and exemplifies their professional aspirations.

Transcript 6. Reflect about the future

Leticia: *What do you want for your daughters in the future?*

Salomé: *All the good things that can happen to them.*

Leticia: *And what do you want for your future?*

Yarezi: *Lawyer.*

Leticia: *What do you like about being a lawyer?*

Gloria: *if you don't know anything*

Salomé: Let her talk

Leticia: Come on. Yes, tell us, tell us.

Salomé: I'm going to check the beans. [She leaves]

Yarezi: I want to be a lawyer because there are many things you have to do, that is. As well as defend, as well as many cases of. I mean, so to speak. How? As well as. Defend people, people.

Leticia: Who would you like to defend?

Yarezi: No, well I would like to defend the ladies who are beaten by their husbands

Leticia: And you?

Gloria: Well, I want to be a doctor.

Leticia: What type of doctor

Yarezi: veterinarian

Gloria: No, a doctor to help people.

In the conversation, Yarezi and Gloria expressed their desire to become a lawyer and a doctor. These two are different professions from what their parents do. Their father works in construction and their mom, Salomé, is a housewife. Their mother got married when she was 18 years old, only finishing middle school. Her father insisted she didn't need high school because she only needed to get married. The reasons given by the girls to choose their profession hint at social problems found in this context such as domestic violence, and gangs that they also comment on in their historization process.

After the intervention, when asking participants about what they could do with the acquired knowledge, their desires for the future can be grouped in three subcategories: apply for business, more STEAM projects, to learn other things. Salomé exemplifies the desire to apply the knowledge they acquired for business: *"I was thinking of getting the soap to make bigger soaps to sell in my dad's shop. I told my dad I can make the soaps and sell them here. He said it's okay. We can put them in bags or in the same molds. We can charge 5 pesos for the big one. That would be less expensive than the cheapest in a shop." (Interview Salomé, Pos 226).*

The acquired knowledge by participants opened the horizon for participants to dream about other possibilities. In the "apply it for business" subcategory, the participant has made her marketing study, selected a place, thought about promotion and products thanks to the soap activity. In the second subcategory, the participant asks for other STEAM projects specifically to be taught to make antibacterial handwash which is connected to the pandemic. Through Hyperlocal, she has re-evaluated the circumstances in her life and sees the possibility of learning to deal with it. In the last subcategory, the participant proposes specific topics of interest for future workshops, for moms to discuss their concern on how children use mobile phones and how to tackle domestic violence. Participants were explicit in terms of the learning agenda they wanted to pursue in the following interventions.

5 Discussion

This study of a Hyperlocal Learning Network in La Campana Altamira exemplifies a digital transformation initiative *for and from* a local community. The community's engagement with STEAM educational activities in a non-formal networked learning context created a dialogic space that propelled participants' creativity and search for solutions, giving them a sense of agency. They developed pride and confidence, not just in being able to complete the tasks but in striving to personalize the designs created and in thinking about future possibilities these new skills and ideas could give them.

In the dialogic space created by individuals within a family and their immediate neighbours, the participants challenged their own goals and practices, and positioned themselves in the world. The main drivers of the learning network were mothers and their children. Mothers realized that the project became an opportunity for the children not to be bored, to create new friendships with the neighbour's child, to gain experience to develop their minds. The adults reflected their own educational aspirations with their children. There is a strong role of the mothers in the education of their children, giving them educational opportunities, so their children are not exposed to the same vulnerable labour markets, such as construction and house cleaning, that these adults have to rely on. Giving opportunities to voice their historicities is an important part for bringing about social change and transformation.

The exchange of traditional teaching-learning roles within families was a further important finding that this intervention brought to light. Cooperation among family members to complete the activities represented a space for them to work towards a common goal and negotiate roles. While in some families, mothers led the sewing process for the masks, with children being more engaged in uploading the content into the MAZI platform for recording and sharing, in other cases children took the teaching role in personalizing the masks and soaps.

Documenting the use of technology showed that the transformation was not only about adopting recent technologies, but rather about the appropriation and combination of other technologies and lived experiences in non-formal settings for educational purposes. For example, one participant used the social network service Tik-Tok to create the videos that they then uploaded to the Hyperlocal network. While social networking services were originally not considered a tool for formal learning by the community, informal dialogic spaces invited drawing on these alternative sources for creativity.

Participants compared their experience of using the Hyperlocal offline network to their use of online networks as being less distracting, focused and faster to access. We believe that understanding this mix and match approach to using offline and online ICTs is valuable in non-formal learning and community settings, which might be more difficult to facilitate in formal school settings [e.g. 45].

We assumed that the community had an interest in sharing the outputs and comments on the Hyperlocal hub. Technology is only used when it is convenient or advantageous to do so. A technical glitch during the setup of the Hyperlocal hubs meant that participants could not upload pictures with a higher resolution than 2 MB in the *Comparte* section, but the phone with which they took images produced images larger than 2 MB. This resulted in participants using workarounds, such as using *Comparte Mas* for images and video only, or sharing the pictures, videos, and comments through WhatsApp or sharing them in person. They also used the street as a shared space for them in which they used it as an extended part of their homes, becoming an arena for dialogue to emerge between them. This arena also became an oasis of social interaction where they also engaged in community gatherings with food, drinks and (often unmasked) conversations around the pandemic confinement and how to creatively face everyday problems. Through these interactions they managed to relate to each other in respectful and cooperative ways to survive the lockdown. Introducing Hyperlocal, with the offline hub, mobile phones, and STEAM activities, became a catalyst for dialogue, and got the community members thinking about extending their personal opportunities. While the interest to 'share' could be observed, again, the community participants used a mixed approach to how they did that.

6 Conclusions

The Hyperlocal intervention has implications for academia and practice. Documenting the participants' experiences offers the opportunity to legitimize the richness of the dialogic space created in a non-formal educational context. It is expected that the family members, with the dialogic space created by this intervention, will continue to historicize their own circumstances, challenging their previous learning and future possibilities, so that they realize that they are more capable than what they initially thought. We hope that the results offer professionals who work with communities' advice on how to create such dialogic spaces. The researchers also positioned themselves as participants of the intervention and started to critically question their educational and research practices, and adopted a decolonial perspective, in which diverse ways of thinking were integrated in understanding the processes of change.

The lenses of dialogism and decolonization were useful for analysing the data collected and discussing the possibilities and challenges of this educational intervention. Dialogism, and in particular, its focus on historicizing, was a productive feature for participants to realize that their capabilities are larger than they initially thought, and that they can creatively design transformative trajectories of their own interest, as well as workarounds to the constraints of tools and activities. As a result, their sense of agency flourished allowing them to define an agenda to next pursue, and to propose their own themes for reflection and learning, such as the production of sanitizing gel and learning to do hairdressing, as ways to sell products and services in the future. This resonates with a decolonial perspective, in which participants reflect about defining their own lifestyles as legitimate within a *Global South* way of living. This project was a seed for reflection and for some more promising transformations that can be achieved by continuing the relationships established between community participants, scholars, and university students. This is a noble way to relate to each other, and to bond in the diversity of roles each participant performed.

References

1. De Sousa Santos, B.: El futuro comienza ahora: De la pandemia a la utopía. Ediciones AKAL, España (2021)
2. Santillan-Rosas, I.M., González-Nieto, N.A.: Future and digital literacies: transformative learning experiences in Northeast Mexico. Texto Livre **13**(3), 334–356 (2020). https://doi.org/10.35699/1983-3652.2020.25075
3. González-Nieto, N.A., et al.: FabLabs in vulnerable communities: STEM education opportunities for everyone. Int. J. Interact. Des. Manuf. (IJIDeM) **14**(4), 1535–1555 (2020). https://doi.org/10.1007/s12008-020-00744-y
4. Ancheta-Arrabal, A., Pulido-Montes, C., Carvajal-Mardones, V.: Gender digital divide and education in Latin America: a literature review. Educ. Sci. **11**, 804 (2021). https://doi.org/10.3390/educsci11120804
5. INEGI homepage. http://en.www.inegi.org.mx/programas/dutih/2019/#Tabular_data. Accessed 15 Dec 2021
6. Cárdenas, S., Lomelí, D., Ruelas, I.: COVID-19 and post-pandemic educational policies in Mexico. What is at stake? In: Reimers, F.M. (ed.) Primary and Secondary Education During Covid-19, pp. 153–175. Springer, Cham (2022). https://doi.org/10.1007/978-3-030-81500-4_6
7. Baptista Lucio, P., Almazán Zimerman, A., Loeza Altamirano, C.A.: Encuesta Nacional a Docentes ante el COVID-19. Retos para la educación a distancia. Revista Latinoamericana de Estudios Educativos **50**(ESPECIAL), 41–88 (2020). https://doi.org/10.48102/rlee.2020.50.especial.96
8. González-Nieto, N.A., Fernández-Cárdenas, J.M.: Innovación educativa ante el Covid-19: Una perspectiva comparada en el contexto mexicano. Revista de Educación Superior del Sur Global-RESUR **11**, 1–21 (2021)
9. Lotz, N., et al.: Co-creating FabLab La Campana: Empowering a marginalised community in the North of Mexico. In: IASDR 2019 The International Association of Societies of Design Research. IASDR, Manchester (2019)
10. Montgomery, C., Fernández-Cárdenas, J.M.: Teaching STEM education through dialogue and transformative learning: global significance and local interactions in Mexico and the UK. J. Educ. Teach. **44**(1), 2–13 (2018)
11. Freire, P.: Paulo Freire's speech given at Claremont Graduate University. Presented at the Honorary Doctorate for Paulo Freire, Claremont, CA (1989)
12. Bautista, A.: STEAM education: contributing evidence of validity and effectiveness (Educación STEAM: aportando pruebas de validez y efectividad). J. Study Educ. Dev. **44**(4), 755–768 (2021). https://doi.org/10.1080/02103702.2021.1926678
13. Damus, O.: Towards an epistemological alliance for the decolonization of knowledge of the global South and the global North. UNESCO's Futures of Education Ideas LAB. https://en.unesco.org/futuresofeducation/ideas-lab/damus-epistemological-alliance-decolonization-knowledge-global-South-global-North. Accessed 1 Dec 2021
14. Freeman, B., Marginson, S., Tytler, R.: The Age of STEM: Educational Policy and Practice Across the World in Science, Technology, Engineering and Mathematics. Routledge, London (2014)
15. Fernández-Cárdenas, J.M., Reynaga Peña, C.G., Hernández Salazar, P., González Nieto, A., Alatorre Cuevas, I.: La práctica social de innovar en un makerspace universitario: Posibilidades y retos. Rev. Mex. Investig. Educ. **IXXVII**(92), 235–258 (2022)
16. Dados, N., Connell, R.: The global south. Contexts **11**(1), 12–13 (2012)
17. Esler, A.: Toward a world-historical definition of the Third World. Int. Soc. Sci. Rev. **58**(4), 195 (1983)

18. Palomino, P.: On the Disadvantages of "Global South" for Latin American studies. J. World Philosophies **4**(2), 22–39 (2019)
19. Mahler, A.G.: From the Tricontinental to the Global South: Race, Radicalism, and Transnational Solidarity. Duke University Press, Durham (2018)
20. Vygotsky, L.S.: Mind in Society: The Development of Higher Psychological Processes. Harvard University Press, Cambridge (1978)
21. Wertsch, J.V.: Vygotsky and the Social Formation of Mind. Harvard University Press, Cambridge (2009)
22. Fernández-Cárdenas, J.M.: Aprendiendo a escribir juntos: Multimodalidad, conocimiento y discurso. Comité Regional Norte de Cooperación con la UNESCO/Universidad Autónoma de Nuevo León. México, México (2009)
23. Wenger, E.: Communities of practice and social learning systems: the career of a concept. In: Blackmore, C. (ed.) Social Learning Systems and Communities of Practice, pp. 179–198. Springer, London (2010). https://doi.org/10.1007/978-1-84996-133-2_11
24. Bruning, R.H., Schraw, G.J., Norby, M.M., Ronning, R.R.: Cognitive Psychology and Instruction, 4a. edn. Merrill/Prentice Hall, Upper Saddle River (2004)
25. Mezirow, J., Taylor, E.W. (eds.): Transformative Learning in Practice: Insights from Community, Workplace, and Higher Education. Jossey-Bass, San Francisco (2009)
26. Freire, P.: Pedagogía del oprimido, 55th edn. Siglo XXI, Mexico (2005)
27. Fernández-Cárdenas, J.M.: El dialogismo: Secuencialidad, posicionamiento, pluralidad e historicidad en el análisis de la práctica educativa [Dialogism: Sequentiality, positioning, plurality and historicity in the analysis of educational practice]. Sinéctica **43**, 183–203 (2014)
28. Fernández-Cárdenas, J.M. (ed.): El dialogismo: Su impacto en la construcción ética del conocimiento en diferentes escenarios educativos, Primera, vol. 6. Porrúa, Mexico (2018)
29. Ching Chiang, L.W.C., Fernández-Cárdenas, J.M.: Analysing dialogue in STEM classrooms in Ecuador: a dual Socioeconomic context in a high school. J. New Approaches Educ. Res. **9**(2), 194–215 (2020). https://doi.org/10.7821/naer.2020.7.529
30. Rogers, A.: The Base of the Iceberg: Informal Learning and Its Impact on Formal and Nonformal Learning. Barbara Budrich Publishers, Opladen (2014)
31. Walsh, C.: The Decolonial for: resurgences, shifts and movements. In: Mignolo, W., Walsh, C. (eds.) On Decoloniality: Concepts, Analytics, Praxis. Duke University Press, Durham (2018)
32. De Sousa Santos, B.: Epistemologies of the South and the Future. Eur. South Transdisciplinary J. Postcolonial Humanit. **1**, 17–29 (2016)
33. Wegerif, R., Major, L.: Buber, educational technology, and the expansion of dialogic space. AI Soc. **34**(1), 109–119 (2018). https://doi.org/10.1007/s00146-018-0828-6
34. Carter, P.: Material Thinking: The Theory and Practice of Creative Research. Melbourne University Publishing, Carlton (2005)
35. Shreeve, A., Sims, E., Trowler, P.: 'A kind of exchange': learning from art and design teaching. High. Educ. Res. Dev. **29**(2), 125–138 (2010)
36. Lyon, P.: Design Education – Learning, Teaching and Researching through Design. Gower Publishing Ltd., Farnham (2011)
37. Swanson, G.: Educating the designer of 2025. She Ji J. Des. Econ. Innov. **6**(1), 101–105 (2020). https://doi.org/10.1016/j.sheji.2020.01.001
38. Jones, D., Lotz, N., Holden, G.: A longitudinal study of Virtual Design Studio (VDS) use in STEM distance design education. Int. J. Technol. Des. Educ. **31**(4), 839–865 (2020). https://doi.org/10.1007/s10798-020-09576-z
39. Gaved, M., Hanson, R., Stutchbury, K.: Mobile offline networked learning for teacher Continuing Professional Development in Zambia. In: Proceedings of mLearn2020: The 19th World Conference on Mobile, Blended and Seamless Learning (2020)
40. Maxwell, J.: Qualitative Research Design, vol. 41. SAGE Publications, New York (2012)

41. Merriam, S., Tisdell, E.: Qualitative Data Analysis. Jossey Bass, Hoboken (2016)
42. Pike, K.L.: Language in Relation to a Unified Theory of Structure of Human Behavior, 2nd edn. Mouton, The Hague (1967)
43. Dietz, G.: Towards a double reflexive ethnography: a proposal on the Anthropology of Interculturality. Aibr-Revista De Antropologia Iberoamericana **6**(1), 3–26 (2011)
44. Harris, M.: "Chapter Two: The Epistemology of Cultural Materialism", in Cultural Materialism: The Struggle for a Science of Culture. Random House, New York (1980)
45. Shrestha, S.: Exploring mobile learning opportunities and challenges in Nepal: the potential of open-source platforms. Ph.D. thesis (2016). https://repository.uwl.ac.uk/id/eprint/2962/

Land, Letšema and Leola: Digital Transformation on a Rural Community's Own Terms

Kgopotso Ditshego Magoro[1,2(✉)] and Nicola J. Bidwell[3,4]

[1] University of the Witwatersrand, Johannesburg, South Africa
kdmagoro@gmail.com
[2] Mamaila Community Network, Johannesburg, South Africa
[3] Aalborg University, Copenhagen, Denmark
[4] International University of Management, Windhoek, Namibia

Abstract. Eurocentric paradigms for technology continue to dominate in Africa yet can impede digital transformation by perpetuating senses of inferiority in societies that have endured colonialism and apartheid. This chapter describes how an African creative pedagogy, Mandhwane, is enabling inhabitants of Mamaila, in rural South Africa, to negotiate the meaning of transformation on their own terms. Since 2018 inhabitants have been establishing their own telecommunications system, or Community Network (CN), to provide local internet access and digital services www.mamailanetwork.co.za/. The CN acts as a "land" where inhabitants freely co-create, which is a vital aspect of Mama Tshepo Khumbane's philosophy of doing Mandhwane for transformation. The first author applied Matshepo's techniques to help inhabitants recognise their existing capability to solve their problems by Letšema, or collective work. Our analysis focuses on designing an app to support Leola, a locally created community scheme in which households collaborate to support bereaved families with funding, equipment and human resources, for funerals and burials. We reflect on the ways that locating design within a rural CN and framing innovation with Mandhwane fosters communal and individualised agency, embeds a social relational ontology in innovation, and can tackle tensions that often arise in digital transformation, such as those that result from differences between older and younger people and between local and externally imposed timescales.

Keywords: Cultural knowledge systems · Decolonising technology · Community Network · Ubuntu · Personhood · Motho ke motho ka batho

1 Introduction

"Help me to transfer scientific knowledge into grassroots level by teaching rural children to play Mantlwantlwane. I am ageing, I no longer have the physical power and the energy to play Mantlwantlwane", Mmatshepo urged Kgopotso when they reunited in 2017. They had first met a decade before when Kgopotso had visited Mmatshepo's farm and

© IFIP International Federation for Information Processing 2022
Published by Springer Nature Switzerland AG 2022
J. Abdelnour-Nocera et al. (Eds.): *Innovation Practices for Digital Transformation in the Global South*, IFIP AICT 645, pp. 59–78, 2022.
https://doi.org/10.1007/978-3-031-12825-7_4

had occasionally and joyfully reconnected in the years in between. This time though, the renowned South African development activist's insistence carried frustration and a sense of betrayal. "Many people wrote about my life. My knowledge has produced professors and consultants", she said, "but they all reduced me to Mama Tshepo who plants vegetables and creates underground water dams. They missed my core philosophy of Mantlwantlwane".

Mantlwantlwane is a traditional pedagogy in many southern African communities, where learning occurs through doing, as people improvise, receive feedback and adapt, but Kgopotso did not know how to respond to Mmatshepo's request that she write a book about it. She began driving the 50 km to the Cullinan farm regularly and, as they processed grapes, lemon, lime and kiwano together and analysed the environmental and weather data that Mmatshepo had collected (Fig. 1), Kgopotso learnt about Mmatshepo's approach. Along with the garlic, kiwanis and rosemary and the aloe and other indigenous plants to grow in her own backyard, she took home recordings of Mmatshepo's stories and an embodied knowing about what those stories mean. At the time Kgopotso was considering a proposal for a PhD and, as she ghost-wrote 'The Spirit of Hope' to reflect Mmatshepo's experiences, she realised her research journey would be about Mandhwane as spelt in Selobedu: a dedication to Mmatshepo and a reclaiming of her own cultural identity.

Fig. 1. Left: Kgopotso (left) learns how to process Aloe vera with Mmatshepo (right). **Right:** Kgopotso explores Mmatshepo's weather data. Both photos: Bophelo Mahlabaseletsi, 2017.

This chapter illustrates the digital transformation enabled by situating technology design, deployment and use in an African creative pedagogy. For the past 3-years, co-author Kgopotso and rural inhabitants of Mamaila have been doing Mandhwane to establish a Community Network (CN), which provides local internet access and innovates new digital services. The word Mandhwane is often used pejoratively to describe systems that lack excellence or structure, yet Mamaila's CN and digital services are avoiding the conceptual mismatches, limited local ownership, early failure and amplified inequality that often emerge when technology and innovation paradigms are imported to the Global Souths (e.g. [12, 27, 59]). Thus, we contribute empirical insights about a decolonial app-roach to innovation in rural Africa by describing the role of Mandhwane in innovating an app to support local practices.

We organise this chapter to convey the richness of the relational ontology that Mand-hwane engages with. We seek to minimise the epistemic violence [55] that occurs when the structure of reports about transformation exclude local contributions and meanings. Mmatshepo recognised that creativity is impeded by diminishing local experiences, val-ues and problem-solving approaches and, as Sect. 2 describes, applied techniques to community development that liberated people from these constraints. Owning an envi-ronment in which to freely co-create is vital to Mmatshepo's techniques and in Sect. 3 we propose that Mamaila Community Network is a place in which inhabitants undertake Mandhwane to innovate and negotiate the meaning of digital transformation on their own terms. Section 4 outlines the African cultural framework for technology that orients Kgopotso's ongoing action research with Mamaila Community Network. Our analy-sis, in Sect. 5, focuses on designing an app to support the cultural practice of Leola, a community scheme that supports bereaved families by contributing to funerals and burials. We describe how Leola depicts local logics and relations and how Mmatshepo's techniques helped inhabitants to recognise their collective resources. We conclude by reflecting on the ways that locating design within a rural CN and framing innovation within Mandhwane tackles some of the tensions that emerge in digital transformation and fosters communal and individualised agency.

2 Mmatshepo's Mandhwane and Mind Mobilisation

Young children in Mamaila still play Mandhwane (Fig. 2). Observations of Mandhwane in other southern African communities, where it is called Mantlwane or Mantlwantlwane (Northern Sotho), Mahundwane (Venda), Mahumbwe (Shona) and Imizi (isiXhosa), suggest learning occurs through doing as children improvise their own versions of their elders' practices. Children learn mathematical skills by constructing "homes" with the stalks of corn left after harvesting, and looking for, preparing and preserving "food" made with leaves and mud [57]. In their miniature village, they also learn the social skills needed to be active and effective members of society. Older children enact the roles of mother and father to the younger ones [46], which in the past developed their proficiency in domestic and family affairs [24]. Sometimes elders gave feedback (e.g. [19]); for instance, when children in the "couple" role sought guidance to resolve a dispute or a "wife" presented a meal to the "mother-in-law" - the actual mother of the boy in the husband role [38, 39]. This supported future relationships if, say, a "couple" married in later life. While the gendered roles rehearsed in Mandhwane have attracted feminist critique, African Womanists argue that the pedagogy aligns with women's pursuit of a sense of completeness through family, home and career [44]. The Balobedu people of Mamaila are, in fact, a matrilineal dynasty [45].

Mandhwane was the primary means for sharing knowledge and learning skills in South Africa before European colonial and Christian missionary exercises introduced their education systems [32]. The customary educational practice supports the principles that, Adeyemi and Adeyinka (2002) [2] propose, characterize African onto-epistemology including communalism, through collective learning; preparationism by role modelling; functionalism by imitating; holisticism through multiskilling; and perennialism by preserving culture. Mandwhane has, however, been underappreciated as a creative pedagogy, or an approach to learning that integrates problem solving and responds to political and psychological as well as the social aspects of people's development. Treating children as human beings who are free to express themselves in settings they create themselves and who know what is right and wrong without paternalism [19], indeed promotes creative agency.

Fig. 2. Children from Mamaila playing Mandhwane. Photo: Hlokomelo Mabogale, 2021.

Recognising the importance of culturally-grounded and socially-supported creative agency, grassroots activist Mama Tshepo Khumbane framed community development in Mandhwane for over forty years. Mmatshepo's experience of apartheid oppression convinced her that the nationally prescribed education system was unhealthy [63]. She believed that people need to accept and confront their situation and control their own lives by doing something constructive with whatever few assets they had, and without relying on government and external aid. With her encouragement, communities made gardens and grew crops, using methods to fertilise organically and retain soil moisture; cleaned springs to purify water; built houses; and, made mud stoves for baking and cooking [8, 20]. Mmatshepo situated scientific knowledge in the work; for instance, as they built and maintained their agricultural and irrigation systems people created rain gauges, monitored weather patterns and logged daily activities in charts.

Mmatshepo argued that "poverty of the mind" prevents people from embarking on constructive activities and sought to enable Black people to liberate their minds and heal the psychological damage of colonisation and apartheid. As a trained social worker, she had adopted the group casework approach, in which all group members actively contribute to mutual support, and learn to understand and build on each other's experiences, situations, problems, dilemmas, perspectives, strengths and weaknesses. She integrated a reflective process into her facilitation practice that recognises that transformation inherently links an individual self to social dynamics. However, beyond appreciating intrapsychic dynamics of group casework, such as the impact of group size, roles, norms, communication patterns, member interaction and influence [33], Mmatshepo's approach was situated in a particular philosophy about personhood, or what it means to be human. Often known by the isiXhosa word Ubuntu, this philosophy assumes being human depends on the simultaneous and dynamic constitution of other humans and neither community or individual is prior. That is, a person exists because of other people, or in Northen Sotho and Selobedu: Motho ke Motho ka Batho. Thus, Mmatshepo's Mind Mobilisation technique engaged people in reflecting on their social, economic, political, and psychological challenges situated within a communal entity that shared norms and value systems.

Mmatshepo's rural upbringing entwined a familiarity with traditional farming methods with rituals, ceremony and stories that reinforced the importance of land in co-creating the social system. "Without all the holding hands together and an environment which has been created by the people themselves and the institutions to allow that to happen it [transformation] will not work" [Kgopotso audio recording, Pretoria, 7 April 2017]. Mmatshepo realised that people had the power to do Mandhwane and freely create solutions and enact plans for their lives provided they form a Community of Practice (CoP) around their own land. Owning land, even a small yard, enables a person to express their creativity without constraint and, within a CoP, gardens contributed to both household income and local food security by distributing surplus harvest.

3   Community Networks in Decolonising Transformation

Kgopotso has been doing Mandhwane in helping to establish Mamaila Community Network since 2018 [35]. CNs, or telecommunication systems that are owned, set up and managed by inhabitants of the areas where they are deployed, have been long proposed as ways to provide communications to people who cannot access alternatives [53]. With increased affordability and usability of equipment, such as solar-powered GSM base-stations to provide mobile telephony and Wi-Fi routers to provide internet connections [4], CNs have proliferated around the world. As we explain next, they offer places for decolonising innovation because their members co-create meanings about technologies embodied in their everyday lives [12] and in settings that they own.

3.1 Decolonising Innovation in Africa

Research in the field of Human-Computer Interaction (HCI) over the past five years describes how technology production within Africa has been shaped by a paradigm that originated in Silicon Valley through digital policies, tertiary and higher education, training in digital projects, and investment in and coordination of tech hubs and start-ups [3, 5, 6, 18]. Along with amplifying existing inequalities (e.g. [26, 59]), this paradigm reproduces imperialist superiorities and racism, which has prompted scholars in Africa to advocate for decolonising technology design [1, 7, 9, 34, 47]. Much of this advocacy, however, focuses on the identities of African HCI researchers and designers in technology production rather than on decolonising innovation within the activities of diverse Africans' everyday lives, such as rural inhabitants.

Generally African rural dwellers express insights to inform software development within activities determined by urban-based technologists and researchers, rather than enabling all participants to co-construct learning in design (e.g. [31]). This tends to reproduce beliefs that an effective society follows certain processes in education, innovation and technology production. Indeed, despite discussions about designing technologies to support African educational traditions, such as learning by doing [41], moral reasoning [42] and the nuances of cooperation [14], there are no published examples of situating design and development within an explicitly African creative pedagogy, such as Mandhwane.

Studies in HCI and the field of Participatory Design (PD) draw attention to the importance of accounting for temporal and spatial relationships in rural Africa [11, 13]. Yet, with few exceptions (e.g. [16]), African land is rarely positioned as a key actor in digital transformation and continues to be occupied [54]. Thus, considerations might be critiqued for not engaging with literal decolonisation [30, 60] or accounting for relations between people's ownership of physical infrastructure and their agency in creating solutions and enacting plans for their own lives.

3.2 Grounding Community Networks in Mandhwane

Local ownership means CNs can offer settings for digital transformation that contrast with environments shaped by universalised design methods and corporate control of telecommunications provision and regulation [11]. Each of the, over 30, CNs that now participate in the annual Summit on Community Networks in Africa [58], emerged in their own local social and spatial contexts [25]. For instance, Bosco provides internet access to many small, self-organised centres across hundreds of kilometres in Uganda's Northern and West Nile regions [12] and PamojaNET's La Différence CN provides free internet during off-peak times, via Wi-Fi and a public access kiosk, to the population of Idjwi Island in the Republic of Congo's Lake Kivu. There are at least five CNs in South Africa, where a few large telecom companies prioritise provision to high revenue urban markets and price their services for people who can afford their tariffs [49]. Several serve urban and peri-urban townships, such as iNethi in Cape Town [48], while others address poor quality telecommunications in rural areas, such as Zenzeleni Networks in the Eastern Cape [50].

Fig. 3. Top left: the tower and dishes that were installed to provide backhaul for Mamaila Community Network, photo: Pardon Mabunda. **Top right:** a permanent ladder was installed to enable accessing the tower. **Lower:** view over Mamaila from the site of the tower.

Mandhwane has shaped the development of Mamaila Community Network in Limpopo Province from the start. While Kgopotso had taken an online course about CNs in 2017, it was insights from her visits to Bosco Uganda and Zenzeleni Networks that inspired her to introduce the concept of CNs to Mamaila's inhabitants. She organised a hands-on workshop in Mamaila where, assisted by Soweto Wireless User Group (SOWUG), participants created their own ethernet cables, assembled a parabolic antenna, configured point-to-point connections and, along the way, learnt the basic set-up of the internet. Encouraged by the workshop, Kgopotso explored the feasibility of a CN by deploying a Wi-Fi, for three months, that provided free internet to a school, a Disability Centre and a church in one of the villages under the jurisdiction of Mamaila Tribal Authority. Community members who had participated in the earlier hands-on introduction attended another workshop to test the Wi-Fi and discuss their experiences, aspirations and network requirements. Insights from the pilot informed the design of Mamaila Community Network and, with seed funding from the Internet Society (ISOC) in the past two years, Mamaila's inhabitants set up wireless backhaul (Fig. 3) and permanent access points in all six villages.

Mamaila Community Network (www.mamailanetwork.co.za/) is now licensed to provide local inhabitants with internet access and digital services, such as offline educational resources. As importantly, and much as Mmatshepo conceived people's use of their own land in Mandhwane, the CN is an infrastructure that enables inhabitants to use the electromagnetic spectrum of their Wi-Fi in Mamaila within a creative pedagogy. Transformation through this Digital Mandhwane [35] cannot be assessed according to externally imposed project plans, metrics or value propositions. Neither quantified outputs, such as the number of people trained or the frequency of inhabitants' technology use, nor measures of project productivity within certain timeframes, can depict the culturally-appropriate agency that emerges in co-creating and enacting plans in a community's own 'digital land'. Thus, as we explain next, Kgopotso sought an alternative paradigm to guide technology design and her action research.

4   An African Cultural Framework: Positionality and Paradigm

Kgopotso's contribution to Mamaila Community Network is best expressed through the proverb "Mmetla shapo la tlala o betla a lebile ga gabo", or anyone who aims to solve social ills must start at home. Kgopotso grew up in one of the six villages under Mamaila Tribal Authority, in the region settled by her ancestors when they migrated from present-day Zimbabwe roughly 400 years ago. Her research for her Masters degree, about the challenges of internet connectivity in Mopani District, Limpopo, motivated her to help establish Zuri Foundation, a women-led Not-for-profit organisation (NPO) that aims to develop capacity and provide internet access in villages. Although based in a city 300 km away, where she works in senior technical management for a government ministry, she returns home to Mamaila regularly. Kgopotso is fluent in Selobedu (also spelt Khelobedu), the marginalised language of the Balobedu tribe, but she did not join in all local practices due to her family's Christian beliefs. As a child she had also observed her cousins and peers play Mandhwane, although she was disinclined to express herself or take orders from her peers in order to join in their play. Thirty-three years later, however, her engagement with Mmatshepo for over four years ignited her appreciation of Mandhwane [36].

Kgopotso's and Nic's positionality contrast. Nic is white, Australian and British, has lived in many countries since starting life in the Sudan and has not yet been to Mamaila. Nonetheless, when we first met, through the African CN movement four years ago, we discovered common commitments to life nourished by the African soil and culturally sensitive approaches to technology innovation and design research. Our account draws on Nic's HCI expertise and experience for 14 years undertaking research while employed in university departments of computing and living in rural South Africa and Namibia, including in the place where Zenzeleni networks began.

Kgopotso interviewed Nic while determining a paradigm to guide technology design in Mamaila and the action research for her PhD. Kgopotso's formative research about rural internet connectivity sensitized her to the importance of culturally-embedded digital transformation and her role as a cultural activist. The Eurocentric paradigms that dominate research and innovation make it difficult to specify what culture actually means within a specific community. Thus, Kgopotso sought to learn from the experiences of people who had worked at the intersection of technology, innovation and cultural knowledge systems in southern Africa and thereby ground her pursuit of a paradigm in Mandhwane. All 19 experts and practitioners that Kgopotso interviewed explained culture using examples of practices and processes rather than defining exactly what culture is. Thus, she conceived an African cultural framework for technology that would engage with social, economic, political, educational, health, justice, identity and heritage practices [37].

Kgopotso's African cultural framework shaped her use of standard research instruments, including surveys, interviews, Focus Group Discussions (FGDs) and workshops. To generate data she prioritizes local cultural practices, often without mentioning technology and, establishes rapport with inhabitants based on a shared cultural identity, for instance by discussing what her family totem means to her. Kgopotso limits the effects of linguistic and epistemic translation by conducting all engagements in Mamaila in Selobedu. However, she transcribes in English to in order to use the tools available for software design and qualitative analysis, such as AtlasTi, and write academic reports. Technology specialists had also recommended that Kgopotso use Design Thinking, a technique conceived in Silicon Valley and promoted as a 'standard' to engage users, determine their needs, identify requirements and design prototypes [29]. However, formulating user needs in certain ways limits holistically locating technical solutions in everyday community practices and does not address social, psychological and political relations of digital transformation, unlike Mmatshepo's techniques.

5 Situating Innovation in Mandhwane

Our account focuses on the ways a particular cultural practice, Leola, guided the design of a digital service that supports local cultural knowledge and values. Leola is a community financial scheme in which participating households collect money and provide bereaved families with funding, equipment and human resources for funerals and burials when needed. Although she wishes to be buried in her village, Kgopotso did not know all aspects of Leola at the start of her research. She only began to consider it in technology endeavours as she collected data and realised that Mmatshepo's philosophy of Mandhwane suited the ways the locally innovated scheme connects households into the broader community.

5.1 Documenting Cultural Practices and Tuning into Leola

Kgopotso started by surveying cultural awareness and practices, as well as digital patterns. She consulted with permanent inhabitants of Mamaila village to fill gaps in

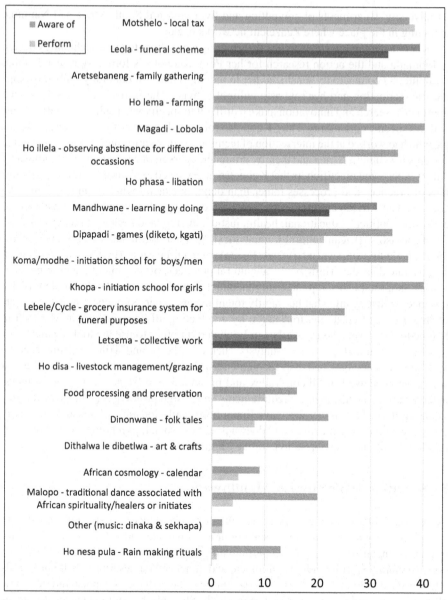

Fig. 4. Frequency of awareness (blue) and performance (orange) of cultural practices in 50 households in two villages in Mamaila. Leola, Mandhwane and Letšema are in darker tones.

her knowledge and co-create closed-ended questions, and two local research assistants administered the survey to households in two villages in Mamaila. The most commonly performed practices mentioned were: Motshelo, or administrative tax paid to the Tribal Office (which performs local government roles); Leola; Aretsebaneng or family gathering; and farming (Fig. 4). Koma, or initiation, is also widely performed, however, while most respondents did not consider that it conflicts with Christian life, unlike earlier converts, its cultural sensitivity makes it difficult to discuss. Nearly half of respondents stated they had performed Mandhwane, although it was not quite as widely known as other common practices.

To further understand intersections between local culture and technology and identify community needs, aspirations and processes that technology could support, Kgopotso facilitated a FGD with representatives of Mamaila Community Development Forum, which handles Mamaila Royal Council's development agenda. Community leaders, in the FGD, emphasised that governance embeds the philosophy of Motho ke motho ka batho, and that digitisation would benefit processes that express Motho, such as Leola. For instance, digital announcements and mobile money transfers might help people who are based in cities for work to ensure they don't miss payments because they are unaware of a death. Thus, Kgopotso focused on Leola because it offered the potential for digitally facilitating social cohesion.

Based on community leaders' suggestions Kgopotso interviewed a representative of one of Mamaila's Leola groups who outlined the history of Leola, the structures supporting it and how Leola interacts with other cultural practices and financial processes within the community. Leola originally emerged when neighbours in one village supported bereaved families and spread as inhabitants observed others, when participating in funerals, and modelled their practice. The scheme embeds the value of honouring the departed with O bolokegile, or "burying in dignity", such that funerals meet communal standards for food supplies, number of people and community support.

While Leola is grounded in common principles, inhabitants are not formally taught about it but learn by doing and evolve their processes along the way. For instance, nine sections, comprising one village, established an executive committee with a formal constitution signed by the Chief. The executive committee enables sharing good practice, discovering solutions to challenges and coaching and mentoring about governance and conflict resolution by drawing on the encouragement and guidance of the Tribal Council (the Chief and his Ndunas/advisors). While people comprising the Leola group's executive committee were born before technology, the representative said that technology could bring benefits to announcements, record-keeping and asset management. However, COVID-19 prevented face-to-face discussions with representatives of all nine Leola groups, which are at different stages of advancement. Thus, Kgopotso sought a more collective conversation that would align with Mandhwane, to validate her findings, further consider how technology currently intersects with cultural practices, identify processes that might benefit from digitization and engage participants in co-creating prototypes.

5.2 Mobilising Minds and Planning to Support Cultural Knowledge

Informed by her preliminary insights Kgopotso hosted a workshop for community representatives at Mamaila Tribal Authority offices. Six women and nine men, aged between 25 and 73 years, participated in the workshop including representatives from Mamaila villages' headquarters, and from the Leola group of one village. Mind Mobilisation began with participants addressing senses of inferiority by recognising their fears and prior knowledge in relation to technology. They recounted stories about their first experiences with the internet. Even elderly people had positive, along with negative, accounts about their daily interactions with technology. Many participants feared online scams; however, they also observed that scamming arises in off-line processes. Kgopotso insisted that the community already demonstrated the capability to address off-line problems by collective work, or Letšema, an economic and social system grounded in the philosophy of Motho. She pointed out, for instance, how a group had crowdfunded a storehouse to store their assets for funerals (Fig. 5) by collecting a brick from each household. Thus, participants discussed local cultural practices to validate collaborative activities listed in survey responses, such as farming, savings groups, initiations, weddings and funerals, and identify collective resources.

Fig. 5. Left: Storehouse for assets built by a Leola group using Letšema. **Right:** Assets lent for funerals

Agricultural activities are prominent collective work and, echoing Mmatshepo's philosophy that land is needed to play Mandhwane, Kgopotso framed the infrastructure of Mamaila Community Network as "land". She referred to the seasonal calendar to prompt linking cultural preservation and collectivity. Unlike conventional modern farming, when most work occurs in planting and harvesting, traditional farming happened throughout the year: Seruthwane, or spring, when the soil and seeds are prepared; Selemo, or summer, the time for ploughing; Lehlabula, or autumn, for harvesting and preserving; and Marega, Initiation season, when food is processed and crops like spinach are planted. Participants often struggled to name the seasons in Selobedu, reflected on loss of cultural memory and the importance of preserving culture for future generations. They referred to a prototype of a heritage website Kgopotso had implemented; noting that it did not depict many local cultural artefacts and recommending content about the names of artefacts, clothing from former eras, and audio recordings of different historical music genres.

Fig. 6. Mind Mobilisation participants review the Leola process documented by Kgopotso. Photo: Joey wa Rabapane, 2021.

Mind Mobilisation revealed how Leola is an innovation that includes inhabitants with varying cultural knowledge. When participants reviewed the Leola processes (Fig. 6), that Kgopotso had documented from the interviews, their only amendment was that some groups in Mamaila deliver funds directly to the bereaved family instead of allowing collection by representatives of the bereaved family. The review prompted discussing different challenges experienced by one Leola group, in which: administrators sometimes lost information stored in books; households do not know how much money is available from the generated files; family members in cities fell behind with contributions because messages were not distributed sufficiently; disputes arose around missing or damaged assets, such as chairs lent for use during funerals; and "scammers" did not always give bereaved families the full amounts the group had collected.

Participants also noted that as Leola had diffused into new settlements, new groups had not adopted the methods that mature groups had evolved and some were dominated by younger members unguided by elders. Thus, new groups do not always adhere to governance processes that promote social cohesion and Leola was exposed to practices that poorly align with the values of Motho, such as by using the collected funds more extravagantly. Participants suggested that technology could help educate people about the values of Leola, address concerns about financial accountability, communication, assets management and knowledge sharing, strengthen social networks, and be used in crowdfunding to solve other community challenges. Some of these ideas fed into their Helicopter Plan, Mmatshepo's technique for visioning, action planning and self-monitoring which emphasised collaboration as a foundation for innovation. Participants agreed on an action-list: to collect information about the cultural artefacts for the heritage website and contribute to developing an app to support Leola.

5.3   Translating Leola into the Mamaila Community App

After the workshop that applied Mmatshepo's techniques Kgopotso translated insights into the basic functionalities of an app to support Leola. User groups included the mostly elderly Leola Administrators who inform members in their sections through meetings by word of mouth; manage assets; collect and record contributions to funerals and fines from members whose payments were late or who damaged assets. Two other user groups comprised household members who contribute Leola payments and report deaths, and Tribal Authority representatives who make announcements to the community. The app enables administrators to announce deaths and meetings, record contributions and fines, and manage an inventory of assets. To support transparency, functionality enables household members to view the total amounts collected, donated to each bereaved household, fines issued and the status of assets. Household members can also report deaths and other incidents that have caused distress, such as robbery, and Tribal Authority representatives can post notices.

Some months later, and following principles of Mandhwane, an elder advised and mentored Kgopotso about introducing the app and suggested that other clan-based funeral schemes could use the app's functionality. Reflection on the elder's insights, and other participants' comments about how Leola might scaffold a process to help people address their economic challenges, prompted 'rebranding' the app to permit future extensions to support other activities, such as developing the website. The resulting Mamaila Community App [40] prioritises the Leola functionality but also enables community members who do not belong to a specific Leola group to report incidents and receive the Tribal Authority's community announcements. Bearing the slogan Motho ke Motho ka Batho and with all interfaces written in Selobedu, the app will run on Mamaila Community Network where users can access it without paying for data and it can stimulate conversations about local digital services. Indeed, the involvement of ten youth who tested the app suggests its potential to motivate youth to create other localised apps. Exchanges on WhatsApp amongst youth as they explored an earlier iteration were punctuated with the emojis for praise, awesome, approval and achievement; "this app could actually make life simple yaz.. i see your vision there wow i give you the hat", one wrote. Their comments suggest the app surpasses expectations about what a home-grown innovation would be "Yoh, its actually nice" and "I'm actually impressed" another youth wrote.

Enthusiasm was reiterated when Kgopotso introduced the app to over 30 people representing Leola groups, the Tribal Office and Mamaila Royal Council (the royal family) in a hands-on workshop recently. Despite enthusiasm, however, participants proposed that manual Leola processes should continue in parallel until everyone is comfortable with the app. Participants were aged up to 73 years old, but approximately a third were aged 25 to 30 years and participated to test the app not because they were members of Leola. The participants who were under 44 years old were particularly quick to express their support of the necessity and simplicity of the app. However, concerns were raised about use by elderly people who don't own smartphones, cannot read and write and may depend on their grandchildren to help them. While supporting the app, one elder implied that such dependency may expose people to scamming by their grandchildren. This sentiment and a youth's response to it indicate different generational perspectives on inclusion. One younger person felt that elders sought to protect and maintain power and, thus, ignored youth's perspectives, and that basing the app and the workshops around Leola, which is currently dominated by men, makes digital transformation exclusive.

Others, however, are hopeful that the app might bridge the gap between elders and youth by building on inhabitants' creativity in innovating their Leola together.

6 Conclusion: Mandhwane in Transformation

The creative pedagogy of Mandhwane is expressed in multiple ways in innovating the app. The non-digital Leola processes spread as the practice emerged, was imitated and collectively adapted when problems arose, based on elders' guidance. Kgopotso's approach also evolved as she consulted experts about their experience in culturally based technology interventions to inform her technology design and action research paradigm; learnt and validated her understandings about Leola; and guided local residents in roles as research assistants. Finally, technical and social aspects of learning and creating entwined, and prioritised relations between domestic, family and community affairs. Thus, we conclude by proposing that applying Mama Tshepo's techniques in a CN can enable rural communities to embed innovation in a local social relational ontology and negotiate the meaning of digital transformation on their own terms.

6.1 Recognising Personhood and Knowledge in Mind Mobilisation

Participants in Mind Mobilisation reflected on the cultural identity expressed in their everyday household and community activities. While swift to state that their non-digital Leola processes were imperfect, Mind Mobilisation framed this critique as an integral part of innovation. Inhabitants improved their Leola by learning from their own and others' mistakes, just as in formal iterative research and design processes, such as Action Research [23] and Prototyping (e.g. [28]). Proponents of PD have long advocated for inclusive problem-solving approaches to improve the accountability and creativity of solutions (e.g. [51]); meanwhile Sen's work [52] shows the need to leverage people's capabilities in transformation. However, Mind Mobilisation, framed inhabitants' Leola innovation within the local creative pedagogy of Mandhwane and emphasised how communal and individualised agency entwine.

Mind Mobilisation recognised Mamaila's inhabitants as creators who innovated their Leola together. Some HCI studies about producing technology in Africa recognise that "methods make people" [5] and the effects of people's subjectivities on methods. These analyses do not tend to focus on the condition of being human, but rather on people's identities based, for instance, on race, gender, professions and education. Personhood, however, is a more culturally located concept that entwines with particular ethics about human relations. For instance, independence and self-maintenance are emphasised in Euroamerican models of personhood more than the social relationality emphasised in Motho.

Prioritising human relations is considered critical to the success of development and economic endeavours in South Africa (e.g. [17, 22, 43]) and studies relate the Ubuntu philosophy to technology design, ICT innovations and operating internet cafes and CNs (e.g. [10, 56, 61, 62]). However, such studies do not specifically consider how Ubuntu is integrated into the mutual shaping of technology and personhood in transformation. Focusing on Mamaila's inhabitants' Letšema, or collective work, and their innovation of Leola oriented digital transformation towards a social relational ontology in multiple ways. For instance, while Kgopotso's goal was a personal PhD when she embarked on her research, neither academic contribution nor credentials can define the knowledge the research has produced. Indeed, our analysis shows that learning that is intractably entwined with a community should not be considered inferior to the structures and generalisations that Eurocentric pedagogies and design and documenting paradigms tend to emphasise.

6.2   The Role of Land in Creative Pedagogy

Kgopotso's African cultural framework for technology imagines innovation in relation to local logics that emerged over centuries and not to 'gaps' determined by transnational ideals about progress, growth and empowerment or by a paradigm of technology production originating in Silicon Valley. While Sankofa teaches that it is not taboo to return to the past for the benefit of the future (e.g. [21]), the framework does not imply designing technologies to mimic times past. Rather, local logics are articulated in practices that evolve with time. For instance, Leola supports the logic of Motho ke Motho ka Batho in various ways, beyond collecting and distributing funds. This includes sharing elders' advice, identifying challenges affecting different parts of the community, determining solutions and coordinating to address them, and networking and liaising with authorities and other institutions. Analysis of the details of Leola enabled mapping local logics and relations and prompted inhabitants to reflect on how these are affected by societal changes.

Exploring the efficacies of a locally innovated and evolving system, such as Leola, and the ways technology can support and improve it, offers resources for negotiating what digital transformation should mean locally. For instance, discussions in Mamaila raised concerns about how elders' oversight can, on the one hand, protect Leola from consumerism and potential scamming but, on the other, exclude youth and reproduce patriarchal power. Intergenerational knowledge is vital to cultural identity; however, digital systems tend to be biased towards communication practices that reinforce differentiations in sharing information between older and younger people [15]. Locating design endeavours within a rural CN can offer, however, particular opportunities to tackle such tensions in digital transformation. For instance, Mamaila Community Network can develop programming skills amongst youth, and in the future children, while involving parents and elders with limited digital literacy. Importantly, the infrastructure of a rural CN, provides the land in which to do Mandhwane. Unconstrained by the expense of commercial telecommunications, inhabitants can adapt their processes and create services according to their own temporal spatial scales, and control and make meaning from the data they generate themselves.

Acknowledgements. We thank Mamaila Royal Council for support and, along with the wider community of Mamaila, contributing to co-creation. We also thank the Internet Society, Zuri Foundation, Kichose Group of companies, Dr Luci Abrahams, Mr Pardon Mabunda and Mr Oscar Mokgola.

References

1. Adamu, S.M.: Rethinking technology design and deployment in Africa: lessons from an african standpoint. In Proceedings of 3rd African Human-Computer Interaction Conference: Inclusiveness and Empowerment (AfriCHI'21), pp. 75–83. ACM (2021)
2. Adeyemi, M.B., Adeyinka, A.A.: Some key issues in African traditional education. McGill J. Educ. **37**, 223–240 (2002)
3. Aludhilu, H.N., Bidwell, N.J.: Home is not Egumbo: language, identity and web design. In Proceedings of the 2nd African Conference for Human Computer Interaction (AfriCHI 2018), ACM (2018)
4. Association for Progressive Communications. Global Information Society Watch: Community Networks. APC (2018). www.apc.org/en/pubs/global-information-society-watch-2018-community-networks
5. Avle, S., Lindtner, S. Design (ing) 'Here' and 'There': tech entrepreneurs, global markets, and reflexivity in design processes. In Proceedings of the 34th Conference on Human Factors in Computing Systems. (CHI 2016), pp. 2233–2245. ACM (2016)
6. Avle, S., Lindtner, S. Williams, K.: How methods make designers. In: Proceedings of the 35th Conference on Human Factors in Computing Systems (CHI 2017), pp. 472–483. ACM (2017)
7. Awori, K., Bidwell, N.J., Shewarga-Hussen, T., Gill, Lindtner, S.: Decolonising technology design panel. In: Proceedings of the 1st African Conference for Human Computer Interaction (AfriCHI 2016), ACM (2016)
8. Baiphethi, M., Hart, T.: Tshepo Khumbane. growing South Africa's women and landscape. Agenda: Empowering Women Gender Equity **22**(78), 156–162 (2008)
9. Bidwell, N.J.: Decolonising HCI and interaction design discourse: some considerations in planning AfriCHI. XRDS **22**(4) 25–30 (2016)
10. Bidwell, N.J.: Moving the centre to design social media for rural Africa. AI&Soc: J. Cult. Commun. Knowl. **31**(1) 51–77 (2016)
11. Bidwell, N.J.: Women and the Spatial Politics of Community Networks: Invisible in the sociotechnical imaginary of wireless connectivity. In: Proceedings of the 31st Australian Conference on Human-Computer-Interaction, pp. 197–208 (2019)
12. Bidwell, N.J.: Decolonising in the gaps: community networks and the identity of African innovation. In: Dunn, H. (ed.) Media, Culture and Technology in the Global South: Reimagining Communication and Identity in Africa and the Caribbean. Palgrave (2021)
13. Bidwell, N.J., Reitmaier, T., Rey-Moreno, C., Roro, Z., Siya, M., Dlutu, D.: Timely relations in rural Africa. In: Proceedings of the 12th International Conference on Social Implications of Computers in Developing Countries. The International Federation for Information Processing (IFIP) WG, vol. 9, no. 4, pp. 92–106. Springer, Cham (2013)
14. Bidwell, N.J., Reitmaier, T., Jampo, K. Orality, gender and social audio in rural Africa. In: Proceedings of the 11th International Conference on the Design of Cooperative Systems (COOP) (2014)
15. Bidwell, N.J., et al.: Designing social media for community information sharing in rural South Africa. In: Proceedings of the Southern African Institute for Computer Scientist and Information Technologists Annual Conference (SAICSIT), ACM (2014)
16. Bidwell, N.J., Winschiers-Theophilus, H.: Extending Connections Between Land and People Digitally. Heritage and Social Media: Understanding heritage in a participatory culture. Routledge, Milton Park (2012)
17. Chilisa, B., Major, T.E., Gaotlhobogwe, M., Mokgolodi, H.: Decolonizing and indigenizing evaluation practice in Africa: toward African relational evaluation approaches. Can. J. Program Eval. **30**(3), 313–328 (2015)

18. Csikszentmihalyi, C., Mukundane, J., Rodrigues, G.F., DMwesigwa, D., Kasprzak, K.: The space of possibilities: political economies of technology innovation in sub- saharan Africa. In Proceedings of the 36th Conference on Human Factors in Computing Systems (CHI 2018), ACM (2018)

19. Daswa, T.J., Matshidze, P.E., Netshandama, V.O., Makhanikhe, T.J., Kugara, S.L.: Mahund-wane: an educational game for Vhavenda youth. Gender Behav. **16**(2), 11623–11637 (2018)

20. De Lange, M., Kruger, E., Stimie, C.M.: Water harvesting for home food security. Int. J. Rural Dev. **4**, 26–29 (2009)

21. Diallo, D.D.: The Sankofa paradox: why black women know the HIV epidemic ends with "WE" (2021)

22. Edozie, R.K.: Pan "Africa" rising: the paradox of culture, third ways, and coproducing global development. In: "Pan" Africa Rising. Contemporary African Political Economy. Palgrave Macmillan, New York (2017). pp 135–165 https://doi.org/10.1057/978-1-137-59538-6_6

23. Gill, A.Q., Chew, E.: Configuration information system architecture: insights from applied action design research. Inf. Manage. **56**(4), 507–525 (2019)

24. Gina, B.: Presenting and re-presenting the past: African childhood recalled. Tydskrif vir Nederlands & Afrikaans 10 de Jaargang (2) (2003)

25. Gwaka, L.T., May, J., Tucker, W.: Towards low-cost community networks in rural commu-nities: the impact of context using the case study of Beitbridge, Zimbabwe. Electron. J. Inf. Syst. Dev. Countries **84**(3), e12029 (2018)

26. Heeks, R. From digital divide to digital justice in the global south: conceptualising adverse digital incorporation. In: Proceedings of the 1st IFIP 9.4 Virtual Conference (2021)

27. Heeks, R.: ICT4D 2.0: The next phase of applying ICT for international development. Computer **41**(6), 26–33 (2008)

28. Ho, M.R., Smyth, T.N., Kam, M., Dearden, A.: Human-computer interaction for development: The past, present, and future. Inf. Technol. Int. Dev. **5**(4), 1 (2009)

29. Irani, L. Design thinking: defending Silicon Valley at the apex of global labor hierarchies. Catal. Feminism Theor. Technosci. **4**(1) 1–19 (2018)

30. Itchuaqiyaq, C.U., Breeanne, M.: Decolonizing decoloniality: considering the (mis)use of decolonial frameworks in TPC scholarship. Commun. Des. Quart. **9**(1), 20–31 (2021)

31. Kanstrup, A.M., Christiansen, E.: Model power: still an issue? In: Proceedings of the 4th Decennial Conference on Critical Computing: between Sense and Sensibility, pp. 165–168 (2005)

32. Krige, E.J., Krige, J.D.: The Realm of a Rain-Queen: A Study of the Pattern of Lovedu Society. Routledge, Milton Park (2018)

33. Kurland, R., Salmon, R.: Group work vs. casework in a group: principles and implications for teaching and practice. Soc. Work Groups **28**(3–4), 121–132 (2005)

34. Lazem, S., Giglitto, D., Nkwo, M.S., Mthoko, H., Upani, J., Peters, A.: Challenges and paradoxes in decolonising HCI: A critical discussion. Comput. Support. Coop. Work (CSCW) **31**(2), 159–196 (2022)

35. Magoro, K.D.: Digital mandhwane driving community networks to connect the unconnected in developing regions for inclusive growth: AN IITPSA #IFIP60 Event, 17 November (2021). https://event.webinarjam.com/register/77/plp6kh45

36. Magoro, K.D.: Cultural knowledge systems, mandhwane and mind mobilisation for rural communities in the digital era. In: Proceedings of the International Conference of the Digital Humanities Association of Southern Africa (2021). https://dh2021.digitalhumanities.org.za/home/proceedings-and-book-of-abstracts/

37. Magoro, K.D.: Social capital and people centred approach. The 10th Virtual African Internet Governance Forum (vAfiGF2021). https://2021.afigf.africa/

38. Makaudze, G.: Africana womanism and shona children's games. J. Pan Afr. Stud. **6**(10), 129–140 (2014)
39. Makaudze, G.: African traditional leadership and succession in the post-colonial Shona novel. South. Peace Rev.-J. **5**(1), 9–19 (2017)
40. Mamaila Community App download: https://play.google.com/store/apps/details?id=com.ree. mizer.communityapp&hl=en_ZA&gl=US
41. Mashiba, M., Asino, T.: Afrikan Pedagogy & Technology-Supported Learning Design. In: Bidwell, N.J., Winschiers-Theophilus, H. (eds.) At the Intersection of Indigenous and Traditional Knowledge and Technology (2015)
42. Mateus, S., Mufeti, T., Bidwell, N.J.: Social network platforms and the oshiwambo practice of eengano. In: Halberstadt, J., Marx Gomez, J., Greyling, J., Mufeti, T.K. (eds.) Resilience, Entrepreneurship and ICT. Latest Research from Germany, South Africa, Mozambique and Namibia. CSR, Sustainability, Ethics & Governance (2021)
43. Mbembe, A.: Democracy as a community of life. In: De Gruchy, J.W. (ed.) The Humanist Imperative in South Africa, pp. 187–192. Sun Press, Stellenbosch (2011)
44. Molehe, R.C., Marumo, P.O., Motswaledi, T.R.: The position of womanism versus feminism in a contemporary world: the African philosophy perspective. Gend. Behav. **18**(4), 16799–16810 (2020)
45. Motshekga, M.K.: The Mujadji dynasty: the principles of female leadership in African cosmology. Emond, M. (ed.). Kara Books (2010)
46. Mutema, F.: Shona traditional children's games and songs as a form of indigenous knowledge: an endangered genre. IOSR J. Hum. Soc. Sci. **15**, 59–64 (2013)
47. Pendse S.R., et al.: From treatment to healing: envisioning a decolonial digital mental health. In: Proceedings of the 39th Conference on Human Factors in Computing Systems (CHI 2022), ACM (2022)
48. Phokeer, A., et al.: iNethi community network: a first look at local and internet traffic usage. In: Proceedings of the 3rd Conference on Computing and Sustainable Societies (COMPASS 2020), pp. 342–344. ACM (2020)
49. Rey-Moreno, C., Pather, S.: Advancing rural connectivity in south africa through policy and regulation: a case for community networks. In: IST-Africa Conference, pp. 1–10. IEEE (2020)
50. Rich, M.J., Pather, S.: A response to the persistent digital divide: Critical components of a community network ecosystem. Inf. Dev. **37**(4), 558–578 (2020)
51. Sanoff, H.: Multiple views of participatory design. Focus **8**(1), 7 (2011)
52. Sen, A.: Commodities and Capabilities. Oxford University Press, Oxford (1999)
53. Siochrú, S., Girard, B.: Community-based Networks and Innovative Technologies. United Nations Development Programme (2005)
54. Smith, C.R., Winschiers-Theophilus, H., Kambunga, A.P., Krishnamurthy, S.: Decolonizing participatory design: memory making in Namibia In: Proceedings of the 16th Participatory Design Conference 2020-Participation (s) Otherwise, no. 1, pp. 96–106 (2020)
55. Spivak, G.C.: Translation as culture. Parallax **6**(1), 13–24 (2000)
56. Tarisayi, K.S., Manhibi, R.: Infancy of internet cafe: the substitute of Ubuntu-padare pedagogy. Indilinga Afr. J. Indigenous Knowl. Syst. **16**(1), 63–72 (2017)
57. Tatira, B., Mutambara, L.H.N., Chagwiza, C.J.: The balobedu cultural activities and plays pertinent to primary school mathematics learning. Int. Educ. Stud. **5**(1), 78–85 (2012)
58. The Internet Society. African Community Networks Summit. https://www.internetsociety. org/events/summit-community-networks-africa
59. Toyama, K.: Geek Heresy: Rescuing Social Change from the Cult of Technology. Public Affairs, New York (2015)
60. Tuck, E., Yang, K.W.: Decolonization is not a metaphor. Decolonization Indigeneity Educ. Soc. **1**(1), (2012)

61. Twinomurinzi, H., Phahlamohlaka, J., Byrne, E.: Diffusing the Ubuntu philosophy into e-government: a South African perspective. In: Janssen, M., Lamersdorf, W., Pries-Heje, J., Rosemann, M. (eds.) EGES/GISP -2010. IAICT, vol. 334, pp. 94–107. Springer, Heidelberg (2010). https://doi.org/10.1007/978-3-642-15346-4_8

62. van Stam, G.: Method of research in a We-paradigm, lessons on living research in Africa. In: Nielsen, P., Kimaro, H. (eds) Information and Communication Technologies for Development. Strengthening Southern-Driven Cooperation as a Catalyst for ICT4D. ICT4D 2019. IFIP Advances in Information and Communication Technology, vol 552, pp 72–82. Springer, Cham (2019). https://doi.org/10.1007/978-3-030-19115-3_7

63. Van Vuuren, L.: Mma Tshepo-celebrating a life dedicated to water. Water Wheel **9**(3), 34–35 (2010)

Adoption of Mobile Applications for Self-healthcare Monitoring by the Youth in South Africa

Macire Kante⬥ and Patrick Ndayizigamiye(✉) ⬥

University of Johannesburg, Johannesburg 2092, South Africa
{mkante,ndayizigamiyep}@uj.ac.za

Abstract. Despite growing recognition of the contribution and availability of mobile applications for self-healthcare monitoring to prevent non-communicable diseases (NCDs), NCDs remain a rising concern amongst the youth in sub-Saharan Africa and South Africa in particular. Indeed, self-healthcare monitoring mobile applications can be used to continuously educate and sensitize people about the need to adopt healthy lifestyles to prevent such diseases. However, the adoption of such applications is influenced by many factors which need to be identified in order to devise strategies to encourage people to adopt such applications. Thus, this study investigated the potential adoption of self-healthcare monitoring mobile applications by the youth in South Africa, using the Unified Theory of Acceptance and Use of Technology (UTAUT) as the theoretical lens. Data, gathered from a convenient sample size of 280 participants, were analysed using the Partial Least Square Structural Equation Modelling. The results revealed that performance expectancy and social influence explained 20.3% of the variance of youth's behavioural intention to adopt self- healthcare monitoring mobile applications in the South African context, while effort expectancy and facilitating conditions did not have a significant effect. Taking the resulting model into account could lead to an increase in the adoption of self-healthcare monitoring applications in South Africa which could assist in the prevention of NCDs. It is recommended that further studies should test the established factors from this study in other contexts.

Keywords: Adoption · Mobile applications · Self-healthcare monitoring · South Africa · Youth · UTAUT · PLS-SEM

1 Introduction and Background

The surge of Non-Communicable Diseases (NCDs) has been widely recognized. More than seventy-five per cent of deaths linked to NCDs worldwide occur in Low and Middle-income countries [1]. In South Africa, it has been argued that youth are the most exposed to NCDs. For instance, De Wet and Frade [2] reported that a considerable percentage of youth suffer from hypertension, diabetes, and obesity amongst other NCDs. These

J. Abdelnour-Nocera et al. (Eds.): *Innovation Practices for Digital Transformation in the Global South*, IFIP AICT 645, pp. 79–96, 2022.
https://doi.org/10.1007/978-3-031-12825-7_5

authors also concluded that NCDs were the predominant cause of mortality. Thus, attention should be paid to the prevention of NCDs amongst the youth in South Africa in particular, as NCDs are no longer attributed to "old age" only [3]. Unhealthy lifestyles such as smoking, excess liquor consumption, lack of physical exercise and skipping breakfast are some of the causes of NCDs in South Africa and globally [4]. One of the ways to prevent NCDs is to sensitize the youth to adopt a healthy lifestyle.

In addition, research has shown that self-healthcare monitoring and the provision of relevant information to the youth amongst others can prevent more than 40% of NCDs-related deaths [5]. Furthermore, Kim et al. [6] argue that healthcare monitoring is crucial in preventing NCDs such as asthma, diabetes and other diseases. Hence, there is a need to foster self-healthcare monitoring with the aim of changing people's unhealthy behaviour, and therefore, lower the risk of NCDs. On the other hand, it has been argued that mobile technology can be used to change people's unhealthy behaviour. Particularly, there is evidence that mobile applications with educational content on healthy lifestyle and self-healthcare monitoring can contribute to the adoption of healthy lifestyles. For instance, a systematic review by Zhao, Freeman and Li [5] has identified studies that link mobile health applications to the improvement of lifestyle, increasing physical activity, weight control, diet control and self-medication management.

In South Africa, Petersen et al. [7] have found that people who suffer from NCDs such as diabetes demonstrate a positive behavioural intention to adopt mobile applications for diabetes self- management. Moreover, mobile phone usage is increasing among South African youth, who are more adept at utilizing technologies than older people [7]. Despite this increase in the use of mobile phones by the youth, recent literature suggests that the adoption of mHealth, including self-healthcare mobile applications is still scanty in South Africa [7, 8] and in developing countries [9, 10]. There are still factors that affect the adoption of mobile applications for self-healthcare monitoring purposes [11] which need to be clearly established. Moreover, there is also a need to establish the effects of these factors on the youth's adoption of mobile applications that may assist them to monitor their health.

The aim of this paper was to investigate the youth's adoption of mobile applications for self-healthcare monitoring purposes in South Africa. The specific objectives of this study were to: establish the factors that could influence the adoption of self-healthcare monitoring mobile applications; and identify the effects of these factors on the adoption of self-healthcare monitoring mobile applications.

2   Literature Review

2.1   Non-communicable Diseases in South Africa

Non-Communicable Diseases are the main causes of deaths in South Africa. The World Health Organization reports that NCDs are estimated to account for 51% of all deaths in the country [1]. Addressing NCDs is critical to improving public healthcare. Researchers have argued that prevention and monitoring of NCDs are some of the best ways to address these diseases. For instance, Hofman [4] highlighted the need for monitoring interventions to effectively prevent premature deaths caused by NCDs. NCDs surveillance needs to be strengthened to provide reliable and robust information for planning and monitoring of health policy [12]. Additionally, the South African National Strategy commission [13] indicates that the South Africa's healthcare system has failed to address the leading diseases such as HIV/AIDS, tuberculosis, hypertension and diabetes. Figure 1 provides an overview of NCDs deaths in South Africa.

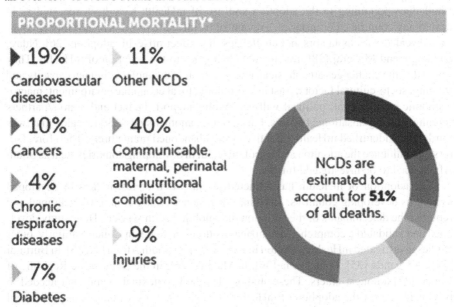

PROPORTIONAL MORTALITY*

▶ **19%**   ▶ **11%**

Cardiovascular   Other NCDs
diseases

▶ **10%**   ▶ **40%**

Cancers   Communicable,
                maternal, perinatal
▶ **4%**   and nutritional
                conditions
Chronic
respiratory
diseases   ▶ **9%**

▶ **7%**   Injuries

Diabetes

NCDs are estimated to account for **51%** of all deaths.

Fig. 1. NCDs proportional mortality source: world health organization (World Health Organization, 2018)

2.2 Mobile Health (mHealth)

Over the past decade, many researchers have investigated mHealth in developing countries [14–19]. Mechael [20] reports that the health community debates whether a specialized field of "mHealth" exists and how to define it. The World Health Organization described mHealth as the utilisation of mobile technologies such as mobile-based applications to realise health objectives [21]. By the end of the year 2021, there were more than 350 000 mHealth applications covering a broad scope of health issues ranging from managing chronic illness to tracking personal fitness [22]. Unsurprisingly, it is often argued that mHealth has the potential to transform healthcare by supporting citizen-centric care which is heralded to result in better care for patients at lower costs and with greater efficiency [23].

On a practical level, mHealth solutions can encourage the adopters to commit to a healthy behaviour and equip them with the information they need to manage their health conditions [21, 24]. In South Africa, it has been reported than over one hundred mHealth applications have been in use [25]. The use of mHealth in developing countries can help foster efficiency and effectiveness in the provision of healthcare [26]. In the same vein, Ndayizigamiye [27] investigated the potential adoption of mobile health technologies for public healthcare in Burundi. He found that mHealth adoption can contribute to disease prevention, disease management and the provision of quality healthcare in Burundi. Thus, mHealth applications, especially self-healthcare monitoring applications, present an opportunity for improving people's health.

However, the benefits of mHealth cannot be realized without its adoption and use. Challenges pertaining to the adoption and use of mHealth have been reported as in developing countries. For instance, a review of 64 mHealth projects in developing countries revealed various factors and challenges that affect mHealth adoption [26]. Ndayizigamiye and Maharaj [28] investigated challenges to the adoption of mHealth. They found that the challenges are: physical access to mobile technology; human capacity and training; socio-cultural factors; trust in technology; local economic environment; macroeconomic environment; political will and public support; budget and donors/partners funding; and organisational barriers. Furthermore, another study [29] revealed that two-thirds of the identified mHealth initiatives were abandoned prematurely. Therefore, factors that influence the adoption and use of mHealth in developing countries such as South Africa need to be investigated further.

The adoption of mHealth has attracted the attention of researchers in developed as well as developing countries. In China for instance, Deng et al. [30] examined and reported the determinants of the adoption of a mobile health service. Their study developed and validated a comprehensive mHealth adoption model in China. Similarly, other studies investigated mHealth adoption in Kenya [31], in South Africa [32, 33], in Burundi [34], in Uganda [35], in Tanzania [36], in Malawi [26], in the Democratic Republic of Congo [37] amongst others. These studies identified contextual factors that needed to be considered for the adoption of mHealth in these countries. Countries have different contextual factors (including culture) that needed to be taken into account [38]. Thus, this study attempts to identify such factors within the context of the youth's adoption of mHealth in South Africa.

2.3 Adoption of Mobile Self-healthcare Monitoring Applications

The choices people make, such as diet, socialization and exercise patterns, have a considerable impact on their health. It has been argued that exercise patterns have an impact on health-related issues such as anxiety, high blood pressure, stress and depression [39]. However, generally, people have little knowledge of these health-related issues. Hence, without adequate knowledge of preventative measures against NCDs, people's unhealthy lifestyles remain unchanged which increase the NCDs-related mortality. On the other hand, mHealth can empower individuals to manage and monitor their personal health [21]. An investigation of the challenges that affect the adoption of ICTs for diabetes self-management in South Africa was conducted by Petersen et al. [7]. The study was qualitative in nature, and hence, could not establish the effects of the factors (drivers and challenges) on the adoption of self-healthcare monitoring mobile applications in the South Africa's context. This points to a methodological gap, as there is a need to investigate the adoption of self-healthcare monitoring applications from a quantitative stance. Thus, this study aimed to fill this gap, to a certain extent, by investigating the adoption of self- healthcare monitoring applications from a quantitative point of view.

3   Theoretical Framework and Hypotheses Formulation

Woosley and Ashia [40] argue that in health IT research, there are three commonly used theories/models: a) Technology Acceptance Model (TAM), b) Diffusion of Innovation Theory (DOI) and c) Unified Theory of Acceptance and Use of Technology (UTAUT). However, UTAUT is more comprehensive than the other theories of technology acceptance [41]. Additionally, UTAUT has been used in various studies pertaining to healthcare (mHealth, eHealth, health) in developing countries [31, 42–44]. It is for these reasons that, the Unified Theory of Acceptance and Use of Technology (UTAUT) [45] was adopted as the theoretical lens underpinning this study.

The UTAUT model aims to explain a user's intention to use an information system and the subsequent use behaviour. The following are the four constructs of UTAUT and their descriptions. Performance expectancy refers to the individual beliefs that a system will improve his/her job performance. Effort expectancy refers to the extent of ease of use of a system. Social influence refers to the extent an individual perceives that 'important others', including his peers, would recommend using a system. Facilitating conditions refer to the extent to which a person believes that technical and organisational infrastructure are available to support the use of a system. The UTAUT model has proved to be a comprehensive framework that can explain a user's intention to use an information system [45]. Venkatesh et al. [45], when testing the model, concluded that other models such as TAM and TAM2 explained approximately 40% of technology acceptance while, on the other hand, the UTAUT model explained 69% of intention to use a technology (Fig. 2).

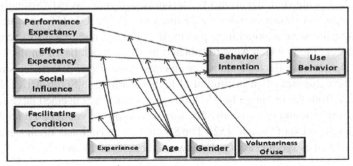

Fig. 2. The UTAUT model [45]

In the context of this study, the four constructs of the UTAUT framework were used to assess factors that may influence the youth to adopt self-healthcare monitoring mobile applications. A study conducted by Nanyombi and Habinka [46] on the factors affecting the adoption of mHealth in both developed and developing countries reported performance expectancy as a driver of mHealth adoption. Hence, this study hypothesizes that:

H1₁ Performance expectancy has a positive effect on behavioural intention to adopt self-healthcare monitoring mobile applications.

Jeon and Park [47] argued that training on using mobile health and technical support had a significant effect on the adoption of mHealth. This points to effort expectancy of the UTAUT. Thus, this study argues that:

H1$_2$ Effort expectancy has a positive effect on behavioural intention to adopt self-healthcare monitoring mobile applications.

Social influence was reported as having an effect on the adoption of mHealth applications in Burundi [43] and in South Africa [8]. Therefore, this study argues that:

H1$_3$ Social influence has an effect on behavioural intention to adopt self-healthcare monitoring mobile applications.

Albabtain [48] suggest that the (high) cost associated with using mHealth applications is a challenge to its adoption. Cost factors are related to the price of the mobile phone, airtime, and data [48]. In the same vein, Petersen et al. [7] have identified the cost of mobile devices and Internet connection costs as the economic factors that affect the behavioural intention to adopt mobile applications for diabetes self-management in South Africa. Furthermore, language has been identified as one of the determinants to mHealth adoption in developing countries [3]. These are facilitating conditions of the UTAUT framework. This study, therefore, hypothesizes that:

H1$_4$ Facilitating conditions have an effect on self-healthcare monitoring mobile applications use behaviour.

H1$_5$ Behavioural intention has an effect on self-healthcare monitoring mobile applications use behaviour.

4　Methodology

This quantitative research used a structured questionnaire with 23 items ranked on a 5-point Likert scale (ranging from (1) "Strongly disagree" to (5) "Strongly agree") to collect data. As shown in Table 1, all measures of the UTAUT constructs within the questionnaire were adopted from previously validated research instruments except facilitating conditions which were formulated by the authors, based on the context of the study. Data were collected from a convenient sample size of 280 students registered at one of the campuses of an institution of higher learning in South Africa. Based on the evidence from the literature [49–51], this sample size was deemed large enough to draw statistically sound conclusions. The sample comprised youth based on the South Africa's classification of "youth" [52]. The South African National Youth Development Agency Act defines "youth" as people between the ages of 14 and 35.

Table 1.　Summary of measurement items

Construct	Items in the questionnaire	Sources
Performance Expectancy (PE)	PE1. Using mobile applications for self-healthcare monitoring will improve the quality of my life PE2. Using mobile applications for self-healthcare monitoring will make my life more convenient PE3. Using mobile applications for self-healthcare monitoring will make me more effective in my life PE4. Overall, I find the mobile applications for self-healthcare monitoring to be useful in my life	[45, 46]

(continued)

Table 1. (*continued*)

Construct	Items in the questionnaire	Sources
Effort Expectancy (EE)	EE1. Learning to operate mobile applications for self-healthcare monitoring will be easy for me EE2. I can easily become skilful at using the mobile applications for self-healthcare monitoring EE3. I can get the mobile applications for self-healthcare monitoring to do what I want them to do EE4. Overall, the mobile applications for self-healthcare monitoring are easy to use	[45, 46]
Social Influence (SI)	SI1. People who influence my behaviour think that I can use mobile applications for self-healthcare monitoring SI2. People who are important to me think that I should use mobile applications for self-healthcare monitoring SI3. People who are close to me think that I must use the mobile applications for self-healthcare monitoring	[47]
Facilitating Conditions (FC)	FC1. I have access to the internet when needed FC2. I have financial resources to purchase mobile data when needed FC3. I have technical knowledge to download mobile applications on a smartphone FC4. I have the technical knowledge to use mobile applications FC5. I have access to a person who can assist me anytime when I encounter difficulties while downloading a mobile application FC6. I have access to a person who can assist me anytime when I encounter difficulties while using a mobile application	Formulated by the researcher
Behavioural Intention (BI)	BI1. I have high intention to use the mobile applications for self-healthcare monitoring BI2. I intend to learn about using the mobile applications for self-healthcare monitoring BI3. I plan to use mobile applications for self-healthcare monitoring to manage my health	[41]
Use Behaviour (AU)	AU1. Using mobile applications for self-healthcare monitoring is a pleasant experience AU2. I currently use mobile applications for self-healthcare monitoring AU3. I spend a lot of time on mobile applications for self-healthcare monitoring	[48]

Basic statistical analysis and data management techniques (frequency analysis, descriptive statistics and data distribution analysis) were performed, using the Statistical Package for Social Sciences (SPSS) software version 20. Thereafter, the authors applied the Partial Least Square Structural Equation Modelling (PLS-SEM) technique, using SMARTPLS version 3.2.9 software to assess the UTAUT model. The PLS-SEM helps to create path models to depict the causal sequence [53]. The PLS-SEM comprises two models, namely the inner or structural model and the measurement model. The inner model displays the relationships among the constructs while the outer model, also known as the measurement model, is used to evaluate the relationships among the indicator variables and their corresponding constructs. Table 2 provides the criteria used for PLS-SEM models assessment.

Table 2. Guidelines when using PLS-SEM [50, 51, 53]

Assessment	Criterion	Description
Indicator reliability	Indicator loading > .600	Loadings represent the absolute contribution of the indicator to the definition of its latent variable
Internal consistency reliability	Cronbach's α > 0.6	Measures the degree to which the measured variables (MVs) load simultaneously when the latent variable (LV) increases
Internal consistency reliability	Composite reliability > 0.6	Attempts to measure the sum of a latent variable (LV) factor loadings relative to the sum of the factor loadings plus error variance
Content validity	Average Variance Extracted (AVE) > 0.5	The degree to which individual items reflecting a construct converge in comparison to items measuring different constructs
Discriminant validity	Heterotrait-Menotrait Ratio (HTMT) < 1	In information Systems research, it is argued that discriminant validity should be assessed by the Heterotrait-Menotrait Ratio (HTMT)
Model predictability	Predictive relevance Q^2 > 0.05	By systematically assuming that a certain number of cases are missing from the sample, the model parameters are estimated and used to predict the omitted values

(*continued*)

Table 2. (*continued*)

Assessment	Criterion	Description
Model validity	$R^2 > 0.100$	Coefficient of determination
Model validity	Path coefficients and critical t-values for a two-tailed test are 1.65 (significance level = 10 per cent),1.96 (significance level = 5 per cent), and 2.58 (significance level = 1%	Structural path coefficients are the path weights connecting the factors to one another

5 Findings

This study's results are reported in the light of the research objectives and compared with the current literature. This study collected 277 usable responses. Most of the respondents (87.73%) were between the ages of 18 and 24, followed by the age group of between 25 and 30 years. Respondents aged 31 and above were the least represented in this study. In addition, 53.8% of the respondents were female while male respondents made up the remaining 46.2%.

5.1 Factors Influencing the Adoption of Self-healthcare Monitoring Mobile Applications

The first objective of the study identified factors influencing the adoption of mobile applications for self-healthcare monitoring. The subsequent (measurement) model of PLS-SEM, as mentioned in the methodology section, is concerned with the validity of the model's constructs. This section assesses the convergent validity and discriminant validity of the latent variables. A latent variable that has convergent and discriminant validity implies that it can be incorporated into the model under study [51].

Convergent Validity
The authors used the following measures to assess convergent validity: composite reliability (greater than 0.8), Cronbach's alpha (greater than 0.8), average variance extracted (AVE) (greater than 0.6) and indicator reliability (greater than 0.7). As depicted in Table 3, the convergent validity was established, as the values of Cronbach's alpha and composite reliability were above the threshold of 0.8 and the average value extracted and indicator reliability above the threshold of 0.6 and 0.7 respectively for all the constructs.

Discriminant Validity

Discriminant validity represents the extent to which the construct is empirically distinct from other constructs; in other words, the extent to which the construct measures what it is intended to measure. There are three means of assessing the discriminant validity: the Fornell-Larcker criterion, the cross-loading criterion and the Heterotrait-Menotrait Ratio (HTMT) [50].

Although the assessment of cross-loadings and the use of the Fornell-Larcker criteria are accepted methods for assessing the discriminant validity of a PLS model, these methods have shortcomings [53]. This was noted by Hair et al. [50] who argued that the lack of discriminant validity was better detected by the Heterotrait-Monotrait Ratio (HTMT) assessment. Thus, we used the HTMT criterion to assess discriminant validity (see Table 4).

Table 3. Convergent validity

Construct	Item	Indicator reliability	Cronbach's alpha	Composite reliability	Average Variance Extracted (AVE)
BI	BI1	0.936	0.885	0.945	0.896
	BI2	0.957	0.806	0.884	0.719
EE	EE1	0.834	0.907	0.954	0.911
	EE2	0.879	0.819	0.892	0.733
	EE3	0.830	0.876	0.922	0.798
FC	FC1	0.936	0.819	0.879	0.710
	FC2	0.973	N/A	N/A	N/A
PE	PE1	0.868	0.885	0.945	0.896
	PE2	0.889	0.806	0.884	0.719
	PE3	0.809	0.907	0.954	0.911
SI	SI1	0.860	0.819	0.892	0.733
	SI2	0.911	0.876	0.922	0.798
	SI3	0.908	N/A	N/A	N/A
AU	AU1	0.850	0.885	0.945	0.896
	AU2	0.916	N/A	N/A	N/A
	AU3	0.753	N/A	N/A	N/A

Table 4. HTMT criterion

	BI	EE	FC	PE	SI	AU
BI	N/A	N/A	N/A	N/A	N/A	N/A
EE	0.333	N/A	N/A	N/A	N/A	N/A
FC	0.093	0.114	N/A	N/A	N/A	N/A
PE	0.478	0.615	0.096	N/A	N/A	N/A
SI	0.300	0.335	0.220	0.343	N/A	N/A
AU	0.227	0.198	0.080	0.196	0.377	N/A

This study concluded that the convergent validity (AVE > 0.5) and discriminant validity (HTMT < 1) of the UTAUT constructs, as presented in this study, were established. Therefore, based on the UTAUT model, factors that could influence the youth's adoption of mobile applications for self-healthcare monitoring were performance expectancy, effort expectancy, facilitating conditions, social influence, behavioural intention and use behaviour. Therefore, the first research objective of this study was achieved.

5.2   Effects of the Factors on the Adoption of Self-healthcare Monitoring Mobile Applications

The second research objective identified the effects of the factors identified through the first objective on the adoption of self-healthcare monitoring mobile applications. In PLS-SEM, the structural or inner model represents the causal model. The primary criterion for the evaluation of the causal model is the coefficient of determination (R^2). The second criterion is the path coefficient (β), the third is the predictive relevance (Q^2), followed by the Standardized Root Mean Square Residual (SRMR) [50]. The last criterion is to test whether there are any moderating variables. The following sections present the results pertaining to the assessment of these criteria.

Coefficient of Determination (R^2)
As shown in Fig. 3, the variance of the first endogenous variable (behavioural intention) is 0.203. This means that performance expectancy, effort expectancy and social influence explain 20.3% of the variance in the behavioural intention to adopt self-healthcare monitoring mobile applications. Furthermore, this R^2 value of 0.203 shows that the model derived from this study is good as it explains more clearly the youth's adoption of self-healthcare monitoring mobile applications.

Path Coefficients (β)
Structural path coefficients are the path weights connecting the model factors to one another (β). On the first endogenous variable, this study found that performance expectancy (PE) has the strongest effect on behavioural intention (0.355), followed by social influence (0.160). The effects size of effort expectancy and facilitating conditions

on the behavioural intention to adopt self-healthcare monitoring mobile applications are 0.070 and 0.059 respectively. Moreover, behavioural intention has the second strongest effect in the model (0.229) on the endogenous variable (use behaviour). The path coefficients β of the model constructs are greater than 0.1 except for effort expectancy (0.070) and facilitating conditions (0.059). Thus, they can be considered as significant.

Using SMARTPLS version 3.2.9, we ran the bootstrapping function as suggested by [53] (Fig. 3). The results of the bootstrapping are reported below in Table 5.

Table 5. Path coefficients

Hypothesis	β	T-statistics	P-values	Comments
PE → BI	0.335	4.51***	<0.001	Supported
EE → BI	0.070	0.88	0.38	Rejected
SI → BI	0.160	2.95***	<0.001	Supported
FC → AU	0.059	0.66	0.51	Rejected
BI → AU	0.229	4***	<0.001	Supported

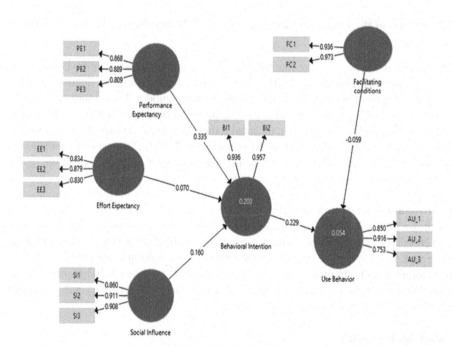

Fig. 3. Model results.

Predictive Relevance (Q^2)

The blindfolding function of SmartPLS 3.2.9 was run, following the recommended guidelines [51, 53]. The results indicated that performance expectancy, effort expectancy and social influence were highly predictive of the behavioural intention to adopt mobile applications for self-healthcare monitoring with a high Q2 (0.16). This assertion was based on the argument provided by Garson [53] who reported that a Q^2 value above 0 indicates that a model is relevant to predicting the set factor(s). Behavioural intention also predicted its endogenous latent variable (i.e. use behaviour with a high Q^2 of 0.03). These results for the model prediction were consistent with the threshold reported in the literature (see Table 2).

Standardized Root Mean Square Residual (SRMR)

The model fit function of SMARTPLS provided SRMR value of 0.04. An SRMR value of less than 0.08 is deemed adequate [53, 54]. Therefore, the model passed the SRMR test.

6 Discussion

This study was designed to establish the determinants of the adoption of self-healthcare monitoring mobile applications in South Africa. In the literature review, the authors found empirical evidence suggesting that performance expectancy, effort expectancy, social influence, facilitating conditions and behavioural intention constructs of the UTAUT framework were determinants of the adoption of mHealth [7, 55]. The results of this study confirmed these findings. As stated by Heeks [56], each (key) stakeholder's behaviour towards the adoption of an Information and Communication Technology for Development (ICT4D) project is important to the success of the project. In the context of healthcare, this means that the behaviour of each stakeholder (such as youth, patients, elders and so on) towards the adoption of mHealth need to be considered in order to convey information that will enable the stakeholder to make informed health-related decisions. In this study, the authors have provided the determinants for the adoption of self-healthcare monitoring mobile applications by the youth; hence, contributing to the understanding of the youth's behaviour towards mHealth adoption in the South African context. Another important finding with regard to the first specific research objective (to establish the factors that can influence the adoption of self-healthcare monitoring mobile applications) is the statistical power of these determinants. The authors argued in the literature review that there is a methodological gap, as a previous similar study conducted in South Africa has used qualitative methods and hence, could not provide statistical value (s) to support the findings. The authors of this paper have filled this gap by providing the Average Variance Extracted (AVE) of each one of the identified determinants. On a practical level, designers of mobile health in general and self-healthcare monitoring mobile applications in particular, should pay attention to these identified determinants.

The second research objective was to identify the effects of these factors on the adoption of self-healthcare monitoring mobile applications. The authors identified that performance expectancy (H1$_1$) and social influence (H1$_3$) have positive effect on behavioural intention to adopt self-healthcare monitoring mobile applications. Additionally, behavioural intention have a positive effect on use behaviour (H1$_5$). However, hypotheses H1$_2$ (effort expectancy has a positive effect on behavioural intention to adopt self-healthcare monitoring mobile applications) and H1$_4$ (facilitation conditions have a positive effect on use behaviour) were rejected. The findings concurred with those of Karuri [31] who argued that, in the context of the adoption of District Health Information Systems 2 (DHIS2) in Kenya, performance expectancy and social influence positively affected the health workers' behavioural intention to adopt the DHIS2, and that behavioural intention positively affected the health workers' intention to use the system. Opoku, Scott and Quentin [57] also confirmed these findings in the context of the adoption of teleconsultations in Ghana.

In this study, effort expectancy did not exert a significant effect on behavioural intention to adopt self-healthcare mobile applications probably because the youth were generally conversant with the use of smartphones and mobile applications. Therefore, they generally did not have difficulty using mobile applications. Consequently, effort expectancy did not influence their decision to adopt self-healthcare monitoring applications.

For self-healthcare monitoring mobile applications designers and managers, it is important to concentrate on the content of their applications so that the youth will easily identify the benefits of using such applications. Additionally, it is important that designers and managers devise awareness interventions to encourage the youth to adopt such applications. These awareness programmes may be ran by youth peers who are regarded as role models, as the young people influence one another to adopt mHealth applications.

7 Conclusion

The purpose of this study was to investigate the determinants of the youth's adoption of self-healthcare mobile applications. The study formulated five direct hypotheses, using the UTAUT framework as its underpinning theoretical foundation. The study firstly aimed at establishing the factors that could influence the adoption of self-healthcare monitoring mobile applications. In this regard, it was found that performance expectancy, effort expectancy, facilitating conditions, social influence and behavioural intention were factors that could influence the adoption of self-healthcare monitoring mobile applications. Secondly, this research proposed to determine the effects of the established factors. In this regard, the results suggested that performance expectancy and social influence have a positive and significant effect on behavioural intention while facilitating conditions and effort expectancy did not exert a significant effect. Lastly, the study proposed a model that explained 20.3% of the variance of use behaviour. The proposed model could be used as a guide for the adoption of self-healthcare monitoring mobile applications in South Africa.

All UTAUT factors evaluated in this study are contextual, as they are dependent on the specific context setup. Hence, further inquiries should be done to assess the established factors from this study in other contexts.

Acknowledgement. The authors would like to thank Tom Cyprian Soni for his involvement in the collection of data for this study.

Definition of Terms. mHealth: mHealth is a term that describes the use of wireless technology and mobile devices for medical care.

Youth: In this study, the term "youth" refers to people who are within the age range of 18 and 35.

PLS-SEM: The Partial Least Squares Structural Equation Modelling (PLS-SEM) is a statistical method that helps determine cause-effect relationships.

UTAUT: The unified theory of Acceptance and Use of Technology (UTAUT) is a theoretical framework used in the field of Information Systems (IS) to explain user intentions to use an information system and subsequent usage behaviour.

Self-Healthcare Monitoring: Self-Healthcare Monitoring refers to the use of mobile applications and wearable devices to monitor and manage one's health.

Heterotrait-Monotrait Ratio (HTMT): HTMT is a statistical technique used to measure discriminant validity in Partial Least Squares-Structural Equation Modelling.

Convergent validity: Convergent validity helps determine whether measures of a construct are related.

Discriminant validity: Discriminant validity helps to determine whether measures that should not be related are indeed not related.

Standardized Root Mean Square Residual (SRMR): Root Mean Square Residual (SRMR) helps ascertain the mean size of residual correlations.

The Coefficient of Determination (R2): R2 helps determine the variation (s) within the dependent variable caused by independent variables.

Average Variance Extracted (AVE): The AVE helps to estimate, on average, the proportion of variation in a construct's items can be explained by the construct or latent variable.

Path coefficient (β): In PLS-SEM, path coefficient (β) helps determine how an independent variable affects a dependent variable in the path model.

References

1. World Health Organization – Non-communicable Diseases (NCD) Country Profiles (2018). https://apps.who.int/iris/handle/10665/274512. Accessed 20 Jan 2022
2. De Wet, N., Frade, S.: Non-communicable disease prevalence among youth in South Africa: the past, present and future. In 2017 XXVIII International Population Conference Proceedings, p. 90. International Union for the Scientific Study of Population (IUSSP), Cape town (2017)
3. Ndayizigamiye, P., Soni, T.C., Jere, N.: Factors motivating the adoption of self- healthcare monitoring mobile applications by the South African Youth. In: 2018 IST- Africa Week Conference (IST-Africa), pp. 1–7. IEEE, Gaborone (2018)
4. Hofman, K.: Non-communicable diseases in South Africa: a challenge to economic development. S. Afr. Med. J. **104**(10), 647 (2014)
5. Zhao, J., Freeman, B., Li, M.: Can mobile phone apps influence people's health behavior change? An evidence review. J. Med. Internet Res. **18**(11), e287 (2016)
6. Kim, K.A., Shin, S.Y., Suh, J.W., Park, C., Cha, E.J., Bae, H.D.: Home healthcare self-monitoring system for chronic diseases. In: 2012 IEEE International Conference on Consumer Electronics (ICCE), pp. 486–487. IEEE, Las Vegas (2012)
7. Petersen, F., Brown, A., Pather, S., Tucker, W.D.: Challenges for the adoption of ICT for diabetes self- management in South Africa. Electron. J. Inf. Syst. Developing Countries **86**, e12113 (2020)
8. Ndayizigamiye, P., Kante, M., Shingwenyana, S.: An adoption model of mHealth applications that promote physical activity. Cogent Psychol. **7**(1), 1764703 (2020)

9. Dwivedi, Y.K., Shareef, M.A., Simintiras, A.C., Lal, B., Weerakkody, V.: A generalized adoption model for services: a cross-country comparison of mobile health (m-health). Gov. Inf. Q. **33**(1), 174–187 (2016)

10. Laxman, K., Krishnan, S.B., Dhillon, J.S.: Barriers to adoption of consumer health informatics applications for health self-management. Health Sci. J. **9**(5), 1–7 (2015)

11. Neill, D., Van Belle, J.P., Ophoff, J.: Understanding the adoption of wearable technology in South African organizations. In: International Conference on Information Resources Management (CONF-IRM), pp. 1–14. Association for Information Systems, Cape Town (2016)

12. Nojilana, B., et al.: Persistent burden from non-communicable diseases in South Africa needs strong action. South African Med. J. **106**(5), 436–437 (2016)

13. National Development Plan 2030. https://www.gov.za/sites/default/files/Executive% 20Summary-NDP%202030%20-%20Our%20future%20%20make%20it%20work.pdf. Accessed 19 Jan 2022

14. Han, S., Harkke, V., Mustonen, P., Seppanen, M., Kallio, M.: Mobilizing medical information and knowledge: some insights from a survey. In: Proceedings of the 13th European Conference on Information Systems, pp.1–13. Association for Information Systems, Turku (2004)

15. Meng, F., Guo, X., Peng, Z., Lai, K., Vogel, D.: The routine use of mobile health services in the presence of health consciousness. Electron. Commer. Res. Appl. **35**, 1–10 (2019)

16. Kante, M., Ndayizigamiye, P.: A systematic mapping of the adoption of Internet of Things to provide healthcare services in developing countries. In: Ndayizigamiye, P., Barlow-Jones, G., Brink, R., Bvuma, S., Minty, R., Mhlongo, S. (eds.) Perspectives on ICT4D and Socio-Economic Growth Opportunities in Developing Countries, pp. 99–126. IGI Global, Hershey (2020)

17. Kante, M., Ndayizigamiye, P.: An analysis of the current status of Internet of Medical Things policies in developing countries. NPG Neurologie - Psychiatrie - Gériatrie **20**(119), 259–265 (2020)

18. Kante, M., Ndayizigamiye, P.: Internet of medical things, policies and geriatrics: an analysis of the national digital health strategy for South Africa 2019–2024 from the policy triangle framework perspective. Sci. Afr. **12**(2021), e00759 (2021)

19. Ndayizigamiye, P., Maharaj, M.: A systematic review of mHealth interventions for public healthcare in East Africa. In: 24th Americas Conference on Information Systems, p. 77. Association for Information Systems, New Orleans (2018)

20. Mechael, P.N.: The case for mHealth in developing countries. Innov. Technol. Governance Globalization **4**(1), 103–118 (2009)

21. Kenny, G., Connolly, R.: Towards an inclusive world: exploring m-health adoption across generations. In: Proceedings of the 25th European Conference on Information Systems (ECIS), pp. 1129–1144. Association for Information Systems, Guimarães (2017)

22. Mobius MD. https://mobius.md/2021/10/25/11-mobile-health-statistics/. Accessed 20 Jan 2022

23. Whittaker, R.: Issues in mHealth: findings from key informant interviews. J. Med. Internet Res. **14**(5), e129 (2012)

24. Cho, J., Park, D., Lee, H.E.: Cognitive factors of using health apps: systematic analysis of relationships among health consciousness, health information orientation, eHealth literacy, and health app use efficacy. J. Med. Internet Res. **16**(5), e125 (2014)

25. Botha, A., Booi, V.: mHealth implementation in South Africa. In: IST-Africa Conference, pp. 1–13. IEEE, Durban (2016)

26. O'Connor, Y., O'Sullivan, T., Gallagher, J., Heavin, C., Hardy, V., O'Donoghue, J.: A mobile health technology intervention for addressing the critical public health issue of child mortality. Electron. J. Inf. Syst. Dev. Countries **84**(1), 1–11 (2017)

27. Ndayizigamiye, P.: Potential adoption of mobile health technologies for public healthcare in Burundi. Doctoral thesis. University of KwaZulu-Natal (2016)
28. Ndayizigamiye, P., Maharaj, M.: Applying bridges framework to investigate challenges to the adoption of mHealth in Burundi. In: IST-Africa Conference, pp. 1–8. IEEE, Durban (2016)
29. Niemöller, C., Metzger, D., Berkemeier, L., Zobel, B., Thomas, O.: Designing mHealth applications for developing countries. In: Twenty-Fourth European Conference on Information Systems, pp. 1–14. Association for Information Systems, İstanbul (2016)
30. Deng, Z., Zhang, J., Zhang, L.: Applying technology acceptance model to explore the determinants of mobile health service: from the perspective of public user. In: Eleventh Wuhan International Conference on e-Business, pp. 406–411. Association for Information Systems, Wuhan (2012)
31. Karuri, J.W.: Determinants of acceptance and use of routine HIS in developing countries: the case of DHIS2 in Kenya. Doctoral thesis. University of Nairobi (2015)
32. Watkins, J.O.T.A., Goudge, J., Gómez- Olivé, F.X., Griffiths, F.: Mobile phone use among patients and health workers to enhance primary healthcare: a qualitative study in rural South Africa. Soc. Sci. Med. **198**, 139–147 (2018)
33. Ndayizigamiye, P., Hangulu, L., Akintola, O.: A design of a mobile health intervention to enhance homecarers' disposal of medical waste in South Africa. In: IEEE Global Humanitarian Technology Conference, pp. 1–6. IEEE, San Jose (2017)
34. Ndayizigamiye, P., Maharaj, M.: Determinants of mobile health adoption in Burundi. Afr. J. Inf. Syst. **9**(3), 171–191 (2017)
35. Nchise, C., Boateng, R., Shu, I., Mbarika, V.: Mobile phones in health care in Uganda: the AppLab study. Electron. J. Inf. Syst. Dev. Countries **52**(1), 1–15 (2012)
36. Kiwanuka, A., Kimaro, H.C., Senyoni, W.: Analysis of the acceptance process of District Health Information Systems (DHIS) for vertical health programmes: a case study of TB, HIV/AIDS and Malaria Programmes in Tanzania. Electron. J. Inf. Syst. Dev. Countries **70**(1), 1–14 (2015)
37. Imaja, I.M., Ndayizigamiye, P., Maharaj , M.: A design of a mobile health intervention for the prevention and treatment of Cholera in South Kivu in the Democratic Republic of Congo. In: 2017 IEEE Global Humanitarian Technology Conference, pp. 277–281. IEEE, San Jose (2017)
38. Albirini, A.: Cultural perceptions: the missing element in the implementation of ICT in developing countries. Int. J. Educ. Dev. Using ICT **2**(1), 49–65 (2006)
39. Stults-Kolehmainen, M.A., Sinha, R.: The effects of stress on physical activity and exercise. Sports Med. **44**(1), 81–121 (2014)
40. Woosley, J.M., Ashia, K.: Comparison of con- temporary technology acceptance models and evaluation of the best fit for health industry organizations. Int. J. Comput. Sci. Eng. Technol. **1**(11), 709–717 (2011)
41. Taiwo, A., Downe, A.G.: The theory of user acceptance and use of technology (UTAUT): a meta-analytic review of empirical findings. J. Theor. Appl. Inf. Technol. **49**(1), 48–58 (2013)
42. Ami-Narh, J.T., Williams, P.A.H.: A revised UTAUT model to investigate E-health acceptance of health professionals in Africa. J. Emerging Trends Comput. Inf. Sci. **3**(10), 1383–1391 (2012)
43. Ndayizigamiye, P., Maharaj, M.: Mobile health adoption in burundi: a UTAUT perspective. In: 2016 Global Humanitarian Technology Conference, pp.1–11. IEEE, Seattle (2016)
44. Bervell, B., Umar, I.N.: Validation of the UTAUT model: re-considering non-linear relationships of exogeneous variables in higher education technology acceptance research. EURASIA J. Math. Sci. Technol. Educ. **8223**(10), 6471–6490 (2017)
45. Venkatesh, M., Morris, G., Davis, G.B., Davis, F.D.: User acceptance of information technology: toward a unified view. MIS Q. **27**(3), 425–478 (2003)

46. Nanyombi, A., Habinka, A.: Factors influencing the adoption of mobile health in Uganda health facilities: a case study of mobile tracking system in Kayunga. Am. Sci. Res. J. Eng. Technol. Sci. **23**(1), 131–145 (2016)

47. Jeon, E., Park, H.: Factors affecting acceptance of smartphone application for management of obesity. Healthc. Inf. Res. **21**(2), 74–82 (2015)

48. Albabtain, A.F., Almulhim, D.A., Yunus, F., Househ, M.S.: The role of mobile health in the developing world: a review of current knowledge and future trends. J. Sel. Areas Health Inf. **4**(2), 1–6 (2014)

49. Benitez, J., Henseler, J., Castillo, A., Schuberth, F.: How to perform and report an impactful analysis using partial least squares: guidelines for confirmatory and explanatory IS research. Inf. Manag. **57**(2), 1–16 (2020)

50. Hair, J.F., Risher, J.J., Sarstedt, M., Ringle, C.M.: When to use and how to report the results of PLS-SEM. Eur. Bus. Rev. **31**(1), 2–24 (2019)

51. Kante, M., Chepken, C., Oboko, R.: Partial least square structural equation modelling' use in information systems: an updated guideline of practices in exploratory settings. Kabarak J. Res. Innov. **6**(1), 49–67 (2018)

52. National Youth Commission Act. https://www.gov.za/sites/default/files/gcis_document/201409/a19-96.pdf. Accessed 20 Jan 2022

53. Garson, G.D.: Partial Least Squares: Regression and Structural Equation Models. Statistical Associates Publishing, Asheboro (2016)

54. Henseler, J., Hubona, G., Ray, P.A.: Using PLS path modeling in new technology research: updated guidelines. Ind. Manag. Data Syst. **116**(1), 2–20 (2016)

55. Ogundaini, O.O., de la Harpe, R.: Integration of mHealth technologies to support service interaction moments in tertiary healthcare of Western Cape, South Africa. In: 2019 International Conference on Information Resources Management, pp. 1–18. Association for Information Systems, Auckland (2019)

56. Heeks, R.: Information and Communication for Development (ICT4D), 1st edn. Routledge, London (2018)

57. Opoku, D., Scott, P., Quentin, W.: Healthcare Professionals' perceptions of the benefits and challenges of a teleconsultation service in the Amansie-West district of Ghana. Telemedicine e-Health **21**(9), 748–755 (2015)

Determinants of the Adoption of Mobile Applications that Help Induce Healthy Eating Habits

Dineo Adolphina Matlebjane⬥, Patrick Ndayizigamiye(✉)⬥, and Macire Kante⬥

University of Johannesburg, Johannesburg 2092, South Africa
215076547@student.uj.ac.za, {ndayizigamiyep,mkante}@uj.ac.za

Abstract. A healthy diet is a critical factor that affects long-term healthcare outcomes. One of the ways to induce healthy eating habits is through the use of mobile applications. To date, there has been little agreement on the determinants of the adoption of such mobile applications in the South African context. Hence, this study investigated the determinants of the adoption of mobile applications that help induce healthy eating habits in the South African context. The study adopted a survey research design and the UTAUT framework as the guiding theoretical framework. Data were collected and analysed using the Partial Least Square Structural Equation Modelling (PLS-SEM). Findings revealed that performance expectancy and social influence have a significant effect on the behavioural intention to adopt mobile applications that help induce healthy eating habits. However, effort expectancy does not significantly influence behavioural intention. Additionally, behavioural intention positively influences the use behaviour of such applications while facilitating conditions do not have a significant effect on the use behaviour. This study recommends that interventions geared towards encouraging the use of mobile applications to induce healthy eating habits should focus on the identified determinants.

Keywords: mHealth · Diet · Mobile applications · Youth · South Africa · Healthy eating habits · PLS-SEM

1 Introduction

A healthy diet is a critical factor that influence long term health outcomes. Claasen, Hoeven and Covic [1] found that the increased consumption of fatty food and food with high sugar content has become a concern among South Africans. Cooper, De Lannoy and Rule [2] further argued that such consumption is one of the major causes of diseases burden among the youth. A study that investigated the determinants of obesity revealed that South Africa has the second highest number of obese women amongst the 22 developing countries that were investigated [3]. In addition, Obesity and being overweight are majorly caused by unhealthy eating habits and can lead to high blood pressure and heart diseases [4]. Furthermore, it was reported that improving the wellness and health

J. Abdelnour-Nocera et al. (Eds.): *Innovation Practices for Digital Transformation in the Global South*, IFIP AICT 645, pp. 97–112, 2022.
https://doi.org/10.1007/978-3-031-12825-7_6

of the youth is not only important for their present well-being but for the South African economy as they constitute more than half of the South African population [5]. Hence, there is a need for interventions to induce healthy eating habits amongst the youth in South Africa. One of the ways to induce healthy eating habits amongst the youth is the use of mobile health applications. Kante and Ndayizigamiye [5] and Abraham [6] indicated that South Africa is one of the leading global adopters of smartphones, with 93% of South Africans having access to smartphones.

Literature suggests that mobile applications can be used to enhance public healthcare [7–11] and to induce healthy eating habits in particular [12, 13]. Ndayizigamiye and Maharaj [7] reported various mHealth interventions that have been piloted in East Africa. Ndayizigamiye et al. [8] on the other hand provided a proof of concept on how mobile applications can be used to support home-carers in South Africa. Ndayizigamiye and Maharaj [9] conducted a study that identified factors related to the Diffusion of Innovation theory (DOI) that have influence in the adoption of mHealth to provide healthcare services in Burundi. Ndayizigamiye [10] investigated the acceptance of mHealth capabilities in Burundi. Imaja, Ndayizigamiye and Maharaj [11] conducted a study that showed how mHealth can be used to combat Cholera in the Democratic Republic of Congo.

Coughlin et al. [13] studied innovative approaches to encourage healthy eating habits and physical activity in young people. They found that mobile diets and exercise applications can encourage young people to lose weight and keep a healthy diet. In addition, Shin [14] synthesized the literature by reviewing 193 papers on the use of smartphone applications for promoting healthy diet and nutrition. They found that smartphone users preferred quick and easy to run mobile applications that offered them better weight management and suggestions on healthy food intake. The review further identified that the use of mobile applications improved dietary intake of low fat, lower calories and high fibre foods, and also resulted in more physical activities. Moreover, Shin [14] found that having a dietitian support enhances the transition from having an intention to exert a certain behaviour, in this case adopting healthy eating habits, to the actual display of the behaviour, that is eating healthy food. The study concluded that the use of smartphones for photographic dietary tracking is not only convenient, but it increases user engagement as well as healthy eating behaviours.

On the other hand, there is a recognized need to focus on the wellbeing of the youth as they form the crust of the South African productive workforce. Particularly, there is a need to devise innovative interventions to encourage the youth to adopt healthy lifestyles in order to limit the burden of non-communicable diseases among the youth. Van den Berg et al. [15] investigated the lifestyles of South African students that are preparing to undertake a career in healthcare. They found that many of the surveyed students were at risk of getting non-communicable diseases. They also revealed that almost 20% of the surveyed students were obese or overweight. Moreover, they argued that the students had adopted bad eating habits as well as regular alcohol consumption. In the same vein, Van Rensburg and Surujlal [16] found that students (whom the majority are youth) are living unhealthy lifestyles and they have risky behaviours, which have consequences on their future health. The current increase in smartphone penetration amongst the youth in South Africa presents an opportunity to devise healthcare interventions targeting the youth. Particularly, encouraging youth to adopt mobile applications that help induce healthy eating habits could be one of the interventions geared towards inducing healthy lifestyles amongst the youth. Therefore, the objective of this study was to propose an adoption model of mobile applications that help induce healthy eating behaviour amongst the South African youth population.

The specific objectives of the study were to: identify factors that can influence the youth to adopt mobile applications that help induce healthy eating habits; determine the effect of these factors on the adoption of mobile applications that help induce healthy eating habits.

2 Literature Review

2.1 Determinants of the Adoption of Mobile Health Applications

There are a number of studies that have been conducted regarding the adoption of mobile applications in the healthcare context. For instance, a study by Zhao et al. [17] reviewed papers published between January 1, 2010, and June 1, 2015. They identified user-friendly design, real-time feedback, individualized elements, detailed information, and health professional involvement as the determinants of the adoption of mobile health applications. Similarly, Coughlin et al. [13] found that lack of awareness, negative perception, complexity, lack of customisation and feedback are some of the challenges that restrain young people to use mobile health applications. In addition, Kang [18] reported that mobile applications must be user-friendly so that they can serve their intended purposes. Furthermore, Cho, Park and Lee [19] identified factors related to health information-seeking behaviours that influence the adoption of mobile health applications. More specifically, they found that perceived usefulness and perceived ease of use affect the adoption of mobile health applications.

In the developing countries' context, Alam et al. [20] found that performance expectancy, social influence, effort expectancy, facilitating conditions and perceived reliability have an effect on the adoption of mobile health (mHealth) services in Bangladesh. Similarly, Hoque and Sorwar [21] reported that performance expectancy, effort expectancy, social influence, technology anxiety, and resistance to change also have an effect on the behavioural intention of users to adopt mHealth services in Bangladesh. They further found that facilitating conditions had no significant effect on the users' behavioural intention to adopt mHealth services. In Malaysia, Lan et al. [22] argued that performance expectancy, effort expectancy, social influence and facilitating conditions have a positive effect on the user's intention to adopt a mobile dietary intake monitoring application called vTracker. Moreover, Ndayizigamiye and Maharaj [23] found that effort expectancy, performance expectancy and facilitating conditions are significantly correlated with mHealth adoption in Burundi. In the South Africa's context, Ndayizigamiye et al. [5] found that awareness, effort expectancy and social influence have an effect on the adoption of mHealth applications that promote physical activity. In the same context, Soni, Ndayizigamiye and Kante [24] found that performance and social influence constructs of the UTAUT framework are the highest predictors of the youth's behavioural intention to adopt mobile applications for self-healthcare monitoring purposes. In addition, another qualitative study [25] indicated that results demonstrability; performance expectancy; savings; social aspects; awareness; connectivity; accessibility; ease of use and access; privacy; user satisfaction and affordability are factors that motivate South Africa's youth to adopt self-healthcare monitoring mobile applications.

2.2 Effects of mHealth Interventions on Food and Nutrient Intake

Soureti et al. [26] assessed the effects of automated web-based planning tools coupled with mobile text reminders on reducing intake of high-fat foods and food portion sizes in England. The primary outcomes revealed that participants in the intervention group were more likely to report eating balanced diet compared to others that did not partake in the intervention. Beasley et al. [27] on the other hand evaluated the capability of a Personal Digital Assistant (PDA)-based self-monitoring diet program (Diet-MatePro) in the United States of America. Participants in the control group were given a paper-based food diary to record their dietary intake while those in the intervention group were given the PDA-based program. The study recorded that diet adherence was higher among the DietMatePro group (43%) compared to the paper-based diary group (28%) (p = 0.039). Kerr et al. (2016) evaluated the effectiveness of tailored dietary text messaging for improving intake of fruit, vegetables and decreasing junk food (unhealthy food or drinks) over a 6-month period. The study findings revealed that men who received dietary feedback only, significantly reduced their energy-dense nutrient-poor (EDNP) intake (mean = 1.4 intake/day, p = 0.02) while women who received dietary feedback only, significantly reduced their intake of sugar-sweetened beverages (SSB) (mean = 0.2 intake/day, p = 0.04) compared with the participants in the control group. They concluded that the use of mobile technology has great potential for healthy diet and healthy weight promotion amongst young adults.

Vakili et al. [28] evaluated the impact of mobile phone short messaging system on healthy food choices among postmenopausal women in Iran. The study revealed that the consumption of vitamin A rich fruits and vegetables significantly increased in the intervention group compared to the control group (P < 0.001). Moreover, more women in the intervention group consumed fish after the intervention (P = 0.02). However, there was no significant increase in the consumption of dairy products within the intervention group. However, there was also a noticeable increase, although not significant, in the consumption of green leafy vegetable within the intervention group.

Atienza et al. [29] conducted a randomized study to evaluate the efficacy of using a Personal Digital Assistant (PDA) to increase the intake of whole-grain and vegetables intake in mid-life and older adults within an 8-week period. The study revealed that vegetables intake significantly increased within the participants in the intervention cluster (1.5–2.5 intake/day; p = 0.02). Furthermore, a trend towards greater intake of dietary fiber from grains was observed from the participants in the intervention cluster (3.7–4.5 intake/day; p = 0.10).

2.3 Effects of mHealth Interventions on Weight Loss

Fjeldsoe et al. [30] evaluated the effect of a text message-based (GHSH) intervention (as a follow up strategy) on people who participated in an intensive lifestyle coaching intervention. Two hundred and twenty-eight (228) participants were randomly selected to be either part of the intervention group or control group. Then, the participants were sent text messages for a period of 6 months based on each participant's preference. The outcomes revealed that participants in the intervention group recorded significant body weight loss (-0.89 kg), and a reduction in waist circumference (-1.34 cm). Weight loss was significantly greater in the intervention group than in the control group.

Haapala et al. [31] investigated the effectiveness of a mobile phone-enabled weight loss programme among overweight adults. One hundred and twenty-five overweight (BMI $= 26$ to 36 kg/m^2) adults (25- to 44-year-old) were randomly assigned either to an intervention (experimental) group or non-intervention group. Through text messages, participants in the intervention group (N $= 62$) who were self-directed dieters, were instructed to report their weight daily and received immediate tailored feedback. The outcomes revealed that participants in the intervention group recorded significant weight loss compared to the control (non-intervention group).

Lin et al. [32] investigated the effects of text messages to support a healthcare intervention for obese African Americans. The study used a randomized controlled trial of 124 adults of which 63 were assigned to the intervention while 61 were assigned to the control group. The intervention group received a standard care and daily tailored text messages for 6 months while the control group received only a standard care. They found that the extent of engagement with the text messages was correlated with weight loss. Participants in the intervention group recorded more weight loss (-2.5 kg after 3 months and -3.4 kg after 6 months) than the control group.

The above literature has revealed that mobile applications are currently used for healthcare purposes. In addition, the literature shows that these applications can help induce healthy habits. Thus, this study seeks to investigate the (potential) of the youth adopting mobile applications that can help induce healthy eating habits in the South Africa's context. The increasing use of smartphones by the youth in South Africa and their proficiency in the use of mobile devices make a good case for such an investigation.

3 Theoretical Framework

Ventkatesh et al. [33] developed the Unified Theory of Acceptance and Use of Technology (UTAUT) model by combining various factors from eight prominent technology acceptance theoretical frameworks based on their effectiveness in predicting anticipated and actual Information systems' use behaviour. The 8 theoretical frameworks that were combined to form the UTAUT were: a) the Theory of Reasoned Action (TRA) [34]; b) Davis' Technology Acceptance Model (TAM) and its extended version (TAM2) [35, 36]; c) the Motivation Model (MM) [37]; d) the Theory of Planned Behaviour (TPB) [38]; e) the Combined TAM and TPB [39] f) the Model of PC Utilization (MPCU) [40]; g) Roger's Innovation Diffusion Theory (IDT) [41] h) social Cognitive Theory [42]. The UTAUT framework holds that there are four key constructs that influence user's behavioural intention and use behaviour, namely, 1) performance expectancy, 2) effort expectancy, 3) social influence, and 4) facilitating conditions (see Fig. 1) [36].

3.1 Theoretical Propositions

Performance expectancy (PE) is defined as the degree to which an individual believes that using a system will help him or her to attain some gains in the job. In this study,

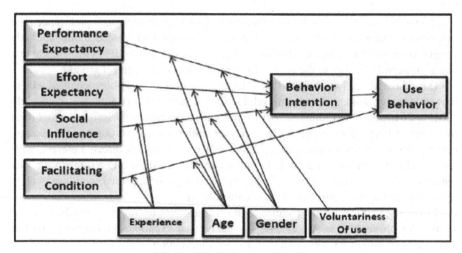

Fig. 1. UTAUT framework [36].

performance expectancy is defined as the degree to which an individual believes that using mobile applications will help him/her induce healthy eating habits. Thus, we hypothesized that:

H1₁. Performance expectancy positively influences the behavioural intention to adopt mobile applications that help induce healthy eating habits.

Effort expectancy (EE) is defined as the extent to which it is easy to use a system. In the context of this paper, effort expectancy is defined as the extent to which mobile applications that help induce healthy eating habits are easy to use. Hence, in this study we hypothesized that:

H1₂. Effort expectancy positively influences the behavioural intention to adopt mobile applications that help induce healthy eating habits.

Social influence (SI) is defined as the degree to which an individual perceives that 'important others' believe he or she should use a new system. This study defines social influence as the degree to which an individual perceives that 'important others' believe he or she should use mobile applications that help induce healthy eating habits. Hence, we hypothesised that:

H1₃. Social influence positively influences the behavioural intention to adopt mobile applications that help induce healthy eating habits.

Facilitating conditions (FC) are defined as the degree to which an individual believes that an organizational and technical infrastructure exist to support the use of a system. In this study, the 'facilitating conditions' construct is defined as the availability and access to the necessary resources and knowledge (skills) to support the use of mobile applications that help induce healthy eating habits. We, therefore, argued that:

H1₄. Facilitating conditions positively influences the behavioural intention to adopt mobile applications that help induce healthy eating habits.

Based on the relationship between behavioural intention and use behaviour in the UTAUT framework, we further hypothesized that:

H1$_5$. Behavioural intention positively influences the use of mobile applications that help induce healthy eating habits.

4 Material and Methods

Data were collected from 89 respondents conveniently sampled from an institution of higher learning in the Gauteng province of South Africa. The study adopted a 5-point Likert scale (1 = strongly disagree, 2 = disagree, 3 = neutral, 4 = agree, and 5 = strongly agree) survey questionnaire as the data collection instrument. Respondents were requested to fill the questionnaires and return them to enumerators. Data were analysed using the Partial Least Square Structural Equation Modelling (PLS-SEM). Partial Least Square Structural Equation Modelling (PLS-SEM) can be used to analyze a small sample size (20 or more respondents) [43–45].

Basic statistical analyses were conducted using SPSS version 20 to identify and deal with missing values and ascertain the multivariate normality. The analysis of missing values revealed that there were 5 questionnaires with a low response rate (missing values higher than 5%), and therefore they were excluded from further analysis as per Carter [46] suggestions. For those responses where the missing values were less than 5%, we applied the mean replacement technique [46]. The multivariate normality was tested through the skewness and kurtosis statistical tests as reported in Table 1. The values of skewness and kurtosis should be between ±1 [47]. However, the distribution of the data collected in this study was not within these acceptable values, indicating a non-normal distribution. However, it is possible to use PLS path modelling with highly skewed data [45] as all Structural Equation Modelling (SEM) techniques are quite robust against the skewness scenario [44].

Thereafter, we applied the Partial Least Square Structural Equation Modelling (PLS-SEM) technique using SMARTPLS 3.2.9 software to assess the UTAUT model. PLS-SEM helps to create path models to depict causal sequence [44]. PLS-SEM comprises two models, namely the inner model, or structural model, and the measurement model. The inner model displays the relationships between the constructs, while the outer model, also known as the measurement model, is used to evaluate the relationships between the indicator variables and their corresponding constructs [45]. Table 2 explains the criteria used for the PLS-SEM model assessment.

5 Results and Discussion

This section discusses the results of the study.

5.1 Demographics Information of the Participants

All participants were between the age of 18 and 35. Hence, they could be categorised as youth according to the South African National Youth Commission Act of 1996 which defines the South African youth as people who are aged between 14 years and 35 years [49]. Most of the participants were females (52.8%).

Table 1. Statistical analysis of the variables

UTAUT constructs	Item	Mean	Std. deviation	Skewness		Kurtosis	
			Statistic	Statistic	Std. error	Statistic	Std. error
Performance expectancy	Using mobile applications that help induce healthy eating habits will increase my chances of achieving my diet targets	3.46	0.83	−0.14	0.26	0.14	0.52
	Using mobile applications that help induce healthy eating habits can help monitor my eating habits	3.70	0.77	−0.71	0.26	1.19	0.52
	Using mobile applications that help induce healthy eating habits can improve my wellbeing	3.75	0.80	−0.51	0.26	0.75	0.52
Effort expectancy	It is easy to learn how to use mobile applications that help induce healthy eating habits	3.71	0.72	−0.10	0.26	−0.20	0.52
	I understand how mobile applications that induce healthy diets work	3.48	1.01	−0.29	0.26	−0.51	0.52
	It is easy to use mobile applications that help induce healthy eating habits	3.59	0.88	−0.23	0.27	−0.03	0.53
Social influence	People who are important to me can influence me to use mobile applications that induce healthy eating habits	3.32	1.09	−0.10	0.26	−0.80	0.52
	People who influence my behaviour can influence me to use mobile applications that help induce healthy eating habits	3.52	0.96	−0.07	0.26	−0.56	0.52
	People whose opinions that I value can influence me to use mobile applications that help induce healthy eating habits	3.68	0.91	−0.40	0.26	0.38	0.52

(*continued*)

Table 1. (*continued*)

UTAUT constructs	Item	Mean	Std. deviation	Skewness		Kurtosis	
			Statistic	Statistic	Std. error	Statistic	Std. error
Facilitating conditions	I have the necessary resources to use applications that help induce healthy eating habits	3.21	1.13	−0.23	0.26	−0.58	0.52
	I have the required knowledge to use applications that induce healthy eating habits	3.36	1.04	−0.37	0.26	−0.36	0.52
	Applications that help induce healthy eating habits are compatible with the technologies I use	3.45	0.88	−0.28	0.26	−0.24	0.52
	I can get help from others when I have difficulties using mobile applications that help induce healthy eating habits	3.54	0.83	−0.38	0.26	−0.43	0.52

5.2 Factors that Can Influence the Youth to Adopt Mobile Applications that Help Induce Healthy Eating Habits

Factors that can influence the youth's adoption of mobile applications that help induce healthy eating habits were identified using the measurement model of PLS-SEM. A latent variable can be a determinant only if its construct validity (convergent and discriminant validity) is established. Using, SMARTPLS software, we assessed the convergent and discriminant validity of the variables.

5.2.1 Convergent Validity

To establish convergent validity, a factor should be unidimensional [50]. A set of variables (factors) presumed to measure the same construct shows convergent validity if their inter-correlations are at least moderate (AVE > 0.5) in magnitude [44]. The Cronbach's Alpha (must be greater than 0.6), the Composite Reliability (must be greater than 0.6) and the Average Variance Extracted (AVE must be greater than 0.5) are reported below in Table 3. As reported in Table 3, all factors within each construct met the recommended threshold. Thus, the convergent validity was established for all the constructs.

5.2.2 Discriminant Validity

Discriminant validity represents the extent to which a construct is empirically distinct from other constructs [44, 45]. Although there are many ways to measure the discriminant validity, however, the Heterotrait-Menotrait (HTMT) Ratio is the recommended way to

Table 2. Guidelines for using PLS-SEM [44, 45, 48]

Type of assessment	Criterion	Description
Indicator reliability	Indicator loading > .600	Loadings represent the absolute contribution of the indicator to the definition of its latent variable
Internal consistency reliability	Cronbach's α > 0.6	Measures the degree to which the measured variables (MVs) load simultaneously when the latent variable (LV) increases
Internal consistency reliability	Composite reliability > 0.6	Attempts to measure the sum of a latent variable (LV) factor loadings relative to the sum of the factor loadings plus error variance
Content validity	Average variance extracted (AVE) > 0.5	The degree to which individual items reflecting a construct converge in comparison to items measuring different constructs
Discriminant validity	Heterotrait-menotrait ratio (HTMT) < 1	In information Systems research, it is argued that discriminant validity should be assessed by the Heterotrait-Menotrait Ratio (HTMT)
Model predictability	Predictive relevance Q^2 > 0.05	By systematically assuming that a certain number of cases are missing from the sample, the model parameters are estimated and used to predict the omitted values
Model validity	R^2 > 0.100	Coefficient of determination
Model validity	Path coefficients and critical t-values for a two-tailed test are 1.65 (significance level = 10%),1.96 (significance level = 5%), and 2.58 (significance level = 1%)	Structural path coefficients are the path weights connecting the factors to one another

validate the discriminant validity [44, 50, 51]. The results of the HTMT test are reported in Table 4. From Table 4, it can be concluded that the discriminant validity is established for all the UTAUT constructs (HTMT < 1).

Table 3. Results of the convergent validity assessment

	Cronbach's alpha	Composite reliability	Average variance extracted (AVE)
Behavioural intention	0.497	0.795	0.661
Effort expectancy	0.8	0.875	0.702
Facilitating conditions	0.544	0.814	0.686
Performance expectancy	0.796	0.877	0.706
Social influence	0.852	0.908	0.767
Use behaviour	1	1	1

Table 4. HTMT results

	Behavioural intention	Effort expectancy	Facilitating conditions	Performance expectancy	Social influence	Use behavior
Behavioural intention						
Effort expectancy	0.42					
Facilitating conditions	0.29	0.64				
Performance expectancy	0.56	0.62	0.43			
Social influence	0.71	0.33	0.56	0.42		
Use behaviour	0.72	0.11	0.15	0.13	0.09	

Since the convergent validity and discriminant validity of effort expectancy, performance expectancy, social influence, facilitating conditions, behavioural intention and use behaviour were established, we can conclude that they constitute valid latent variables that can affect the adoption of mobile applications that help induce healthy eating habits.

5.3 Determinants of the Adoption of Mobile Applications that Help Induce Healthy Eating Habits

The coefficient of determination (R^2), the path coefficient (β), and the Predictive relevance (Q^2) are the criterion used to evaluate the causal model of the Structural Equation Model [45]. The results of the assessment of these criteria are reported below.

5.3.1 Coefficient of Determination (R^2)

R-square (R^2), also known as the coefficient of determination is the overall effect size measure for the structural model. Figure 2 shows the model explains 27.4% of the variance of the behavioural intention (BI) to adopt mobile applications that help induce healthy eating habits. Garson [44] argues that an R^2 within the range of 0.67, 0.33 and 0.19 is "substantial", "moderate" and "weak" respectively. Hence, the R^2 of our model is considered to be of moderate strength.

5.3.2 Path Coefficient (β), and Q^2

Structural path coefficients (loadings), illustrated in the path diagram (Fig. 2), are the path weights connecting the factors to each other [45]. The path coefficients should be between 0 and 1 [44]. In our model, social influence has the strongest effect on the first endogenous variable (behavioural intention) with a value of 0.389, followed by performance expectancy (0.181) and effort expectancy (0.08). The effort expectancy construct, although it has the lowest effect in the model was maintained as its construct validity was established and is within the rage of 0 and 1. In addition, the behavioural intention construct has the strongest effect (0.522) on use behaviour. However, the 'facilitating conditions' construct did not have any significant effect on use behaviour.

We ran the blindfolding function of SmartPLS 3.2.9 and we determined that the Q^2 of the first dependent variable (behavioural intention) was 0.144 and hence greater than the threshold of 0. Additionally, the second dependent variable (use behaviour) had a Q^2 value of 0.249. As these values are all above 0, therefore, as recommended by Garson [44], we argued that our model predicted the adoption of mobile health applications that help induce healthy eating habits.

5.3.3 Hypotheses Validation and Discussion

The first hypothesis $H1_1$: Performance Expectancy -> Behavioural Intention was supported. This means that the degree to which an individual believes that using mobile applications will help him/her induce healthy eating habits influence the behavioural intention to adopt these applications. This finding concurs with Alan et al. [20] who found that performance expectancy had an impact on the behavioural intention towards the adoption of mobile health applications in Bangladesh. The second hypothesis $H1_2$: Effort Expectancy -> Behavioural Intention was rejected. This can be explained by the fact that youth are proficient in the use of smartphones. This means that effort expectancy may not have an influence on them as they will find it naturally easy to adopt mobile applications that help induce healthy eating habits. The third hypothesis $H1_3$: social Influence -> Behavioural Intention was supported, meaning that the degree to which an individual perceives that 'important others' believe he or she should use mobile applications that help induce healthy eating habits influence the behavioural intention to adopt these applications. This finding concurs with Neill et al. [52] who found that social influence affects the behavioural intention to adopt wearable technologies in healthcare. $H1_4$: Facilitating Conditions -> Use Behaviour was rejected. Similarly, Hoque and Sorwar [21] reported that facilitating conditions did not have a significant effect on the behavioural intention to adopt mobile health applications. Our last hypothesis argued that behavioural intention positively influences use behaviour, which was supported. In our model, behavioural intention affects significantly the adoption (use behaviour) of mobile applications that help induce healthy eating habits. Table 5 displays the confirmed and rejected hypotheses of the model.

Table 5. Hypotheses validation

Hypothesis	Path coefficient (β)	T statistics	Model
H1₁. Performance expectancy -> behavioural intention	0.181	1.753*	Supported
H1₂. Effort expectancy -> behavioural intentions	0.079	0.79	Rejected
H1₃. Social influence -> behavioural intentions	0.389	3.514***	Supported
H1₄. Facilitating conditions -> Use behaviour	0.035	0.362	Rejected
H1₅. Behavioral intentions -> Use behaviour	0.522	6.096***	Supported

Critical t-values for a two-tailed test are 1.65* (significance level = 10%), 1.96** (significance level = 5%), and 2.58*** (significance level = 1%).

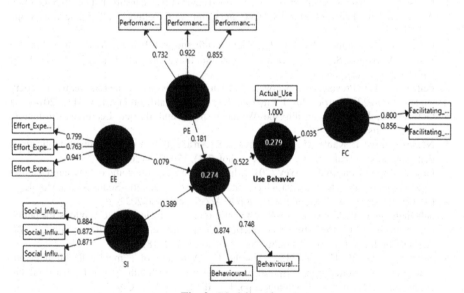

Fig. 2. Model results

6   Conclusion

This study identified factors that influence the adoption of mobile applications that help induce healthy eating habits. In addition, the study determined the effect of these factors on the adoption of these applications. The study concluded that performance expectancy and social influence have a positive and significant effect on the behavioural intention to adopt mobile applications that help induce healthy eating habits while effort expectancy does not exert a significant influence on behavioural intention. In addition, facilitating conditions do not have a significant effect on use behaviour of these applications. Behavioural intention on the other hand, has a significant and positive influence on use behaviour.

Hence, the study advocates that interventions geared towards encouraging the use of mobile applications to induce healthy eating habits should focus on the performance expectancy and social influence factors as this study determined that they exert a significant effect on the behavioural intention to adopt these mobile applications. However, these findings cannot be generalised due to the small sample size. Additionally, we did not test the moderating variables of the UTAUT model. Future research should investigate the adoption of mobile applications that help induce healthy eating habits using a much more representative sample. Moreover, it is suggested that an extended study should be carried out to identify the effect of the moderating variables of the UTAUT framework on the adoption of mobile applications that help induce healthy eating habits.

References

1. Claasen, N., van der Hoeven, M., Covic, N.: Food environments, health and nutrition in South Africa, Working Paper 34. PLAAS, UWC and Centre of Excellence on Food Security, Cape Town (2016)
2. Cooper, D., De Lannoy, A., Rule, C.: Youth health and well-being: why it matters? In: De Lannoy, A., Swartz, S., Lake, L., Smith, C. (eds.) South African Child Gauge 2015, pp. 60–68. University of Cape Town (2015)
3. Peltzer, K., et al.: Prevalence of overweight/obesity and its associated factors among university students from 22 countries. Int. J. Environ. Res. Public Health 11(7), 7425–7441 (2014)
4. Golanty, E., Edlin, G.: Health and Wellness. Jones and Bartlett Learning, Burlington, Massachusetts (2015)
5. Ndayizigamiye, P., Kante, M., Shingwenyana, S.: An adoption model of mHealth applications that promote physical activity. Cogent Psychol. 7(1), 1764703 (2020)
6. Global Mobile Consumer Survey (2017). https://www2.deloitte.com/content/dam/Deloitte/za/Documents/technology-media-telecommunications/ZA-Deloitte-South-Africa-Mobile-Consumer-Survey-2017-Mobile_090718.pdf. Accessed 21 Jan 2022
7. Ndayizigamiye, P., Maharaj, M.: A systematic review of mHealth interventions for public healthcare in East Africa. In: 24th Americas Conference on Information Systems, p. 77. Association for Information Systems, New Orleans, LA (2018)
8. Ndayizigamiye, P., Hangulu, L., Akintola, O.: A design of a mobile health intervention to enhance homecarers' disposal of medical waste in South Africa. In: IEEE Global Humanitarian Technology Conference, pp. 1–6. IEEE, San Jose, CA (2017)
9. Ndayizigamiye, P., Maharaj, M.: Determinants of mobile health adoption in Burundi. Afr. J. Inf. Syst. 9(3), 171–191 (2017)
10. Ndayizigamiye, P.: Potential adoption of mobile health technologies for public healthcare in Burundi. Doctoral Thesis. University of KwaZulu-Natal (2016)
11. Imaja, I.M., Ndayizigamiye, P., Maharaj, M.: A design of a mobile health intervention for the prevention and treatment of Cholera in South Kivu in the Democratic Republic of Congo. In: 2017 IEEE Global Humanitarian Technology Conference, pp. 277–281. IEEE, San Jose, CA (2017)

12. Ludwig, B.J., Galluzzi, C.: Mobile diet and exercise apps for adolescent weight loss. Am. Nurse Today **13**(8), 41–42 (2018)
13. Coughlin, S.S., Whitehead, M., Sheats, J.Q., Mastromonico, J., Hardy, D., Smith, S.A.: Smartphone applications for promoting healthy diet and nutrition: a literature review. Jacobs J. Food Nutr. **2**(3), 021 (2015)
14. Shin, J.: Modeling and evaluating mobile-based interventions for food intake behavior change. In: Proceedings of the 2018 ACM SIGMIS Conference on Computers and People Research, pp.185–186. ACM, New York (2018)
15. Van den Berg, V.L., Abera, B.M.M., Nel, M., Walsh, C.M.: Nutritional status of undergraduate healthcare students at the University of the Free State. S. Afr. Fam. Pract. **55**(5), 445–452 (2013)
16. Van Rensburg, J.C., Surujlal, J.: Gender differences related to the health and lifestyle patterns of university students. Health SA Gesondheid **18**(1), 1–8 (2013)
17. Zhao, J., Freeman, B., Li, M.: Can mobile phone apps influence people's health behavior change? An evidence review. J. Med. Internet Res. **18**(11), e287 (2016)
18. Kang, S.: Factors influencing intention of mobile application use. Int. J. Mobile Commun. **12**(4), 360–379 (2014)
19. Cho, J., Park, D., Lee, H.E.: Cognitive factors of using health apps: systematic analysis of relationships among health consciousness, health information orientation, eHealth Literacy, and Health App Use Efficacy. J. Med. Internet Res. **16**(5), e125 (2014)
20. Alam, M., Hu, W., Barua, Z.: Using the UTAUT model to determine factors affecting acceptance and use of mobile health (mHealth) services in Bangladesh. J. Stud. Soc. Sci. **17**(2), 137–172 (2018)
21. Hoque, R., Sorwar, G.: Understanding factors influencing the adoption of mHealth by the elderly: an extension of the UTAUT model. Int. J. Med. Informatics **101**, 75–84 (2017)
22. Lan, O.T., Baharudin, A.S., Karkonasasi, K.: VTracker: impact of user factors on users' intention to adopt dietary in-take monitoring system with auto workout tracker. arXiv:1806. 06684 (2018)
23. Ndayizigamiye, P., Maharaj, M.: Mobile health adoption in Burundi: a UTAUT perspective. In: 2016 Global Humanitarian Technology Conference, pp. 1–11. IEEE, Seattle, WA (2016)
24. Soni, T.C., Ndayizigamiye, P., Kante, M.: Determinants of the adoption of self-healthcare monitoring mobile applications. In: Fortieth International Conference on Information Systems (ICIS), Association for Information systems, Munich (2019)
25. Ndayizigamiye, P., Soni, T.C., Jere, N.: Factors motivating the adoption of self-healthcare monitoring mobile applications by the South African youth. In: 2018 IST-Africa Week Conference (IST-Africa), pp. 1–7, IEEE, Gaborone (2008)
26. Soureti, A., Murray, P., Cobain, M., Chinapaw, M., van Mechelen, W., Hurling, R.: Exploratory study of web-based planning and mobile text reminders in an overweight population. J. Med. Internet Res. **13**(4), e118 (2011)
27. Beasley, J.M., Riley, W.T., Davis, A., Singh, J.: Evaluation of a PDA-based dietary assessment and intervention program: a randomized controlled trial. J. Am. Coll. Nutr. **27**(2), 280–286 (2008)
28. Vakili, M., Abedi, P., Afshari, P., Kaboli, N.E.: The effect of mobile phone short messaging system on healthy food choices among Iranian postmenopausal women. J. Midlife Health **6**(4), 154–159 (2015)
29. Atienza, A.A., King, A.C., Oliveira, B.M., Ahn, D.K., Gardner, C.D.: Using hand-held computer technologies to improve dietary intake. Am. J. Prev. Med. **34**(6), 514–518 (2008)
30. Fjeldsoe, B.S., et al.: Evaluating the maintenance of lifestyle changes in a randomized controlled trial of the 'get healthy, stay healthy' program. JMIR Mhealth Uhealth **4**(2), e42 (2016)

31. Haapala, I., Barengo, N.C., Biggs, S., Surakka, L., Manninen, P.: Weight loss by mobile phone: a 1-year effectiveness study. Public Health Nutr. **12**(12), 2382–2391 (2009)
32. Lin, M., et al.: Tailored, interactive text messages for enhancing weight loss among African American adults: the TRIMM randomized controlled trial. Am. J. Med. **128**(8), 896–904 (2015)
33. Venkatesh, V., Morris, M.G., Davis, F.D., Davis, G.B.: User acceptance of information technology: toward a unified view. MIS Q. **27**(3), 425–478 (2003)
34. Fishbein, M., Ajzen, I.: Belief, Attitude, Intention and Behavior: An Introduction to Theory and Research. Addison-Wesley, Reading, Massachusetts (1975)
35. Davis, F.D.: Perceived usefulness, perceived ease of use, and user acceptance of information technology. MIS Q. **13**(3), 319–340 (1989)
36. Venkatesh, V., Davis, F.D.: A theoretical extension of the technology acceptance model: four longitudinal field studies. Manage. Sci. **46**(2), 186–204 (2000)
37. Davis, F.D., Bagozzi, R.P., Warshaw, P.R.: Extrinsic and intrinsic motivation to use computers in the workplace. J. Appl. Psychol. **22**(14), 1111–1132 (1992)
38. Ajzen, I.: The theory of planned behavior. Encycl. Health Behav. **50**(2), 179–211 (1991)
39. Taylor, S., Todd, P.A.: Understanding information technology usage: a test of competing models. Inf. Syst. Res. **6**(2), 144–176 (1995)
40. Thompson, R.L., Higgins, C.A., Howell, J.M.: Personal computing: toward a conceptual model of utilization. MIS Q. **15**(1), 125–143 (1991)
41. Rogers, E.M.: Diffusion of Innovations. Free Press, New York (2003)
42. Bandura, A.: Social Foundations of Thought and Action: A Social Cognitive Theory. PrenticeHall, Englewood Cliffs, New Jersey (1986)
43. Hair, J.F., Ringle, C.M., Sarstedt, M.: PLS-SEM: indeed a silver bullet. J. Mark. Theory Pract. **19**(2), 139–152 (2011)
44. Garson, G.D.: Partial Least Squares: Regression & Structural Equation Models. Statistical Associates Publishing, Asheboro, North Carolina (2016)
45. Kante, M., Chepken, C., Oboko, R.: Partial least square structural equation modelling' use in information systems: an updated guideline of practices in exploratory settings. Kabarak J. Res. Innov. **6**(1), 49–67 (2018)
46. Carter, R.L.: Solutions for missing data in structural equation modeling. Res. Pract. Assess. **1**(1), 1–6 (2006)
47. Gupta, S.: SEM for experimental designs: an information systems example. Electron. J. Bus. Res. Methods **12**(1), 27–40 (2014)
48. Hair, J.F., Risher, J.J., Sarstedt, M., Ringle, C.M.: When to use and how to report the results of PLS-SEM. Eur. Bus. Rev. **31**(1), 2–24 (2019)
49. South African National Youth Commission Act (1996). https://www.gov.za/sites/default/files/gcis_document/201409/a19-96.pdf. Accessed 21 Jan 2022
50. Henseler, J., Hubona, G., Ray, P.A.: Using PLS path modeling in new technology research: updated guidelines. Ind. Manag. Data Syst. **116**(1), 2–20 (2016)
51. Henseler, J., Ringle, C.M., Sarstedt, M.: A new criterion for assessing discriminant validity in variance-based structural equation modeling. J. Acad. Mark. Sci. **43**(1), 115–135 (2014). https://doi.org/10.1007/s11747-014-0403-8
52. Neill, D., Van Belle, J.P., Ophoff, J.: Understanding the adoption of wearable technology in South African organizations. In: International Conference on Information Resources Management (CONF-IRM), pp. 1–14. Association for Information Systems, Cape Town (2016)

Sociotechnical Dimension of Trucking in India: Possibilities for Digitalization

Vivek Kant$^{(\boxtimes)}$ ⓘ, Arun Babu, Varun Vikash Karthikeyan, and Nishant Sharma

IDC School of Design, Indian Institute of Technology Bombay, Mumbai, India
vivek.kant@iitb.ac.in

Abstract. India as a country is rapidly changing due to an influx of Information and Communication Technologies (ICTs). The impact of ICTs has been felt on far-flung areas ranging from agriculture to industry. In this chapter, we highlight possible ways in which ICTs can be included in the trucking sector from the bottom-up. In order to accomplish our goal, we present an ethnography with a sociotechnical dimension. Specifically, we recognize that large-scale social systemic challenges shape individual actions in the technological trucking sector. The ethnographic study comprised of semi-structured interviews with over 30 stakeholders, was conducted in the metropolitan port city of Mumbai, India. It was aimed at understanding the functioning of the sector, current practices, roles of stakeholders involved, and the challenges faced by them. The results are followed by a discussion that deals with the impact new information technology is having on the sector and identifies areas for future intervention.

Keywords: Digitalization · Sociotechnical Systems · Ethnography · Symbolic Interactionism · Mumbai

1 Introduction

"Truckers are, after all, the blood vessels that course through the body of our nation, ferrying the oxygen of essential goods on the arteries that are our highways. And yet their problems had not so much as received a diagnosis, forget diagnosis, their symptoms had not been recorded. Countless reams of newsprint have been consumed in op-ed articles on the economy that discuss interest rates, fiscal deficits and other such arcane macroeconomic indicators. But what is this 'economy' they talk about, but an assemblage of countless transactional relations anchored in a system of mutual acceptability, i.e., money changing hands... I believed that the lived reality of truckers, their experiences of the road, would be a useful barometer of the economic health of our nation. The nature of their encounters with state officials would shine a light on the reality of rule of law in our country. It would be helpful in understanding what the 'cost of logistics' actually means in the course of routine transport."

– Rajat Ubhaykar. [1, p. 7–8]

© IFIP International Federation for Information Processing 2022
Published by Springer Nature Switzerland AG 2022
J. Abdelnour-Nocera et al. (Eds.): *Innovation Practices for Digital Transformation in the Global South*, IFIP AICT 645, pp. 113–129, 2022.
https://doi.org/10.1007/978-3-031-12825-7_7

Digital transformation in the trucking sector in India can take place along two different directions simultaneously. First, the trucking infrastructure will change due to embedded technology and sensors manifested in the form of improved combustion efficiency, reduction of emissions, monitoring the health of parts, and others. While improvements in this area happen with the development of technology, this approach towards digitalization is primarily manufacturer-driven. In the second direction, existing technology can be augmented through the change in the digital habits of the humans associated with this sector. In this direction, the focus is on how humans in the trucking sector adapt to and make use of the ICTs. Specifically, in a country like India, the use of IT through mobile phones plays a major role in the adoption of digital services and in changing the trucking sector.

This chapter explicates how the trucking sector operates in India in relation to the various roles involved in the trucking industry such as drivers, brokers(*mehtas, seths*), owners, and helpers (*khalassis*). This understanding of the sector provides an opportunity to gain a sense of digitalization starting from a bottom-up fashion. The chapter is divided into six sections: Sect. 2 lays out the challenges of trucking and digitalization in India. Section 3 provides the theoretical backdrop of Sociotechnical systems and frames the direction for the fieldwork in the next section. Section 4 lists the details of the fieldwork and Sect. 5 presents the results. The chapter concludes with Sect. 6, a discussion of possible avenues for digitalization of the trucking sector.

2   Trucking and Digitalization in India

India as well as other low and middle income countries are undergoing a rapid transformation in the area of information technology. In the future, with the development of cheap electronic hardware, it is expected that several technologies such as sensors will be embedded in everyday objects transforming everyday interaction with devices. Some of this transformation is depicted in the form of cellphones which is transforming the Indian masses towards digitalization and use of ICT. Given this milieu, there is a need to understand how the trucking sector will deal with this sociotechnical transition of ICT. The trucking sector in India involves a few fundamental challenges. Here, we list a few major challenges and how they need to be contended with in terms of addressing the socio-technical dimension of this sector.

First, the trucking sector involves three major categories of service providers — large companies with a line of trucks; small fleets ranging from 5 to 40; and small-scale truck owners having less than five trucks. While major truck companies have the means to embrace information technology, medium-scale and small-scale truck operators will face significant challenges.

Second, many stakeholder segments in the sector have low literacy. A recent study [2], indicates that a majority of truck drivers are educated up to grade 10 of high school or less. The helpers who are in the truck and are involved in sundry roles, also have low-literacy levels. In most cases, the small-scale truck owners may also have low literacy.

Third, barring the large companies, the sector is highly dependent on the restricted flow of information in terms of receiving and providing services. For example, the "*mehtas*" and "*seths*" are information and service brokers who act as mediators between the clients and truck owners. Thus, prices, routes, and movement of goods are heavily dependent on the information flow in this sector.

Fourth, with the growth of cheap cellphone technology, this sector like many others in India is changing in the way it communicates. In a country such as India, due to the low level of technological development and adoption among the masses, Information Technology in the form of computers never constituted a major wave of digitalization. However, with the advent of cheap cellphones, the Indian is rapidly up taking digital tools and practices in their everyday lives. The Government of India recognizes this change and has set up steps to bring digitalization close to the everyday lives of Indians. In terms of the cellphone, it serves as a primary means of communication along with media consumption and economic transactions, making the cellphone an enabling technology in the life of an everyday Indian. In the trucking sector, the cellphone serves as the major route of the transformation for negotiating deals and prices.

While the list of challenges to digitalization can be extended, this chapter aims to recognize digitalization as a sociotechnical endeavor. Specifically, the aim is to understand how the trucking sector works so as to provide pathways for digitalization. Towards this end, the chapter focuses on human knowing and acting in the trucking sector using a conjoined theoretical approach of socio-technical studies and symbolic interactionism developed in Sect. 3. The aim of the analysis will be to use an ethnographic approach using symbolic Interactionism (SI) while being mindful of the four tenets derived from STS theory in the next Sect. 3.

3   Theoretical Backdrop of Sociotechnical Systems and Symbolic Interactionism

Sociotechnical Systems (STS) theory has a wide history and multiple usages developed across almost the past five decades [3]. There is no one specific direction in which the growth of STS can be charted; multiple viewpoints still exist in the literature. One direction in which STS theory has been developed is derived from British researchers and the Tavistock institute [4, 5]. This school of thought provided a key idea which was, to understand and improve tasks related to technologies, the context of work and the social dimensions of the activity were necessary. These researchers developed STS theory in several milieu ranging from coal mining to textile manufacturing. This approach to STS was also prominent amongst macro ergonomics, work psychology, and human factors researchers and still remains an active area of research [6–8].

A second direction was derived from risk management and systems engineering [9, 10]. In this approach, the key idea is to recognize that technical systems involve people and technologies along with social entities such as teams, organizations, and institutions at several levels of abstraction. Therefore, to comprehend and optimize STS all these together as a unified construct. As a result, this direction in STS emphasizes that any construal of an STS involves the social as having an impact on the technical. Therefore, any analysis of behavior should involve an understanding of broader aspects of social, economic, and political dimensions of the work domain under consideration.

A third direction of STS analysis derives from the history and sociology of technology [11, 12]. In this direction, the key idea is to treat STS as a hybrid of social and technical entities. In this thread similar to the previous direction, the social and political dimensions are recognized to be necessary. However, in this direction, the social is treated not as separated but conjoined and mutually constitutive of the technical. In other words, technology has evolved based on choices people have made in light of their relevant social groups. Therefore, while there is a technical trajectory, there is co-shaping by a social trajectory that together defines have been co-constructed socially.

While all these three approaches provide different aspects to the construal of the human-technology interaction in STS, a final direction is needed to comprehensively understand how people interact with technology in context. In the field of Human-Computer Interaction (HCI), researchers have turned towards micro-sociological theories to understand how human behavior can be addressed in human technology interaction. One approach has been that of Symbolic Interactionism (SI) and is particularly important for HCI. SI was developed in the discipline of sociology at the beginning of the nineteenth century to understand how people make sense of themselves and the world around them. It rests on three basic premises that provide a basis for how human beings interact with their surroundings (which in our case is the social and technological context).

> "Symbolic interactionism rests in the last analysis on three simple premises. The first premise is that human beings act toward things on the basis of the meanings that the things have for them. Such things include everything that the human being may note in his world—physical objects, such as trees or chairs; other human beings, such as a mother or a store clerk; categories of human beings, such as friends or enemies; institutions, as a school or a government; guiding ideals, such as individual independence or honesty; activities of others, such as their commands or requests; and such situations as an individual encounters in his daily life. The second premise is that the meaning of such things is derived from, or arises out of, the social interaction that one has with one's fellows. The third premise is that these meanings are handled in, and modified through, an interpretative process used by the person in dealing with the things he encounters"
>
> – Herbert Blumer [13, p. 2]

Further, to fully comprehend these meanings, we need a qualitative approach to capture and comprehend how these meanings evolve over interaction with technologies. This qualitative approach is obtained through an ethnographic process that aims towards comprehending the meanings and values of people and their relevant social groups as viewed from their own viewpoint.

Based on the above discussions, four key insights can be summarized for developing this chapter. In the rest of the chapter, these four key insights will be used to guide the ethnography in the trucking sector in India:

1. The social and interpersonal dimensions of human behavior are important for comprehending human-technology interaction in STS.
2. Humans in technological environments are constrained by macro-social dimensions of organizational institutions in any particular sector.

3. Human technology interaction involves a conjoined understanding of both the social and technical dimensions of the system as they are hybrid entities.
4. Finally, to understand human-technology interaction, we need to understand how interaction is shaped through meanings and values in a given social milieu.

4 Details of Fieldwork

4.1 Setting

Mumbai is a major port city and serves as the western conduit to the Arabian Sea. Therefore, Mumbai serves as a major hub for the transfer of goods to and from inland India. The fieldwork was conducted at the truck yards in *Vashi* and *Wadala* (Cotton green) in Mumbai suburban region. These locations were chosen for study as they are the primary trucking spots that connect Mumbai to the rest of the country.

Wadala truck yard is situated at the edge of Cotton Green railway station on a barren strip of land with a lot of warehouses. There are 6 different lanes with multiple entrances to them and each entrance is manned by parking lot officials. Different lanes are for trucks from different locations. The trucks in this yard are those that mostly run within Mumbai and the yard also happens to be a warehouse for a steel company.

Vashi truck yard is located 4 km away from the *Vashi* railway station is a well-organized place, unlike the *Wadala* truck yard. It has only one entrance and one exit. It has an integrated petrol pump and food joints in the vicinity. One can also find a lot of truck repair shops in the yard, making this a perfect place for drivers to stay for a long time safely. The trade-off is a higher parking fee. In the *Vashi* truck yard, long-haul trucks were predominant.

4.2 Participants

The research study was granted ethics clearance from the Institute Ethics Committee, Indian Institute of Technology Bombay (ID: IITB-IEC/2020/021). In all, there were more than 30 participants which included a wide variety of drivers, brokers (*mehtas*, *seths*), parking officials, transport agency personnel, among others. For example, the drivers whom the researcher met at the truck yards in Mumbai hailed from all across India and they took consignments all across the country as long as they saw profit in it. These included far-flung areas such as the southernmost state of India- Kerala, and the northernmost tip of the country- the union territory of Jammu & Kashmir. They cover almost all regions in India except for the extreme North East.

4.3 Duration and Process

The entire fieldwork lasted for around two months and was conducted from Jan-Mar, 2020. Semi-structured interviews and observations were used as a primary means of data collection. The first two weeks were spent observing and having informal discussions with the participants to understand the whole ecosystem of the trucking industry in Mumbai. Once there was a clear picture of the trucking industry as a whole, a more detailed set of interviews were conducted for the remaining period.

The time frame for interviews varied from a few minutes to one hour depending on the interviewee's availability. There were days in which the researcher interviewed just a single person and there were days where he could interview 6–7 people. Finally, there were also days that were spent completely on observing the activities instead of interviewing. With the permission of the interviewees, some discussions were recorded in audio format. This proved to be fruitful especially during casual group chats with drivers, where it was impossible to take mental note of everything and write it down later. When it seemed possible, drivers were probed to reveal their little secrets. The insights derived from the participants were gleaned using categorization and coding. Codes were developed bottom-up from the notes and interviews. The key idea in ethnographic research is to start from individual instances and, based on the data, inductively provide generic themes and insights for this sector. Based on this analysis, the major generic themes are developed in Sect. 5 as results.

The entire fieldwork was conducted by one field researcher. This ensured that a more reliable and clear engagement with primary sources. These insights were interpreted with the help of two mentors and another researcher (also authors in this chapter) who have been working in this sector, as well as, supplemented by secondary literature currently present about this sector.

4.4 Engagement

"I used to casually talk to the drivers and a major breakthrough happened one day when a driver actually invited me to join in for a tea break along with other drivers. That chat session lasted for an hour and from the conversations between the people, I understood a great deal about their view of the world/system and the problems they face. On another such occasion, I happened to be with a group of drivers who were getting the papers cleared by a *mehta* for a trip. That day, I understood the social hierarchy and the limited control/information drivers have about their consignments."

— Field researcher, *Reflections on fieldwork*.

A primary challenge during the study was that people were not ready to open up to discuss the details once they heard that this was a "formal research study". A major challenge with conducting research in this sector is that, in general, a number of participants do not wish to be recorded (audio and visual) or even give their signatures on consent forms. They provided verbal consent and provided their insights in length but were unwilling to sign forms. As a result, the major focus was on taking down notes which was then used for data analysis to highlight general themes depicted as results in Sect. 5.

Further, a significant reason for this was the language barrier and distrust of any outsider who does not provide any monetary value. Most people would say that they are not at all interested to talk after being given a brief introduction about the research. However, after an initial fallow period, contacts were made and this made the detailed set of interviews possible. Once a general sense of the trucking sector was obtained, the interviews were structured and as the study progressed, questions were more in the form of probes to get more ideas about specific aspects. This method was continued throughout the remaining period of the study and slowly a unified picture emerged.

5   Results: Trucking as Sociotechnical Processes

The sector deals with literally anything that can be moved— food, machinery, hardware, or any other miscellaneous items. Truckers traveling within a particular state tend to carry vegetables, perishables, or other similar FMCGs. Long haul trucks ferry a range from raw materials and machinery to organic materials, which perish within 2–3 days. There are a few trucks with cold storage and they carry goods like ice-creams and other beverages. Based on the delivery priority, goods can be classified into:

1. Express delivery (to be delivered within 2–3 days)
2. Normal delivery (delivered within 1–1.5 weeks; timeline varies when heavy machinery or fragile equipment are involved, as driving speed is lower in such cases)

The kind of clients the sector encounters range from someone who wants to send two boxes to companies that ship multiple truck loads. Similarly, on the truck ownership side, there is a lot of diversity with a lot of small players involved. Hence, there is a need for an intermediary whom the parties on both sides can rely on for continued business. This role is taken up by 'transport agencies' through which all flow of goods take place. Only in 2–3% cases do clients directly deal with a truck owner [14].

5.1   Transport Agencies and the Functioning of the Sector

Transport Agencies. Transport agencies in this sector are quite diverse. They can be broadly classified into:

1. Corporate entities: They have their own truck fleets that can be as large as 5000 trucks, their own warehouses and full-time drivers with fixed salaries.
2. Medium-sized transport agencies: They do not have their own trucks and are dependent on a network of middlemen/brokers to find trucks for the consignments. Some of them do have their own warehouses/storage areas.
3. Tea-stall sized transport agencies: They own neither a truck nor a warehouse and due to the low volumes, deal directly with the drivers of the trucks.

While the corporate players offer end-to-end services, they form a small portion of the market share with only 10% of all trucks belonging to players owning more than 20 trucks [15, 16]. As a result, it is the domain of the smaller players that has gained our attention.

Functioning of the Sector. In a typical scenario, a client calls up a transport agency and gives them the details of the consignment that needs to be shipped. The goods are collected and stored at the warehouse/office of the transport company. In the meantime, one can find a lot of trucks at the truck yard that have registered themselves as 'available for a trip' with the transport company and are waiting for a consignment. Once the consignment is assigned to one of these trucks, they pick up the goods and leave for the destination. In case a transport agency does not have storage space, the goods are directly picked up from the client's *godown* (warehouse).

In the event of the drivers not getting a consignment that is not a full load, they try to take multiple consignments on a single trip. The field researcher, for example, met drivers from Kerala who were willing to wait 2–3 days to get one more consignment if a single consignment does not fill up the cargo space. After delivering the goods, the truck usually returns empty as they would not be able to find a return trip immediately (also see [14] for a similar point). Moreover, the drivers of these trucks are usually paid based on the income generated by the truck; hence, the faster a driver can return home and get registered with a transport agency for the next trip, the more money he makes. It is also possible that a single truck can be registered at more than one transport agency. For the time during which the truck is at the yard waiting for a consignment, which might take days together, a 'parking fee' is levied on a per-day basis. Hence, in many ways, time is directly linked to money in the everyday functioning of this sector.

5.2 Stakeholders and the Social Hierarchy

Truck Owners. Among the trucks at the yard, one can find the following variety in ownership:

1. Trucks of corporate logistics companies
2. Owned by *maliks* (owners having small fleets of 10–50 trucks)
3. Partnerships between *maliks* and individuals
4. Owner-cum-driver

While large companies that have their fleet of trucks often involve an impersonal system of management, smaller owners like the *Maliks* generally tend to be someone related to the trucking industry in some form like an ex-driver, a mechanic, a broker, a business person who regularly needs a truck to transport things or someone for whom it is their family business. Over 70% of owners have been associated with the sector for more than 10 years [2, p. 11]. There also exists a class of drivers who own their own trucks and make up for 6% of total truck ownership [2, p. 3]. These drivers are aware of the technicalities of the sector, the truck and its components, but might not be comfortable with abstract technical terms. Although the truck owners have greater power compared to drivers, they do not interfere much in the administrative or monitoring activities of the sector and leave it to the driver to take care of the day-to-day activities. The truck owners' level of education can vary from primary school to sometimes even a university degree, though the average stands around a secondary or higher secondary school education (Fig. 1).

Mehta (broker 1). *Mehtas* are clerks who are responsible for clearing all the paperwork for a consignment which includes road permission, luggage insurance, and other documents like bills. All these documents (insurance included) have been made mandatory

Fig. 1. Truck owner categories

by the government and the goods can even be seized by law enforcement for not carrying them. Usually, *Mehtas* are freelancers and may work for more than one transport agency. They are the ones who are in direct contact with the client and are responsible for connecting the consignment with a truck.

Seth (broker 2). *Seths* are middlemen between the *mehtas* and the drivers. They are usually veteran drivers who have extensive contacts with the drivers visiting the yard. The *mehta*, who is more towards the client side of things might not have the proper contacts with the drivers. Therefore, *seths* take over the responsibility of acting as a liaison. In most cases, a new driver who comes to the truck yard has to get in touch with the local *seth* to get introduced to *mehtas* for getting a consignment.

Drivers. Drivers are hired based on recommendations from acquaintances or other drivers and drive the same truck. They stay with the truck even when the truck is waiting at the truck yard. When on a trip, they tend to drive for long periods continuously, eating at roadside eateries and sleeping either inside or under their trucks.

They are given a certain amount of money for the trip from which they can draw for fuel, food, tolls, among other miscellaneous expenses [2]. They are required to maintain a logbook to keep track of expenses during the trip that will serve as documentation and be verified by the *mehta* as to what was done with the money that was given for the trip. While drivers working with corporate fleets who have fixed salaries earn between 12,000 to 17,000 INR (Indian Rupees), their counterparts driving individual trucks whose salaries are based on the economic functioning of the truck (often called "truck running" (sic)) in the sector, make about 7,000 to 10,000 INR a month.

Due to the spending long periods away from home, harsh working conditions, and lower social status, there are not many newcomers into the profession which has led to a shortage of drivers across the country. The government, in an attempt to tackle this issue, has lowered the educational requirement to get a driving license from Class 10 (high school) to Class 8 (middle school), which gives an insight into the low levels of educational qualifications of the drivers.

> "overall 37.1% of truck drivers were educated up to primary level (until Class 5th), 44% were educated up to high school level (until Class 10th) while 8.8% were illiterate." [2, p. 9].

Khalassi (Helpers/Cleaners). *Khalassis* are assistants of drivers who are mostly youngsters. Their role is to help the driver with reversing, taking sharp turns, cleaning the windshield, and other supportive tasks. In many cases, these *khalassis* work as apprentice to the drivers and learn to drive and become future drivers. The shortage of drivers has also led to the role of helper becoming almost non-existent in recent times. The drivers also prefer it that way as they get some extra money for running without a helper.

5.3 Everyday Challenges in Trucking

Flow of Information and Money. Since *mehtas* are the people who deal with the client, as they are the ones who receive money for the shipment. After taking a cut from it, they hand it over to the *seths* who in turn take a cut for themselves before finally handing over the payment to the driver. This leads to an interesting scenario wherein at each level the person does not know how much money was actually received by the person at the higher level.

> User interview 1: "After deducting the logistics company's profit, the drivers would be eligible to get a sum of say 12000 per trip. The instruction first goes to Seth and Mehta. They could take 2000 each and tell us that the final amount is 8000. These kinds of cheatings happen all around the place. But nobody will know whether it has happened"
>
> — Gopal (name changed), co-driver of a truck running within Mumbai suburban.

When the company is ready for a consignment, the intermediary *mehtas* and *seths* do not notify the driver about the financial side of things. A consignment might be worth 11000 rupees. But the *seths* and *mehtas* can easily grab a fair amount from this amount and tell the driver that the consignment's value is 8000 rupees. The important issue is that the drivers will never know if they are being cheated like this albeit being aware of such practices. In addition, bribery remains rampant in the sector and does not go in any official records. Drivers ultimately pay the bribe as there is no other way to escape from this. As this amount is unaccounted, drivers find it really difficult to convince the

Seths about incidents as there is no proof. *Seths* argue that drivers could easily lie about an incident and snatch the amount. Further, *seths* claim that drivers steal goods and fuel and sell them to make extra cash. Nobody trusts anyone and that seems to be the core issue in the industry. Only a solution that ensures transparent data flow can solve this trust issue (Fig. 2).

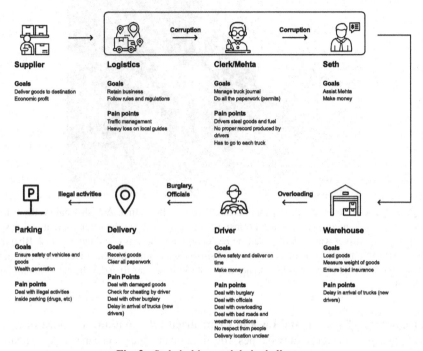

Fig. 2. Stakeholders and their challenges

Overloading of Trucks. In a reciprocal manner, *mehtas* may collaborate with the client to overload a truck with more weight than what is mentioned on the bill. Trucks are not usually equipped with a gauge to measure the weight of cargo on the bed and thus drivers would not know whether the truck is overloaded or not. For example, a consignment might say that it is 15 *tonnes* on paper. But the company/*mehtas* can take advantage of drivers and load the truck up to 15.5–16 *tonnes*. This will effectively affect fuel consumption and drivers end up paying for the extra fuel. Most of the time drivers ignore this extra amount as it may not exceed INR 500 per trip; however, considering the fact that the company/ warehouse might be involved with a large number of trucks makes one imagine the economic benefit that is gained. The National Highway Authority of India (NHAI) is in the process of installing technology such as electronic weighing machines at various toll stations to curb this malpractice. However, this issue still persists for trucks that do not take a route with such a toll booth (Fig. 3).

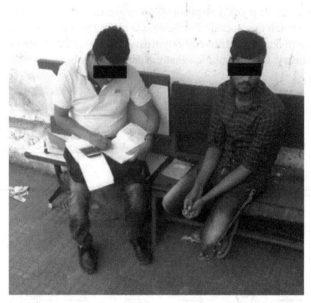

Fig. 3. A truck driver getting his papers cleared from Ashish Bhai. Ashish Bhai (yellow shirt, name changed), a *mehta* working for a transport company clearing the truck journal and passes for a truck. The driver was patiently waiting beside him and he was convincing Ashish Bhai that he lost some amount due to bribery. However, Ashish Bhai claims that the driver is to be blamed. Ashish Bhai works for 5 companies and he earns 5000INR per day. In a day, he clears a minimum of 3 trucks."

Consignment Allocation and Lack of Centralized Information. The idea of a preferred consignment can be of two types – destination and the good carried. A destination preference might be due to the driver being from a particular part of the country and a trip to that part meaning that they will get to visit their family members. In terms of preference of good carried, some drivers might not be willing to take glass or other fragile items in small quantities as it does not allow them to load their truck with an additional consignment due to the nature of the good involved.

After having registered with a transport agency and waiting at the yard, the driver may face a possible challenge. For example, it is possible that some other transport company might have a more favorable consignment that is not in the driver's awareness. While it is possible that one truck can be registered at more than one agency, with the plethora of agencies present, it is simply impossible to have visibility into all of them resulting in a lapse of smooth functioning of the sector.

Further, it is possible that a driver could get a preferred consignment from another company but as he is not registered with them, he will not know about such a consignment; this challenge of communication is quite rampant in this sector. These situations result in financial loss in such a business where time is of utmost importance. This is an issue faced by drivers who own their own trucks. Such private trucks would be registered with only one or two transport companies and most of the time they would wait for 5–7 days for a consignment. Some of the drivers had waited for more than 10 days (Fig. 4).

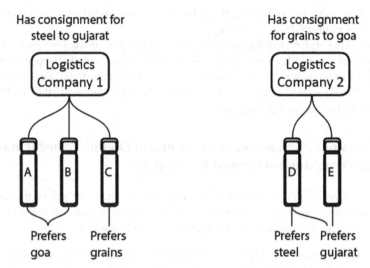

Fig. 4. Truck consignment problem

Further, when registered with a transport agency, drivers have no information on how many people have registered before or after them. This has given rise to practices like *mehtas* and *seths* favoring their more acquainted drivers by giving them consignments ahead of the queue. It is also due to this lack of accessible information and lack of coordination among the transport agencies that the freight rates haven't been able to keep in touch with the level of increase in trip expenses to the point that they are artificial and not a true reflection of a free-market [17, 18]. This is because, currently, if an agency quotes higher prices, they will have difficulties in finding clients and hence the status quo remains unchallenged. These artificially low prices are often manifested in the form of lower income for those at the lower levels of the hierarchy or in the poor condition of the trucks.

"truck operators, whether large or small, are "price takers" in the industry. Due to tough competition and fragmentation, truck owners cannot dictate freight rates" [14, p. 12].

5.4 Challenges on the Road – Burglary and Natural Calamities

There are occasions when trucks are robbed when the area they have parked is not safe enough. There are also incidents where running trucks were looted by armed mercenaries and because of the advantage in numbers, they could easily get away. Drivers pray for their own lives, as they keep on driving the truck being looted. Drivers report having faced random burglary in remote and isolated roads. This usually happens in *ghats* (hill valleys), for example, in the Indian state of Madhya Pradesh and truckers are often advised to pass through such regions as a fleet of trucks. One of the drivers described a burglary that he faced. All he could do at that time was to keep on driving while thugs were stealing goods from a running truck. He was accompanied by his co-driver but they were heavily outnumbered by the thugs.

Along with burglary, natural calamities also wreak havoc on trucking routes, truckers had been stuck for 2–3 days on roads due to landslides which usually happen in the *ghats* of Southern India as well as mountainous regions of northern India. Drivers would be unaware of these natural calamities and without taking a bypass route they will head on to the affected region and get trapped.

6   Discussion: Avenues for Sociotechnical Digital Transformation in the Trucking Sector and Key Insights

The past sections highlighted some basic challenges in terms of lack of transparency, power hierarchy, and flow of information. In this section, we present avenues of how digitalization can ameliorate some basic challenges in this sector.

Business Generation. While the current system of registering with transport agencies has to live with the limitations of the reach of the agency, new-age services like *BlackBuck* (an uber-like platform for inter-city trucking), through digitization, are trying to expand the pool within which one can look for trucks and also making it possible to find loads for return trips as well. With this model where all demand is aggregated together, it is also possible to merge smaller consignments and present them as a single consignment to the trucker, eliminating the waiting time to achieve a full load. Apart from making it easier to find orders, such services also facilitate a dynamic pricing model based on the market [19]. This can help solve the issue of artificially low freight charges that are a byproduct of the decentralized brokerage system where the owners do not have much of a choice in negotiating prices. In addition, they facilitate the acquisition of payment or insurance digitally.

Key Insight 1. In the future of the digitalization, artificial low freight rates can be combatted effectively through transparent technology. This avenue requires a conjoined understanding ("joint optimization") of socio-dynamics of business and technology.

Driver Well-Being. To help drivers from spending long periods away from home, tech startup *Rivigo* has introduced the concept of driver relay that creates a network of 'pit stops' across the country where drivers can be switched to ensure that they do not spend more than 5–6 h straight behind the wheel and can return home within 24 h [20]. This would also increase the attractiveness of the profession of driving. While this is primarily focused towards larger fleets, the pit stops thus created can serve as proper rest or refreshment spots for drivers where they can even sleep properly when the truck is parked safely without fear of burglary. The rise of digital payments can not only facilitate getting insurance or receiving payment digitally, it can also ensure that the people in the lower levels of the hierarchy get their fair share by eliminating the multiple levels payment has to pass through currently.

Key Insight 2. The future of digitalization can only be ensured in the trucking sector, if the social capital of the trucking sector is enhanced. This includes improvement in well-being by creation of infrastructure which specifically focuses on work-rest services that is linked to digital economics.

Fleet Management. The arrival of GPS & smartphone-based tracking solutions has brought in a lot of visibility to make it possible for the owner as well as the end customer in terms of whether the shipment is on course for timely delivery. It also helps the owner keep a check on over speeding, unwanted stoppage, or deviation from the designated route. Further extending the use of GPS tracking, it would be possible to observe whether drivers are driving long hours at a stretch. If this data is made public, it can help law enforcement enforce regulations in this regard if necessary. Fuel cards (a kind of debit card for fueling alone) that have been introduced some years ago are becoming more commonplace and provide a fool-proof way to keep track of fuel expenses, which account for up to 25–30% of total trip expenses [21], as compared to manual logging.

It is even possible today to monitor for fuel theft by systems that continuously monitor fuel levels and check for anomalies on their own. Currently, firms like *Locus, FarEye* are working on generating optimized routes based on real-time traffic data that can ensure faster pass-through in times of traffic congestion, road construction, and even accidents or calamities, thereby saving time and fuel. Further, with the help of IoT sensors, it would be possible to ensure the quality and quantity of shipment intact. For example, a temperature sensor could monitor perishables, make auto-corrections [22] and trigger an alert when not possible. A weight sensor can ensure that it is brought to the notice of the driver and other stakeholders when contents are disturbed or removed, at unexpected times Another possible area of intervention that can go along with route optimization is optimizing where and how much fuel is to be filled along the route as fuel prices can vary across states.

Key Insight 3. Transparency can be introduced in the system by digital services and monitoring of key parameters involved in the functioning of the trucks as well as fleets. In terms of the sociotechnical basis of driving, these include large-scale changes at regulatory levels of the trucking sector, considered as a sociotechnical system.

Infrastructure. In recent times, the introduction of digital services at the policy level such as *Fastag* (RFID based on-the-move toll transactions) and *e-way bill* (an electronic bill that can be directly verified online by police at check posts) have facilitated having lower stoppages before the trucks reach the destination [23]. This also reduces the avenues for harassment or bribery. The boom in e-commerce has already created an increased demand for trucking and warehousing. With large growth being predicted in the ready-to-cook, ready-to-eat space, the demand for cold storages and trucks capable of transporting them is predicted to increase as well. At present, the amount of fresh fruits and vegetables shipped via cold storage trucks is a meagre 4% as compared to 80–85% in the USA [21]. This presents a new space for the average owner who currently deals with only the 'normal' trucks.

Key Insight 4. The current changes in digitalization in India will bring about further changes in terms of purchasing power of technology for the small-scale truck owner, who currently focus on "normal" trucks. With the growth of digitalization newer form of technology-enhanced trucks will be available at the grasp of the truck-owner. In the long-run, this provides an understanding of adoption and diffusion of advanced technology in the trucking sector.

7 Conclusion

In this chapter, we have tried to understand the trucking sector in India as a sociotechnical system, by first addressing the current state with a bottom-up viewpoint. This was achieved through an ethnographic study that highlighted challenges related to the flow of information, lack of transparency, along with the social hierarchical setup of the sector. Based on these insights, we presented current and future avenues for digitalization in this sector.

References

1. Ubhaykar, R.: Truck de India!: A Hitchhiker's Guide to Hindustan, pp. 7–8. Simon & Schuster India, New York (2019)
2. SaveLIFE foundation: status of truck drivers in India. SaveLIFE Foundation, Mumbai (2020). Accessed https://savelifefoundation.org/wp-content/uploads/2020/02/design-single-page-27th-feb-2020.pdf
3. Baxter, G., Sommerville, I.: Socio-technical systems: from design methods to systems engineering. Interact. Comput. **23**(1), 4–17 (2011)
4. Trist, E.: The Evolution of Socio-Technical Systems: a Conceptual Framework and an Action Research Program. Ontario Quality of Working Life Centre, Toronto (1981)
5. Trist, E., Murray, H.: The social engagement of social science, a Tavistock anthology, Volume 2: The Socio-Technical Perspective. University of Pennsylvania Press, Pennsylvania (1993)
6. Clegg, C.: Sociotechnical principles for system design. Appl. Ergon. **31**(5), 463–477 (2000)
7. Carayon, P.: Human factors of complex sociotechnical systems. Appl. Ergon. **37**(4), 525–535 (2006)
8. Waterson, P.E., Older Gray, M.T., Clegg, C.W.: A sociotechnical method for designing work systems. Hum. Fact. J. Hum. Fact. Ergon. Soc. **44**(3), 376–391 (2002)
9. Rasmussen, J.: Risk management in a dynamic society: a modelling problem. Saf. Sci. **27**(2–3), 183–213 (1997)
10. Rasmussen, J., Svedung, I.: Proactive risk management in a dynamic society. Swedish Rescue Services Agency, Karlstad (2000)
11. Bijker, W.E., Hughes, T.P., Pinch, T.J.: The Social Construction of Technological Systems. New directions in the Sociology and History of Technology. Anniversary edition. MIT Press, Cambridge (2012)
12. Vermaas, P., Kroes, P., van de Poel, I., Franssen, M., Houkes, W.: A Philosophy of technology: from technical artefacts to sociotechnical systems. Synth. Lect. Eng. Technol. Soc. **6**(1), 1–134 (2011)
13. Blumer, H.: Symbolic Interactionism: Perspective and Method. University of California Press, Berkeley (1986)
14. International institute for sustainable development: the impacts of India's diesel price reforms on the trucking industry. International institute for sustainable development, New Delhi (2013). Accessed. https://www.iisd.org/gsi/sites/default/files/ffs_india_irade_trucking.pdf
15. Raghuram, G., Sanghani, P.: An overview of the trucking sector in India: Significance and structure (No. W.P. No. 2015-12-02). Ahmedabad: Indian Institute of Management Ahmedabad (2015). Accessed. http://vslir.iima.ac.in:8080/jspui/bitstream/11718/20289/1/WP_2015_12_02.pdf
16. Roy, D., Raghuram, G., Jain, R., Tripathi, S., Sharda, K.: Trucking Business Management: Cases and Concepts. McGraw Hill Education, New Delhi (2016)

17. TCI, IIM-C: operational efficiency of freight transportation by road in India, 2014–15, 3rd Edition, (2016). Accessed www.tcifreight.in/pdf/study-reports/TCI-IIM-Report.pdf
18. NITI Aayog: goods on the move: efficiency and sustainability in Indian logistics. (2018). Accessed www.movesummit.in/files/Freight_report.pdf
19. Atasoy, B., Schulte, F., Steenkamp, A.: Platform-based collaborative routing using dynamic prices as incentives. Transp. Res. Rec. J. Transp. Res. Board. **2674**(10), 670–679 (2020)
20. Raghuram, G., Sanghani, P.: Rivigo. Indian institute of management Ahmedabad. (2017). Accessed https://doi.org/10.1108/CASE.IIMA.2020.000023
21. RSM: RSM India white paper: optimising supply chain cost – road transportation. (2019). Accessed https://www.rsm.global/india/insights/consulting-insights/rsm-india-white-paper-optimising-supply-chain-cost-road-transportation
22. Kim, W.R., Aung, M.M., Chang, Y.S., Makatsoris, C.: Freshness gauge based cold storage management: a method for adjusting temperature and humidity levels for food quality. Food Control **47**, 510–519 (2015)
23. NETC: FASTag Card. (2021). Accessed. https://www.npci.org.in/what-we-do/netc-fastag/productoveview#:~:text=FASTag%20is%20a%20RFID%20passive,stopping%20for%20any%20toll%20payments

Role of Digital Platforms in Entrepreneurial Processes: The Resource Enabling Perspective of Startups in Pakistan

Hareem Nassar[(✉)] [iD] and Fareesa Malik

National University of Sciences and Technology, Islamabad, Pakistan
hareemnassar@gmail.com, fareesa.malik@nbs.nust.edu.pk

Abstract. The recent infusion of digital platforms into different aspects of innovation and entrepreneurship has supported digital entrepreneurship; however, the altered entrepreneurial processes are yet to be explored. This chapter aims to explore the role of digital platforms as external enablers in the entrepreneurial processes. It focuses on digital platform-based startups of Pakistan and draws on entrepreneurial bricolage theory to understand the enabling external resources. The authors followed multiple qualitative case study approach and collected data through semi-structured interviews from six startups operating solely on digital platforms, 1) XYLEXA, 2) Toycycle, 3) PaakHealth, 4) DadaJee.com, 5) Qurbani App and 6) PriceOye. The findings show that entrepreneurial process is a continuous process. Digital platforms have made entrepreneurial processes less bounded i.e., the products and services keep on evolving even after they have been endorsed to the end user. Moreover, platform-based startups having limited resources can pass through the entire entrepreneurial process by combining available resources efficiently and effectively. Entrepreneurial bricolage helps as a catalyst in successfully developing and exploiting the opportunity with existing resources.

Keywords: Digital platforms · Entrepreneurial processes · Digital entrepreneurship · Entrepreneurial bricolage theory · External enablers

1 Introduction

The entrepreneurial literature has considerably paid attention to the entrepreneurial processes, the discovery and exploitation of entrepreneurial opportunities and the role of concerned individuals (Shane and Venkataraman 2000; Srinivasan and Venkatraman 2018). A key emphasis has been on understanding the nature and sources of uncertainty that underlie entrepreneurial pursuits and the ways by which entrepreneurial actions unfold during such uncertainty (McKelvie et al. 2011; Nambisan 2016). However, the recent infusion of digital platforms into different facets of innovation and entrepreneurship has transformed the nature of uncertainty inherent in the entrepreneurial processes and the

J. Abdelnour-Nocera et al. (Eds.): *Innovation Practices for Digital Transformation in the Global South*, IFIP AICT 645, pp. 130–148, 2022.
https://doi.org/10.1007/978-3-031-12825-7_8

ways of dealing with such uncertainty (McKelvie et al. 2011; Srinivisan and Venkataraman 2018). It attracts the scholars 'attention towards an emerging research direction at the intersection of digital platforms and entrepreneurship i.e., digital entrepreneurship, which considers digital platforms and their distinctive features in influencing entrepreneurial pursuits. The digital platforms are enabling numerous entrepreneurial opportunities that are breeding a new generation of startups (Du et al. 2017). Digital platforms have not only shaped the entrepreneurial processes (opportunity generation, opportunity development and opportunity exploitation) but have also brought changes in innovation, competences, control, financing, institutions and ecosystems. Digital entrepreneurship includes transforming existing businesses or new ventures with the help of digital technologies which then serve as a catalyst for social and economic development. It is viewed as a vital pillar for development in the digital economy (Shen et al. 2015).

Businesses operating on digital platforms are quite different from the traditional businesses in terms of building trust, governance, resources and entrepreneurial processes. The study explores this through the theoretical lens of entrepreneurial bricolage which explains how entrepreneurship can be done through minimal resources (Baker and Nelson 2005; Garud et al. 2003; Phillips and Tracey 2007; William et al. 2011; Guo et al. 2015; Steininger 2019). Entrepreneurial bricolage can be a feasible path for platform-based startups or SMEs, having limited resources, to help in facilitation of entrepreneurial processes.

Even though, a considerable number of entrepreneurs and businesses are using digital platforms to tap the opportunities, research is still at nascent stage (Gregoire and Shepherd 2012; Shen et al. 2015). This knowledge gap in understanding the novel usage of digital platforms by entrepreneurs has been highlighted in several review articles (Kiss et al. 2012; Mainela et al. 2014; Shepherd et al. 2015; Shen et al. 2015). von Briel et al. (2018) also emphasized that the role of digital platforms in shaping the entrepreneurial opportunities, decisions, actions and processes has largely been neglected in the existing literature. Furthermore, the scholars have acknowledged the need to bring more discipline-specific theories into the interdisciplinary research stream of Information Systems and Entrepreneurship (Steininger 2019). Thus, the authors' choice of theory of entrepreneurial bricolage to sensitize this research can enable the next stage of investigations on the topic. Since many digital platform-based startups have started operating in Pakistan and various SMEs are also shifting their businesses on platforms, the authors found an interesting context to understand the characteristics of digital platforms and how they play a crucial role in shaping the entrepreneurial processes.

1.1 Purpose and Objectives

The research explores the role of digital platforms as facilitators of various resources for startups in the entire process of entrepreneurship. It also highlights the resource challenges that platform-based startups face in the execution and implementation of business ideas. As consequence, potential implications of this research for startups operating on digital platforms are discussed. The research focuses on the following research question:

'How do digital platforms act as external enablers in the entrepreneurial processes?'

To find answers to this, the authors have conducted multiple qualitative case studies. The authors selected six platform-based startups incubating in the National Science and Technology Park (NSTP) Islamabad, Pakistan: 1) Toycycle, 2) XYLEXA, 3) Paak Health, 4) PriceOye, 5) Qurbani App and 6) DadaJee.com.

2 Literature Review

2.1 Digital Platforms

Digital platforms provide an infrastructure to users (producers and consumers) to carry out a wide range of activities, thus resulting in the formation of entire ecosystems for creation and capturing of value (Kenney and Zysman 2015). They are a distinct type of information technology artefact with distinct properties and are characterized as a sociotechnical grouping which includes the technical elements of software and hardware as well as the organizational processes and principles (Koskinen et al. 2021; De Reuver et al. 2018). They are a shared and common set of services and architecture that provides help in hosting complementary offerings. For instance, iOS platform of Apple and Android platform of Google allow apps to run on their respective smartphones (Nambisan 2016). The success of digital platforms is based on the ecosystem in which the platform is embedded. The digital platforms share three basic features: 1) technologically mediated, 2) enabling interaction between user groups, and 3) allowing user groups to perform tasks (Koskinen et al. 2021; Cusumano et al. 2019; de Reuver et al. 2018).

Digital platforms help new startups to expand their specialization while offsetting their production, marketing, and distribution abilities (Nambisan 2016). They can serve to be infrastructure, marketplace and ecosystems at the same time i.e., Facebook and Google are digital platforms which provide social media interaction and search but at the same time, they also serve to be the platforms on which other platforms can be built. Amazon, e-Bay and Etsy are some of the platforms that are existing as marketplace. These diverse digital platforms are contributing to reorganizing of markets and value generation (Kenney and Zysman 2015). They have flourished as engines of innovation for other firms to build complementary products and services in the ecosystems like PCs, video games, smartphones and newer webs orchestrated by Facebook, YouTube, Twitter etc. Thus, success of such digital platforms is also dependent on important roles of complementary innovators (Boudreau and Lakhani 2009; Srinivasan and Venkatraman 2018). Digital platforms can be made customizable, which are shared by many companies within same or different industry and can also take the form of business community platforms, which are personalized for usage by all the members of a particular business community (Markus and Loebbecke 2013).

Modular systems have led to the development of platform architectures that partition the industry ecosystem into a stable platform and a complementary set of modules that are encouraged to diverge and grow (Tiwana et al. 2010; Srinivasan and Venkatraman 2018). Increased modularity of digital systems has released an extensive wave of entrepreneurial firms that innovate and launch modules (of compatible applications) to align with specific platform architectures. In digital platform settings, there is a strong interdependence between entrepreneurial firms that launch specific modules and platform firms for whom the modules are launched. Platform firms spend substantial resources to attract third-party developers to their platforms. In order to get greater support from third-party complementors, platform firms attempt to attract a significant number of users to their platforms and, in the process, build a higher installed base which creates enticements for entrepreneurs to introduce more complementary modules (Armstrong 2006; Evans and Schmalensee 2008; Srinivasan and Venkatraman 2018). Digital platforms having large user base is more valued by entrepreneurs as they offer the biggest potential market for their complementary products (Venkatraman and Lee 2004; Srinivasan and Venkatraman 2018). They create indirect network effects (Cennamo and Santalo 2013; McIntyre and Srinivasan 2017; Srinivasan and Venkatraman 2018) which is a foundation of competition in digital platform settings. An entrepreneur's choice to support the platform is greatly influenced by the network effects for the platform. The presence of network effects and installed base advantages are vital elements of success in platform industries and often lead to the introduction of new platforms and new competitors (Venkatraman and Lee 2004; Srinivasan and Venkatraman 2018).

Digital platforms have added various new functionalities which has changed the overall environment, thus increasing competition and reforming the traditional organizational strategies and processes (Shen et al. 2015). Since there is rapid pace of technology transformation in digital platforms and intense rivalry, the ability to distinguish one's offerings and rapid adaptation to technological change becomes necessary for success and survival (Srinivasan and Venkatraman 2018). This has led to new ways of communicating and collaborating with stakeholders, orchestrating resources and designing goods and services (Markus and Loebecke 2013; Shen et al. 2015). They have restructured various parts of the global economy by altering organizational processes, resetting barriers to entry, introducing more open communication and new ways of creating and capturing value (Kenney and Zysman 2015). Resultantly, the entrepreneurial processes have been reshaped.

2.2 Entrepreneurial Processes

The entrepreneurship process is an activity which processes the opportunities. It goes through the process of opportunity generation (creation and discovery), opportunity development and opportunity exploitation by attaining, assembling and deploying resources with the objective to transform an opportunity into a viable venture and thus, achieve success [see Fig. 1]. So, it becomes important to understand the nature of opportunities and how they enter and move up the entire entrepreneurial process in order to achieve success. There have been recent arguments in literature by theorists for the significance of opportunity as an explanatory concept (Shane 2000; Jeff et al. 2011).

Entrepreneurial opportunities are situations in which new products, services and markets are introduced through new means and ends (Shane 2000; Jeff et al. 2011). As depicted in Fig. 2, Shane (2000) has argued that the entrepreneurial process begins with entrepreneurial opportunities which are discovered by an entrepreneur on the basis of prior knowledge acquired through education, work experiences and personal events,

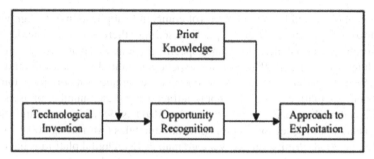

Fig. 1. The entrepreneurial process (Jeff et al. 2011)

rather than through active search. Prior knowledge allows an entrepreneur to use technology in different markets, serve them in different ways and cater to different problems by providing solutions. It also helps in exploitation of opportunity by selecting markets and catering to customer needs and concerns.

However, some scholars are of the view that opportunities exist prior to the entrepreneurial process, while some argue that opportunities are recognized or discovered by entrepreneurs to start the process of entrepreneurship. When an entrepreneur displays behaviors like recognizing, scanning, searching, discovering or constructing, it leads to the emergence of opportunity generation. The entrepreneurial process moves from opportunity generation to opportunity development when a decision is made by the entrepreneur to commit time and effort to the opportunity so that it can be turned into a viable venture. The development stage includes engaging entrepreneurs in internal search of their web of 'knowledge corridors' for information that is applicable to that particular opportunity as well as scanning surrounding environment for available resources which can provide aid in the exploitation of the opportunity. Entrepreneurs require a catalyst for easy facilitation in their progression from opportunity generation to opportunity development. This role of catalyst can be best served by bricolage as it allows applying prior knowledge and orchestrating available resources which can greatly shape the development of an opportunity and help an entrepreneur to progress. As the development stage progresses, bricolage helps in strategy formation and allows entrepreneurs to see novel resources which can be combined and applied immediately to a particular situation on hand and move the venture to the exploitation phase. Having prior knowledge of markets and customer needs and problems is crucial for the exploitation stage. Inventories of existing resources is another important link between the development and exploitation stage as it provides an entrepreneur with tangible means to prepare their developed opportunities for exploitation (Jeff et al. 2011).

Previous studies on innovation and entrepreneurship as well as the present theories on product life cycle, architectural innovation and product development process have assumed constant and discrete boundaries for ideas relating to new product or service that underlie an entrepreneurial opportunity (Davidsson 2015; Short et al. 2010; Nambisan 2016). However, infusion of digital technologies has made these boundaries more permeable as the scope, attributes and value of product or service keep evolving even after the idea has been endorsed. For instance, Tesla has introduced various new

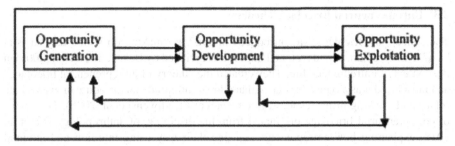

Fig. 2. Shane's (2000) conceptual model of entrepreneurial process

functions and features in its cars even after they have been endorsed to the market, simply by modifying digital artifacts or components. With digital technologies and platforms, entrepreneurial processes have also become less bounded mainly in terms of their temporal arrangement as they allow product ideas and business models to be formed, endorsed, amended and restructured rapidly e.g., 3D printing (Ries 2011; Nambisan 2016). The scalability of digital platforms (e.g., cloud computing and mobile networking) i.e., the capability to promptly increase performance at low cost and with ease, also causes variations in entrepreneurial activities. For instance, Airbnb started with its initial focus on meetings and events for which hotel space was required. Later, it catered to the demand for affordable accommodation which the hotels were unable to meet thus, rapidly scaling up its services enabled by cloud computing services. Thus, digital technologies enable a greater level of fluidity and variability into entrepreneurial processes. These changes in entrepreneurial processes enabled by digital platforms lead to change in behaviors and actions of entrepreneurs in the digital arena. Digitalization of entrepreneurial processes has also helped in breaking down the boundaries between various phases along with bringing greater levels of unpredictability and nonlinearity into how they fold (Nambisan 2016).

With traditional models and frameworks on entrepreneurship assuming fixed and stable boundaries for an entrepreneurial opportunity, a more evolving stream in entrepreneurship research presents alternate views regarding opportunity creation and enactment that reflects fluid boundaries for entrepreneurial processes. For instance, the perspective of 'opportunity creation' is of the view that opportunities are emergent, and the entire creation process is evolutionary (Garud 2003; Nambisan 2016). Likewise, the 'effectuation' perspective suggests that the entrepreneur continuously re-evaluates all the available means and shape the offering (Nambisan 2016; Saravsathy and Dew 2005). These perspectives indicate that there are fluid boundaries with respect to entrepreneurial processes.

Thus, it is concluded that alternative concepts and theories are necessary for integrating new ways of evaluation of entrepreneurial success and inform on all those factors that are linked with progression of entrepreneurial processes. Digital platforms can play a major role in shaping such liminal entrepreneurial processes (Nambisan 2016).

2.3   Entrepreneurial Bricolage Theory

The concept of Bricolage was introduced in 1967 as "making do with whatever is at hand" which remained undeveloped until it was revisited by Baker and Nelson (2005) in the context of entrepreneurship. They created the "theory of entrepreneurial bricolage" and introduced it as a type of resource that allows entrepreneurs to endure or even create robust and growing firms despite scarce resources (Tindiwensi et al. 2020). The theory of entrepreneurial bricolage originated from the discipline of anthropology (Yu et al. 2018) explaining how entrepreneurs can find their way using intuition and minimal resources. This theory can help illuminate the dynamic business model development processes of founders with scarce resources (Baker and Nelson 2005; Steininger 2018). It is concerned with the application of unique combination of resources at hand to new problems and opportunities (Baker and Nelson 2005; Yu et al. 2018). In other words, entrepreneurs can build available resources in an innovative manner into new products or services rather than merely accepting their current potential (Baker and Nelson 2005; Yu et al. 2018). The theory involves extensive decision-making and combines thoughts and actions (Fan et al. 2019). The theory of entrepreneurial bricolage has three important features. The first feature involves action and active engagement with the problem to assess whether an effective outcome can be generated from what is available at hand. The second is combining and orchestrating resources in an innovative manner for new applications rather than only using them for purposes for which they were originally intended or used. The third is using available resources rather than looking for new resources (Yu et al. 2018).

Most of the existing research on entrepreneurial bricolage theory has been done in the context of SMEs where resource scarcity is a common issue. SMEs are generally very resilient, flexible and creative but their limited network and scarce resources pose to be a great challenge for them. They have many unrecognized and under-utilized resources (Di Domenico et al. 2010). With the help of this theory, SMEs can discover many new prospects by taking advantage of these unrecognized and under-utilized resources and overcoming difficulties in resource acquisition (Phillips and Tracey 2007; Guo et al. 2016; Yu et al. 2018). They can leverage bricolage to transform limitations and constraints into opportunities, resolve catastrophes and lift boundaries (Hsiao et al. 2014; Hsiao, Ou and Su 2017; Hsiao, Ou and Wu 2017; Fan et al. 2019). Since SMEs generally need to make quick decisions, execution to find the right resources and combining them to solve their prevailing problems is necessary (Baker and Nelson 2005; Hsiao, Ou and Wu 2017; Fan et al. 2019). Entrepreneurial bricolage combines both resource-based theory and dynamic capabilities theory to describe the effective arrangement of resources. Entrepreneurial bricolage theory also complements with the resource-based view (RBV). RBV is of the view that a firm can achieve competitive advantage if it possesses resources that are rare, distinctive, and not easily imitated by competitors. However, it may not be readily applicable in the context of SMEs as it is quite difficult for startup SMEs to acquire novel strategic resources in open market. Thus, entrepreneurial bricolage complements RBV by stating that apart from searching for external strategic resources, SMEs can take benefit from existing under-utilized resources by combining them in unique ways to achieve competitive advantage (Yu et al. 2018).

Based on the nature of resources, entrepreneurial bricolage has been classified into three types: input bricolage, market bricolage and institutional bricolage (Baker and Nelson 2005; Desa and Basu 2013; Yu et al. 2018). (1) Input bricolage applies combinations of physical (e.g., materials) and human (e.g., labor and skillset) resources in an innovative manner and apply them to new problems and opportunities. Due to the disadvantage of being new and small, it becomes expensive for SMEs to seek and acquire new and costly resources from stakeholders. This is where input bricolage allows combining available resources which can prove to be beneficial for providing supporting infrastructure and less expensive labor. This also lowers operational, management and marketing costs. Input bricolage also increases operational efficiency when startups have very limited financial resources or have to react instantaneously to the demands of their customers. It helps platform-based startups in recombining available resources, creating unanticipated products and improving sales performance by broadening the distribution channels, providing infinite shelf space and targeting new audience (Garud and Karnoe 2003; Yu et al. 2018). It also assists platform-based startups in expanding niche markets and creating new market demand. (2) Market bricolage transforms existing network of entrepreneurs (customers, friends, suppliers and competitors) to create new customers from the market in which rivals operate. Existing networks are resources at hand for entrepreneurs and successful entrepreneurs are those who fully utilize their existing networks to create new markets. In platform businesses, many customers begin as or become friends. Suppliers become customers and vice versa. Such shifts and expansion of roles deepens the understanding of customer needs and receiving feedback from them which allows iterating products at a low cost. Market bricolage enables digital platform-based startups to broaden their product and service combinations at low cost through economies of scale as they are often limited with storage capacity and small amount of available funds which has a negative impact on market expansion. It also helps platform-based startups in developing trust and committed relationships between business partners. Customers formed through market bricolage are more likely to try new products and services, thus leading to repeated purchases (Baker and Nelson 2005; Garud and Karnoe 2003; Yu et al. 2018). (3) Institutional bricolage involves working around symbolic principles, rules and norms to bring about an institutional change. There are three pillars of an institution i.e., regulative, normative and cognitive. Institutional bricolage comprises of two stages. The first is to socially reconstruct the available resources which is possible only by being unlocked from existing practices of using certain type of resources. The second stage involves normalizing any institutional deviance in order to set up new institutions. There is no intention violation of existing policies and rules on behalf of the entrepreneur. Rather, platform-based startups are an emerging phenomenon so existing standards and regulations do not prove to be sufficient for them. Institutional bricolage enhances the acceptability of novel products by forming new institutions, rather than fitting into new ones (Desa and Basu 2013; Baker et al. 2005; Yu et al. 2018).

3 Research Methodology

The authors adopted a qualitative multiple case study approach to investigate the role of digital platforms in entrepreneurial processes of platform-based startups in Pakistan as it is context-based research (Gustafsson 2017). Considering the early stage of establishment of the startups, multiple case study approach was more suitable to develop an in-depth understanding of the phenomena than a single case and to explore the answers of 'how' questions for theory building. The evidence created from a multiple case study is strong and reliable and similarities and contrasts can be made. Moreover, this approach creates a more convincing theory when the suggestions are intensely grounded in several empirical evidence, thus allowing for a wider exploration of our research question and theoretical evolution (Saunders et al. 2016).

The authors selected six digital platform-based startups 'Toycycle', 'XYLEXA', 'PaakHealth', 'Qurbani App', 'DadaJee.com' and 'PriceOye' incubating in Pakistan's National Science and Technology Park (NSTP). NSTP aims for stimulating innovation-led economic growth of the country and the region and supporting emerging local startups and SMEs that are seeking to develop and export diverse technology-based products and services.

(1) Toycycle is an online platform for buying and selling of preowned items including baby gear (strollers, highchairs, bouncers and carriers), clothes and toys (games, puzzles, electronic toys and wooden toys). It provides full-service consignment where toys and baby gear are picked from the owner's place, sorted out and sold on the platform. Once the items are sold, the owner gets paid.

(2) XYLEXA is an online platform for provision of diagnostic services to caregivers using AI and image processing techniques. The platform serves as a decision support system for radiologists by providing medical image diagnosis and disease and is also involved in R&D for timely diagnosis of cancer.

(3) PaakHealth is an online platform for the provision of services related to setting up appointments with doctors, hospitals, home delivery of prescribed medicines ordered through their app and emergency portal for finding blood donors.

(4) Qurbani App is an online marketplace that facilitates the buying and selling of animals by connecting farmers, mandi (market) owners, traders and vets on a single platform. Their services include Sadqah, Aqiqa and Ijtimae Qurbani as well as developing drones for the surveillance of livestock.

(5) DadaJee.com is an online B2B platform for selling a wide range of toys (cars, dolls, helicopters etc.) in all materials.

(6) PriceOye is an e-commerce platform for price comparison and purchase of electronics products online. It aims in finding authentic, latest and lowest prices product by catering to Pakistan's 210 million consumers with a business model similar to China's JD.com.

In order to maximize the flexibility of this research study, data collection and analysis occurred simultaneously across 2 phases. The authors also established various mechanisms to ensure reliability and validity of our findings [See Table 1]. Phase 1 began in October 2020 when the manager of NSTP provided support for obtaining access to digital platform-based startups at NSTP. However, this phase was an introductory phase focused on creating linkages with the digital startups and finalizing our research sample. The next phase (phase 2) began in March 2021 in which the interviews with the startups' founders were conducted. All the six startups were at the post-incubation stage. The authors stopped aiming for more startups after the interviews started to repeat themselves and failed to unveil more themes.

Table 1. Mechanisms to ensure reliability and validity

Mechanisms to Ensure Reliability	Mechanisms to Ensure Validity
✓ Ensured statement from one respondent is supported by another respondent. ✓ Studied Pakistan's innovation landscape and entrepreneurial ecosystem in order to contextualize the findings.	✓ Ensured that our study was supported by both interview data and existing literature.

The primary data was collected through informal chats and semi-structured interviews with founders, co-founders and employees of all the startups. Thirteen semi-structured interviews were conducted from founders (8 interviews – all males), co-founders (3 interviews – 2 males and 1 female) and employees (2 interviews – both males) of the startups. Regarding interview procedures, all interviews started with open-ended questions such as "What does your startup do?" and "How did you come up with this platform-based idea?" Later, the interviews moved on to those questions that were very focused and specific to our research question e.g., how they reshaped their products and services once they had been introduced to the end user. For resource enabling perspective, our interview questions were focused on what technological, financial and social network resource challenges were encountered and how were they overcome. The interviews were analyzed in real-time. While the informants were busy answering the initiated question, the authors jotted down main points of the informant's response, interpreted it, identified themes and then redirected questions around those themes.

All interviews were recorded with the permission and transcribed lately. Three interviews were in Urdu language had to be translated to English language while some interviews were completely conducted in English. The transcriptions and translations were thoroughly gone through several times in order to ensure their validity. The transcriptions were read multiple times for coding and thematic analysis. During the process, the authors compared the interview data and prior literature to ensure that the study is supported by both interview data and existing literature. When a new theme emerged but data relevant to that theme was insufficient, a follow-up interview took place. This iteration between data collection and follow-up interviews lasted about 4 months, until the findings reached theoretical saturation, at which point the newly collected data failed to reveal new or contradictory themes. The concepts of ICT and entrepreneurial bricolage theory helped in making sense of the data. The themes were finalized after extensive discussion within the team.

4 Findings

This section summarizes the research findings in three themes to explain the role of digital platforms as resource enabler in entrepreneurial processes.

4.1 Input Bricolage: Combining Internal and External Resources

Building a platform-based startup is challenging in Pakistan. The digital landscape of Pakistan is still in the developing phase which leads to technological and its acceptance issues due to inadequate know-how of using technology. Apart from this, startups also face the issue of resource scarcity due to limited resources in the beginning. But maximum utilization of available internal and external resources helps them in easy facilitation throughout the entire entrepreneurial process.

Majority of the respondent startups started with a subjectivist perspective. They discovered and created opportunity through their personal knowledge rather than through active search. They completely utilized their internal resources like skills, experience, education, personal events and knowledge base for market selection and identifying customers' problems along with categorizing and evaluating information received from the environment. This also helped them in identifying the use of technology in different markets, serving a particular market in different ways and providing solutions to new and different problems. Improvised resources were orchestrated for novel usage using just-in-time strategy in order to reduce costs. Only two startups followed an objectivist perspective by tapping unexplored opportunities and gaps which did not have close linkage with their knowledge base. So, they had to adapt their knowledge and resources according to them. As explained by one respondent with a subjectivist perspective:

'Market research was very critical in the start as we had to get it right to let our customers buy from us. However, I have been in this industry for about 16 years, so I am already familiar with the market and I addressing potential customer voices and concerns' [R 3, XYLEXA Co-founder].

External resources were also acquired by startups from external stakeholders and recombined for use. Those external resources included technological and financial resources. Financial resource constraints were a huge challenge in the beginning for most of the startups as they had developed viable prototypes but lacked the required resources to turn it into a tangible product ready for commercialization. The financial resource challenges were mainly overcome by financial bootstrapping, financial rounds and funding received from accelerator programs. These accelerator programs were willing to provide funding for new and 'out of the box' ideas in the country and since platform concept is an emerging phenomenon in developing countries like Pakistan, these startups were easily provided with adequate funding.

'We started with bootstrapping in the beginning. Now since we are growing, we have shifted our focus on financial rounds' [R 6, Qurbani App Founder].

Another respondent also articulated this: 'We raised two pre-seed rounds for this financial challenge. As a result, now we are close to our break-even' [R 4, Toycycle Founder].

Technological resource challenge was another big issue in the development of the platform. Hiring appropriate developers and passing through the procedure of domain registration was not an easy task. Moreover, the target user base of these startups was not tech savvy, so it was a challenge in providing them with adequate training to operate the apps. Language barrier was overcome by offering the feature of Urdu language on the platform.

'When we started our platform, we faced technological resource issues related to domain and hosting registration, hiring skilled developers and contacting software houses for provision of services. After that, we shifted to WhatsApp business in which our website got blocked as we did not read technological terms and conditions thoroughly. So, after this experience, we had to start all over again which increased our cost' [R 12, DadaJee.com Founder].

All these internal (knowledge base and skills) and external (financial and techno-logical) resources were a necessity at the opportunity generation stage. While moving forward towards the development stage, internal search of knowledge corridors and environmental scanning was also important. Potential strategic alliances, personal contacts, partnerships and joint ventures were needed to obtain the required R&D, manufacturing and marketing capabilities and other related support and to gain quick access to vital markets in which the startups had little or no experience.

'We did partnerships with mobile payment and telecommunications companies to get access to easy payments and with one non-profit organization for distribution of our products on our platform' [R 7, Qurbani App Founder].

Another respondent also highlighted this:

'We did joint ventures to get hosting and technological support' [R 13, Dada-Jee.com Co-founder].

Due to their newness and smallness, it was very expensive for startups to seek and acquire resources from their stakeholders. But with the startups operating on third-party digital platforms, friends and family resources came in handy to lower the operational costs by bringing in supportive infrastructure, less expensive labor and flexibility.

'We brought in consultants who were relevant in areas of Artificial Intelligence (AI) and Machine Learning to come in and help the team at different stages where they get stuck. They were expensive resources, but we were able to negotiate a very good package with them so that they can provide guidance to the team' [R 2, XYLEXA Co-founder].

The involvement of family and friends allowed these digital startups to explore leveraging resources at hand and to increase the probability of creating new market demand as quality and participation level of social network resource allows emerging startups to make full use of the resources at hand. However, it was important to retain the labor and every effort was made in order to retain them. As one respondent mentioned:

'In order to retain our employees, we offered them trading, a good working environment, the interesting product that we were making and the cutting-edge technology
that we are using. We took care of our employees and gave them a chance to learn
and grow and not make empty promises to them. We are sitting in the same office,
working on the product and funding. So, they have seen the progress themselves
and they are committed to what we are doing' [R 1, XYLEXA Founder].

4.2 Market Bricolage: Enhancing Customer Base and Building Trust

Market bricolage served as a catalyst in developing and exploiting opportunities. Function of the entire business network was changed; non-business relationships were
changed into business relationships and startups created new markets and new customers by transforming their existing network of entrepreneurs i.e., customers, friends,
suppliers and competitors. Customers became friends, suppliers became customers and
vice versa.

'We did partnerships with relevant suppliers and startups to enhance our customer
base' [R 5, Toycycle Employee].

'We created a new market by making sure that we have enough customers who
would be our referential customers who helped us grow and expand our system in
Pakistan and globally' [R2, XYLEXA Co-founder].

Obtaining large user base was a challenge because advancement in digital technologies in Pakistan is still at an early stage, either because of adequate technological
knowledge or high costs. The startups initially started with referential customers but
when it came to enhancing customer base, the target market was hardly tech savvy. They
did not have much know-how in operating the apps and they were resistant to change.
Trainings had to be provided to them so that they can operate the app. Moreover, it was
ensured that the platform is user friendly and cheap in order to attract more customers.
Word-of-mouth also played a major role in attracting new user base.

'Not a single hospital in Pakistan is using Computer Aided Diagnosis (CAD)
system. It is not that they do not know about it. It is just that they cannot afford it.
So, we had to make it very comparative in terms of price and entry where they do
not have to invest any dollars in capital investment. There is no expense, and they
only have to pay for what they use. So, we are creating a new market by making
sure that we have enough customers who would be our referential customers and
that will help us grow and expand our system in the hospitals of Pakistan and
globally' [R 2, XYLEXA Co-founder].

Another respondent also reported:

'Only 5 to 7% of our user base was educated. So, we had to offer local language on
our platform and make it user-friendly along with providing trainings to operate
app and instilling privacy and sense of security in our customers to retain and
expand our network' [R 7, Qurbani App Founder].

Such shifts and expansion of roles to transform the network facilitated in establishing multiplex ties which deepen the understanding of customer needs and concerns and allowed the platforms to iterate the products at lower costs. New products were iterated after receiving feedback from end users. As platforms are virtual and geographically dispersed, it becomes convenient to receive feedback from customers regarding the product. Moreover, the network formed via market bricolage further helps iterate the products at lower cost. Through digital platforms, it was easier to shape the offerings (i.e., the products and services) even after they had been introduced to the end users simply by modifying digital artifacts or components. As customer requirements change with time, entrepreneurship process becomes ongoing and continuous. This greatly helped in retaining customers and attracting new ones. One respondent mentioned:

'We generally go through a product management process. We have built a base product; we have requirements coming in from customers whether they are related to user experience or new functionality. We go through a standard release process. We prioritize them and implement them' [R 2, XYLEXA Co-founder].

Other respondents also commented:

'We keep our eyes on whether our old product design is up to date and working properly, if we can improve our conversion and customer acquisition' [R 4, Toycycle Founder].

'We modify our offerings everyday through continuous improvement. What is not worthy is shelved' [R 8, PriceOye Founder].

These emerging digital startups also faced low level of trust and governance issues as well as less committed relationships between customers and business partners because reputation and trust building take a lot of time and plays a crucial role at both commercial and social levels. Particularly in the context of digital startups, it was very important to establish trust and good reputation among customers as consumer behavior and purchase decisions were relying greatly on electronic word of mouth. Since the startups had referential customers in the beginning and friends who were early adopters, this immensely helped them in obtaining active transaction records of products with many favorable and positive reviews to their profiles. Moreover, their transformed network formed via market bricolage also voluntarily purchased new products and services, thus leading to repeated purchases. Another trust building mechanism included products and services going through an entire process of trial and error and receiving feedback from customers. Based on this, startups went from concept to proof of concept and the Minimum Viable Product (MVP) was released in the market. The needs and concerns of the customers were received, and those customer feedbacks were incorporated in the beta product.

'At this stage, it was very important to build trust. Since I had already been in the industry for 16 years, so our customers were all referral customers. This helped us in building trust among them comparatively easily' [R 3, XYLEXA Co-founder].

Another respondent also demonstrated:

'We developed trust among users through communication, word of mouth and mind reading. We also developed an effective helpline and feedback mechanism which facilitated both sides of our platform. But overall, communication was the key element in instilling trust among customers' [R 6, Qurbani App Founder].

4.3   Institutional Bricolage: Institutional Orders and Institutional Transformation

Institutional bricolage helped the startups in socially reconstructing the available resources by deferring from existing practices of using certain types of resources. Since digital platforms are an emerging phenomenon in Pakistan, existing business standards and regulations were not fully sufficient in guiding the startups and supportive institutions were not strong and efficient.

'We had our first startup in the US because the current market and existing business regulations were not enough in Pakistan. But as the platform concept is growing locally, more business rules and regulations are available now which are sufficient for us' [R 9, PriceOye Founder].

Legitimacy to existing structures and outcomes was more focused on stability. So, normalization of institutional deviance was necessary for re-purposed resource combinations and deployment practices to bring change and form new institutions. Startups did not conform to cultural myths and symbols because it promotes the public legitimacy necessary for organizational startup but deviates them in the development of goals and actions that may not be their core technical mission. Considering the institutional orders, the cultural and behavioral values differ with respect to religion, family, the bureaucratic state, the capitalist market, democracy and community. However, it could not be stated which norms were more salient than others because the startups were more centered in one or more of the institutional orders than others.

PriceOye blended the market and corporation. The founders observed that the traditional e-commerce models like Daraz do not cater to all the gaps in the market. Their research showed this demographic of Pakistan having the fastest growing middle-class population who would be very inclined towards an idea of comparing prices of different products and purchasing them at an affordable rate. Their research also showed the demographics of Pakistan and India are similar, so they went to India and later to China to learn about their ecosystem and have a knowledge of their markets and corporations. From there, they implemented this idea which was similar to Indonesian startup ecosystem. Thus, they transposed and blended practices from the market and corporate management to create new ways to set e-commerce standards that focused on outcomes and purchasing decisions of customers.

Similarly, Toycycle also blended the market and corporation. It was observed by the founder that traditional marketplaces like Daraz and e-Bay do not offer full-service consignment. Since the houses were very compact in the US and the babies outgrew from the baby gear very quickly, it was troublesome to store the baby gear in the house. So, he came up with the idea of full-service consignment where the item was picked from the houses and sold on the platform. For this, he blended practices from the market and corporation after observing and studying the US startups which were working on the same idea.

DadaJee.com blended family, market and corporation. The founder was working as a corporate employee in his family's trading business which focused only on local markets. In this changing era, he recognized the need to make it digitized in order to target a wider set of user base. For this, he began with collecting investment and approaching accelerator programs but could not receive funding from them as they were only interested in funding 'out of the box' idea. So, what he needed was a blend of family capitalism with market and corporate management.

Qurbani App blended religion, community and corporation. With the past corporate experience and practices, the founder focused on executing the idea which was committed to community values and ideology and sources of legitimacy of importance of faith in the society.

PaakHealth segregated family and blended market and profession. The founder did not follow the traditional family values but rather went for the idea in which he excelled. He wanted to change the traditional mindset of his family and people in his area who only believed in visiting local hakims (herbal medicine practitioners) for any kind of treatment. He shifted from family capitalism to market and personal capitalism and from status in household to status in market and profession. He shifted his sources of legitimacy from unconditional loyalty to personal expertise.

This led to better positioning to garner resources by creating new and reconfiguring institutions. Institutional bricolage helped the startups in implementing innovative approaches to employ available resources. Individualized and customized services were made available to the end users and open source was used to build components and add new functionalities. These platform-based startups have become pioneers in their area by introducing novel products in the market. As a result, the perception of people has changed to some extent. They are adopting new technology-based products. The startups have also experienced first-mover advantage.

5 Discussion and Conclusion

The study seeks to make contribution to research and practice in digital entrepreneurship. It offers novel insights into digital entrepreneurship literature by exploring role of digital platforms as facilitators of various resources for startups.

The answer to the research question – "How digital platforms act as external enablers in entrepreneurial processes?" has been examined with the help of entrepreneurial bricolage theory. Digital platforms serve to be infrastructure, marketplace and ecosystems at the same time (Kenney and Zysman 2015). They help in continual updating of entrepreneurial processes. Our findings concur with the literature that digital platforms create fluid boundaries of the entire entrepreneurial process as the products and services keep getting modified even after they have been introduced in the market and to the end user. This is done through modification in digital artifacts or components (Nambisan 2016).

The limited resources are an important challenge that almost all small startups face. They have the required skillset, social network and creativity but are unable to have access to costly new resources (Di Domenico et al. 2010). Having enough finances to turn a viable prototype into a tangible product is a challenge for which funding from incubation and accelerator programs is needed. Combining available resources (internal and external), indulging in partnerships and seeking help from the limited social network can help in operationalization, improving sales performance and efficiency and creating customers. Moreover, normalizing institutional deviance rather than legitimacy to existing structures and outcomes should also take place. Technological challenges are also common in Pakistan where technology is still in its nascent stage. It is somewhat challenging to enhance platform user base in Pakistan as customers are at times less familiar with the technology either because it is expensive or due to less adequate technological knowledge. Making the technology comparative in terms of price point and entry and allowing the customers to pay only for what they use can help platform-based startups in overcoming technological resource challenges throughout the entrepreneurial process.

Startups in developing countries like Pakistan are more inclined towards operating on digital platforms as it enables entrepreneurship even in resource constraint environment. Scarce resources are a huge challenge and people in developing countries tend to have technology acceptance issues. However, combining available resources in an effective manner and taking help from existing network of family and friends can help in operationalizing the startups. Moreover, digital platforms charging customers only for what they use becomes a major solution to cater to the technology acceptance issues and enhancing user base. New business standards and regulations are also coming in place to facilitate the operationalization of platform-based startups.

In this chapter, the authors attempt to bring the attention of IS scholars towards exploring the interaction of digital platforms and entrepreneurial processes. It is the right time to focus on digital entrepreneurship as the entire world is moving towards digitization. In developing countries, startups and small enterprises can catalyst the economic and social development. This initial level research identifies the need of future research to unpack the various stages of entrepreneurial process from input, market and institutional resources facilitated by digital platforms in developed and developing countries. These theoretical and practical insights will not only contribute into emerging literature of digital entrepreneurship but will also assist in flourishing the entrepreneurial ecosystems in developing countries where resources are scarce.

References

Armstrong, M.: Competition in two-sided markets. RAND J. Econ. **37**(3), 668–691 (2006)

Baker, T., Nelson, R.: Creating something from nothing: resource construction through entrepreneurial bricolage. Adm. Sci. Q. **50**(3), 329–366 (2005)

Baron, R.A.: Opportunity recognition as pattern recognition: how entrepreneurs connect the dots to identify new business opportunities. Acad. Manag. Perspect. **20**(1), 104–119 (2006)

Boudreau, K., Lakhani, K.: How to manage outside innovation: competitive markets or collaborative communities? MIT Sloan Manag. Rev. **50**, 69–75 (2009)

Cennamo, C., Santalo, S.: Platform competition: strategic trade-offs in platform markets. Strategic Manag. J. **34**(11), 1331–1350 (2013)

Cusumano, M.A., Gawer, A., Yoffie, D.B.: The Business of Platforms: Strategy in the Age of Digital Competition, Innovation and Power. Harper Business, New York (2019)

Davidsson, P.: Entrepreneurial opportunities and the entrepreneurship nexus: a reconceptualization. J. Bus. Ventur. **30**(5), 674–695 (2015) de Reuver, M., Sørensen, C., Basole, R.C.: The digital platform: a research agenda. J. Inf. Technol. **33**, 124–135 (2018). https://doi.org/10.1057/s41265-016-0033-3

Desa, G., Basu, S.: Optimization or bricolage? Overcoming resource constraints in global social entrepreneurship. Strateg. Entrepreneurship J. **7**(1), 26–49 (2013)

Di Domenico, M., Haugh, H., Tracey, P.: Social bricolage: theorizing social value creation in social enterprises. Entrepreneurship Theory Pract. **34**(4), 681–703 (2010)

Du, W., Pan, S., Zhou, N., Ouyang, T.: From a marketplace of electronics to a digital entrepreneurial ecosystem (DEE): the emergence of a meta-organization in Zhongguancun, China. Inf. Syst. J. **28**(6), 158–1175 (2017)

Evans, D., Schmalensee, R.: Markets with two-sided platforms. Issues Competition Law Policy **20**, 667–693 (2008)

Fan, W.S., Huang, K.C., Chiang, P.Y.: An empirical application of entrepreneurial bricolage theory to resource integration using data from small and medium-sized enterprises in Taiwan. Int. J. Bus. Soc. Sci. **10**(7), 65–77 (2019)

Garud, R., Karnoe, P.: Bricolage versus breakthrough: distributed and embedded agency in technology entrepreneurship. Res. Policy **32**(2), 277–300 (2003)

Garud, R., Giuliani, A.: A narrative perspective on entrepreneurial opportunities. Acad. Manag. Rev. **38**(1), 157–160 (2013)

Gregoire, D.A., Shepherd, D.A.: Technology market combinations and the identification of entrepreneurial opportunities. Acad. Manag. J., 753–758 (2012)

Guo, H., Su, Z., Ahlstrom, D.: Business model innovation: The effects of exploratory orientation, opportunity recognition, and entrepreneurial bricolage in an emerging economy. Asia Pacific J. Manag. **33**(2), 533–549 (2015). https://doi.org/10.1007/s10490-015-9428-x

Gustafsson, J.: Single Case Studies vs. Multiple Case Studies: A Comparative Study, pp. 1–15 (2017)

Hsiao, R., Ou, S., Chen, H.: Innovating under disadvantages: bricolage behaviors in Van Gogh art curation. Sun Yat-Sen Manag. Rev. **22**(2), 323–367 (2014)

Hsiao, R., Ou, S., Su, Y.: Inversing the powerful: process of resource construction through bricolage. NTU Manag. Rev. **27**(4), 1–32 (2017)

Hsiao, R., Ou, S., Wu, Y.: Making-do within adversity: resource constraints as a source of innovation. Sun Yat-Sen Manag. Rev. **25**(1), 219–268 (2017)

Jeff, V., Winkel, D., Malewicki, D., Dougan, W.L., Bronson, J.: Varieties of bricolage and the process of entrepreneurship. New Engl. J. Entrepreneurship 53–66 (2011)

Kenney, M., Zysman, J.: Choosing a Future in the Platform Economy: The Implications and Consequences of Digital Platforms. Kauffman Foundation New Entrepreneurial Growth Conference, pp. 1–23. Florida (2015)

Kiss, A.N., Danis, W.M., Cavusgil, S.T.: International entrepreneurship research in emerging economies: a critical review and research agenda. J. Bus. Ventur. **27**(2), 266–290 (2012)

Koskinen, K., Bonina, C., Eaton, B., Gawer, A.: Digital platforms for development: foundations and research agenda. Inf. Syst. J. **31**(6), 869–902 (2021)

Mainela, T., Puhakka, V., Servais, P.: The concept of international opportunity in international entrepreneurship: a review and research agenda. Int. J. Manag. Rev. **16**(1), 105–129 (2014)

Markus, L.M., Loebbecke, C.: Commoditized digital processes and business community platforms: new opportunities and challenges for digital business strategies. MIS Q. **37**(2), 649–653 (2013)

Martin, K., Todorov, I.: How will digital platforms be harnessed in 2020, and how will they change the way people interact with brands? J. Interact. Advert. **10**(2), 61–66 (2013)

McIntyre, D., Srinivasan, A.: Networks, platforms and strategy: emerging views and next steps. Strateg. Manag. J. **38**(1), 141–160 (2017)

McKelvie, A.H.: Unpacking the uncertainty construct: implications for entrepreneurial action. J. Bus. Ventur. **26**(3), 273–292 (2011)

Nambisan, S.: Digital entrepreneurship: toward a digital technology perspective of entrepreneurship. Entrepreneurship Theory Pract. **41**(6), 1029–1055 (2016)

Nambisan, S., Sawhney, M.: Orchestration processes in network-centric innovation: evidence from the field. Acad. Manag. Perspect. **25**(3), 40–57 (2011)

Phillips, N., Tracey, P.: Opportunity recognition, entrepreneurial capabilities and bricolage: connecting institutional theory and entrepreneurship in strategic organization. Strateg. Organ. **5**(3), 313–320 (2007)

De Reuver, M., Sorensen, C., Basole, R.C.: The digital platform: a research agenda. J. Inf. Technol. **33**(2), 124–135 (2018)

Ries, E.: The Lean Startup: How Today's Entrepreneurs Use Continuous Innovation to Create Radically Successful Businesses. Crown Publishing, New York (2011)

Santarelli, E., D'Altri, S.: The diffusion of e-commerce among SMEs: theoretical implications and empirical evidence. Small Bus. Econ. **21**, 273–283 (2003). https://doi.org/10.1023/A:102 5757601345

Sarasvathy, S.D., Dew, N.: New market creation through transformation. J. Evol. Econ. **15**, 533–565 (2005). https://doi.org/10.1007/s00191-005-0264-x

Saunders, M., Lewis, P., Thornhill, A.: Research Methods for Business Students. Pearson Education Limited, Essex (2016)

Shane, S., Venkatraman, N.: The promise of entrepreneurship as a field of research. Acad. Manag. Rev. **25**(1), 217–226 (2000)

Shane, S.: Prior knowledge and the discovery of entrepreneurial opportunities. Organ. Sci. **11**(4), 448–469 (2000)

Shen, K., Lindsay, V., Yunjie, X.: Special issue on: digital entrepreneurship. Inf. Syst. J. (2015)

Shepherd, D., Williams, T., Patzelt, H.: Thinking about entrepreneurial decision making: review and research agenda. J. Manag. **41**(1), 11–46 (2015)

Short, J., Ketchen, D., Shook, C., Ireland, R.: The concept of "opportunity" in entrepreneurship research: past accomplishments and future challenges. J. Manag. **36**(1), 40–65 (2010)

Srinivasan, A., Venkatraman, N.: Entrepreneurship in digital platforms: a network-centric view. Strateg. Entrepreneurship J. **12**(1), 54–71 (2018)

Steininger, D.M.: Linking information systems and entrepreneurship: a review and agenda for IT-associated and digital entrepreneurship research. Inf. Syst. J. **29**(2), 363–407 (2019)

Tindiwensi, C., Munene, J.C., Abaho, E., Serwanga, A., Dawa, R.: Farm management skills, entrepreneurial bricolage and market orientation. J. Agribus. Dev. Emerg. Econ. **10**(5), 717–730 (2020)

Tiwana, K.A., Bush, A.A.: Platform evolution: coevolution of platform architecture, governance and environmental dynamics. Inf. Syst. Res. **21**(4), 675–687 (2010)

Van de Kaa, G., Van den Ende, J., de Vries, H.J., Van Heck, E.: Factors for winning interface format battles: a review and synthesis of the literature. Technol. Forecast. Soc. Change **78**(8), 1397–1411 (2011)

Venkatraman, N., Lee, C.: Preferential linkage and network evolution: a conceptual model and empirical test in the US videogame sector. Acad. Manag. J. **47**(6), 876–892 (2004)

von Briel, F., Davidsson, P., Recker, J.: Digital Technologies as external enablers of new venture creation in the IT hardware sector. Entrepreneurship Theory Pract. **42**(1), 47–69 (2018)

William, L., Bronson, J., Winkel, D., Malewicki, D.: Varieties of bricolage and the process of entrepreneurship. New Engl. J. Entrepreneurship 53–66 (2011)

Yu, X., Li, Y., Chen, D.Q., Meng, X., Tao, X.: Entrepreneurial bricolage and online store performance in emerging economies. Electron. Mark. **29**, 1–19 (2018). https://doi.org/10.1007/s12 525-018-0302-9

The Chronicles of Kunene: The Lion, the Omuhimba and the Drone

Chris Muashekele[1]([✉]), Heike Winschiers-Theophilus[2], Kasper Rodil[1],
Colin Stanley[2], and Hina MuAshekele[3]

[1] Aalborg University, Fredrik Bajers Vej 7K, 9220 Aalborg Øst, Denmark
cpa@create.aau.dk
[2] Namibia University of Science and Technology, 13 Jackson Kaujeua Street,
Windhoek, Namibia
[3] University of Namibia, 340 Mandume Ndemufayo Avenue, Windhoek, Namibia

Abstract. Many technology projects are driven by (hidden) agendas which prioritize the one or the other stakeholder or the technology itself, thereby creating tensions and compromising important perspectives. In the field of digital conservation and wildlife management, the focus has often been on safeguarding wildlife (the lion), not incorporating socio-economic factors of communities (the Omuhimba), by exploiting technologies concerned with wildlife data collection only (the drone). Concerned with reconciling heterogeneous perspectives the authors present the development and conceptualisation of an integrated wildlife monitoring system in Southern Africa. The authors postulate that a community-based co-design approach, grounded in the Ubuntu philosophy, leads to novel and innovative technology designs embracing ecocentrism.

Keywords: African indigenous knowledge system · Community-based co-design · Innovation · Conservation technologies · Human-wildlife conflict · Rural communities · Chronicles of kunene · Digital platform · Southern Africa · Innovation practices

1 Introduction

Many a time technology projects are driven by (hidden) agendas which prioritize the one or the other stakeholder or the technology itself, thereby neglecting important points of views and needs. In the field of digital conservation and wildlife management, the focus has often been on safeguarding wildlife (the lion), not incorporating socio-economic factors of communities (the Omuhimba), by exploiting technologies concerned with wildlife data collection only (the drone). The authors are concerned with reconciling those different viewpoints within an integrated ecological approach.

Framed in an ecocentric paradigm, the authors postulate that a community-based co-design (CBD) approach, grounded in the Ubuntu philosophy considering local indigenous practices, leads to novel and innovative technology designs

J. Abdelnour-Nocera et al. (Eds.): *Innovation Practices for Digital Transformation in the Global South*, IFIP AICT 645, pp. 149–164, 2022.
https://doi.org/10.1007/978-3-031-12825-7_9

embracing multiple perspectives. Thus the objective of this chapter is to demonstrate that a participatory approach, such as CBCD contributes towards a digital transformation of indigenous communities in the global south, embracing ecocentrism and yielding in novel locally situated technology developments.

In this chapter, the authors present a case study demonstrating the tensions between communities, technologies and animals as well as the conceptualisation and development of an integrated wildlife monitoring system in Southern Africa, considering heterogeneous perspectives. The case study was part of a recently concluded multinational and multidisciplinary project in Iona National Park (Angola), and adjacent to the Skeleton Coast National Park in Namibia that form part of Iona-Skeleton Coast Transfrontier Conservation Area (TFCA). The project aimed "to strengthen cross-border ecosystem management and wildlife protection through co-designing and implementing conservation monitoring technology with the park authorities and surrounding communities" [36].

2   Theoretical and Methodological Framing

Ecocentrism in alignment with African indigenous perspectives builds this case studie's theoretical frame deploying a community-based co-design methodology.

2.1   Ecocentrism

Ontologically, humanist approaches view design as an exclusively human endeavour, therefore amplifying human values and perceptions [58]. However, it is imperative to think beyond anthropocentrism, and evaluate the inclusion of other species [2] and objects, at least conceptually. The de-centring from the human is referred to as posthumanism [18], rooted in the fundamental ecocentric entanglements with the world [58].

Ecocentrism, as a philosophy, builds on the accentuation of non-human nature, with specific emphasis on decision making diverging from an anthropocentric stance [31,45]. Ecocentrism goes above the advocacy of living things, as prescribed by biocentrism, to include the entire ecosystem and its abiotic nature [31]. According to Payne [39], "ecocentrism provides a way into making meaning of the many moral stances, value positionings and existential conditions we ordinarily occupy or create as pedagogues, researchers, scholars and policy-makers". Mainstream technology design has not yet mastered the inclusion of other beings [2]. Aspling [2] maintain that the involvement of nonhuman species in technology design contexts leads to novel concepts and possibilities. To bask in the current and future possibilities of ecocentrism, futuring is endorsed. According to Homan et al. [19], futuring is the active process of imagining the future, in which we find a conglomerate of approaches that are concerned with "future alternatives" [26]. Specifically, design futuring approaches seek to re-envision and envision optimum futures and alternatives [26,32], including ecocentric futures.

2.2   African Indigenous Perspectives

African philosophy accords itself with biocentrism and ecocentrism [16]. Indigenous worldviews are holistic, wherein all species are interconnected, as opposed to an individualistic perspective that views the world in separate spectrums [3]. Indigenous communities place great emphasis on living harmoniously with the environment [48]. This is articulated in the African philosophy of *Ubuntu*, a word derived from the *Nguni languages* which means "humanness" [14], in its wider sense. Ubuntu is well-known for the short phrase: *Umuntu ngumuntu ngabantu* which translates to "A person is not a person without other people" [33], emphasizing the interconnectedness. Innately, Ubuntu is more than a word, it is an African way of living, in kindness, harmony, consideration, respect, peace, love and care - embedding sharing, altruism, social maturity and sensitivity, virtuosity and striving for conciliation [29]. Thus, local indigenous communities have formed inseparable relationships with different species that inhabit the same physical contexts as them [28]. As a result, indigenous communities have gained an understanding of wildlife behaviour, phenology and abiotic indicators, allowing for effective conservation and sustainable use of natural resources, and organisation of ecological knowledge [1,15,25,57]. It is imperative to leverage this indigenous knowledge and local expertise in the development of ecological strategies, tools and technologies through the involvement of indigenous community members [25,34,69].

2.3   Community-Based Co-design

Community-based co-design (CBCD), conceptualised by Winschiers-Theophilus et al. [63], is based and refined on empirical work with indigenous and marginalised communities in Southern Africa [64], framed within an Afrocentric research paradigm [35] and Ubuntu epistemology [54]. CBCD is methodologically derived from action research and participatory design. The fundamental embodiment of CBCD is based on the established premise of co-creating locally appropriate applications [64], enabling designers and stakeholders to work in tandem as co-designers while developing solutions that address local challenges [51].

CBCD focus on community values, and a realization that communities are organised by protocols and culture. Any collaborative technology effort with a community in the Global South necessitates a continuous negotiation of how the collaboration must respect local views and values [62]. Kapuire et al. [23] observe that Ubuntu values, such as togetherness and care are practised by local African communities, and therefore can and should be incorporated into technology design processes simply by respecting and acknowledging communities design inputs. Through embracing Ubuntu in CBCD, technology developers are 'being participated' by immersing in the community, following local and newly negotiated protocols thereby incorporating local values and practices Winschiers-Theophilus et al. [62]. Blake [4] further suggest a paradigm shift, integrating

Ubuntu values in Software Engineering methods through allowing for and learning from unintended uses of software by communities. Ssozi-Mugarura et al. [50], working on ICT enabled water management in Uganda stated: "CBCD has offered us a basis for continuous engagement with communities to understand their context, their needs and aspects in their environment that easily affect technology adoption and use." CBCD encompasses what Crabtree et al. [9] call "invisible work", where the respect for local protocols is essential to ensure collaboration and technology adoption [38]. Of significance in CBCD is the concept of reciprocity [6], ensuring all stakeholder benefit from the participation. Rizzo et al. [44] specifies how an approach such as CBCD facilitates an environment where technology appropriation, in essence technology innovation, can occur, as users are given a voice in design activities. CBCD has found many applications in the technology and service sector [12], allowing for situated innovation practices.

3   Case Study Context

3.1   Communities

The majority of TFCA inhabitants are of the Ovahimba tribe. The Ovahimba are semi-nomadic pastoralists who place emphasis on ownership of substantial numbers of livestock. It is common practice for a patriarch in the Ovahimba community to own herds of more than a thousand goats and cattle. The Ovahimba live in conservancies, which were gazetted by the Namibian government. Conservancies are land zones implemented to enable the protection and growth of natural resources such as wildlife and plants [7]. Administration of the conservancies is in the form of Community Based Natural Resource Management (CBNRM), on the basis that communities who are dependent on natural resources for their livelihoods are usually motivated to conserve such resources [22,69].

3.2   Tensions and Challenges

CBNRM has had ambivalent results, considering some communities have not been able to fully comprehend the management of their conservancies [52]. The challenges include inconsistent and negligible data collection through an array of tools and practices that are not intuitive. Additionally, limited technical skills, insufficient wildlife monitoring mechanisms, drought, illegal plant and tree felling, encroachment, lack of diversified livelihood alternatives, dwindling species populations, and primarily Human-Wildlife Conflict (HWC), further escalate the diminution of wildlife and biodiversity populations [42,60,66].

Non-lethal methods such as translocation of animals, livestock guarding dogs and herding are used to mitigate HWC [46]. However, such methods tend to be one-sided and ineffective, as wildlife continue to suffer the obstructive consequences of human growth and development [59]. Equally current policies have not taken into consideration the perspectives, desires, capabilities, environment, as well as previous and current undertakings of the affected communities [36].

With an obvious conflict of habitats between wildlife and humans and the consequent tensions in strategies prioritizing the one over the other, the authors postulate that an ecocentric paradigm should be applied in the development of technologies mitigating HWC.

3.3 Wildlife Monitoring

The task of wildlife protection is tedious, taxing, and requires tremendous human effort together with computed oversight to be effective [56]. It requires systematic and effective monitoring, collection of data and responsiveness [30]. Specific understanding of fundamental ecological factors such as animal habitat use, animal movement and activities, through wildlife monitoring and data collection, is necessary to address HWC and other resounding environmental challenges that persist, resulting in the preservation of endangered species [37].

However, there is a lack of monitoring methods that offer long term, real-time and efficient data [27]. Traditional methods of monitoring usually require researchers and game guards to walk extensive distances, to track animals and collect desired data [37]. While monitoring technology such as camera traps exist, they require exacting manual data collection [11]. Hence, for enhanced and convenient use, wildlife monitoring systems should allow for a collective configuration and integration of technologies as per the needs, values and ecological perspectives of conservationists [40]. .

3.4 Towards an Integrated Wildlife Monitoring System

The authors argue that an integrated wildlife monitoring system, needs to reconcile the aspects of protecting wildlife with socio-cultural practices of the community as well as a sustainable deployment of appropriate technologies. Although, the design actions described in this chapter appear anthropocentric, they were framed within ecocentrism and Ubuntu recognizing interconnectedness of living beings and their environment, including technologies. To this effect, *Okuwonga* was conceptualised and partially implemented. In the local indigenous Otjiherero language, '*Okuwonga*' means collection. *Okuwonga* is an integrated digital wildlife monitoring and data collection system, which is comprised of a custom digital data collection mobile application, known as Wildlife Activity Recording (WAR) app, drones and camera traps. *Okuwonga* intends to facilitate and enable harmonious coexistence between local communities and wildlife living in community-managed conservancies, therefore curtailing HWC. This is achieved through the constant non-obstructive collection and dissemination of wildlife data and continuous monitoring, providing insight and consciousness on environmental patterns such as movement and presence of predators. In addition to providing an empirical and fundamental premise onto which a rural digital system can be established, the conceptualisation of *Okuwonga* provides a blueprint on the integration and interface of mainstream and emerging technologies within a rural indigenous space, focusing on the prioritisation of local community and wildlife peculiar use cases and the necessary appropriation of technology to fulfil the use cases.

3.5   Development Approach

In the pursuit of appropriate and intuitive technological solutions for challenges faced by communities that manage conservancies, the authors employ, affirm and extend Community-Based Co-Design (CBCD) [64] as a design practice and interface to stimulate and propel meaningful innovations. Local rural indigenous communities, through CBCD, were involved in a series of technology design and appropriation activities, transforming established yet inefficient practices and processes, and informing design with their vivid and inestimable knowledge and viewpoints. Their viewpoints, unconventional and novel, beget innovative designs, concepts and use cases that broaden the applicability and successful integration of mainstream and emerging technologies [55]. A revolving emphasis is placed on how the intentional and coordinated involvement of indigenous rural communities and their encompassing ecological views have invoked innovative novel use cases that are explicit and appropriate for rural contexts. In practice, the use cases offer technology developers insights, as they expand initial design and use to actual rural end users [10,11,61].

4   Co-design of *Okuwonga*

The co-design activities begin with a contextual inquiry focusing on local practices and the human perspective, followed by the design of technology encompassing the aim of wildlife protection. The last step includes an exploratory design of emerging technologies to complete the integrated system, *Okuwonga* (Fig. 6) (Fig. 1).

4.1   The Omuhimba

Indigenous Communities in the TFCA have over time developed several conservation practices partially influenced by their own indigenous practices, such as game patrols. Game guards roam around a conservancy in search of any signs of illegal activities or predator sightings [66]. They use a range of techniques to track intruders and predators, such as inspecting footprints and paws, and detecting animal carcasses either as traps or remains of a predator attack. Additionally, herding is practiced, as a preventative measure practiced for livestock protection. It is a treasured ancient custom dating millenniums, whereby herders stringently supervise, guide and support livestock as it roams and grazes to prevent predatory attacks [47]. Kraals are used as shelter and barriers to prevent livestock from roaming unsupervised, in addition to shielding livestock from predators [49]. There are instances, especially during droughts, where predators obtrude local villages in search of prey. To this effect, they pose a danger to humans and

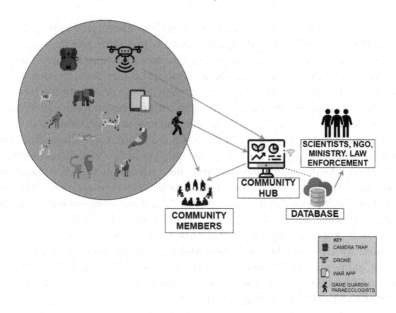

Fig. 1. Okuwonga digital data collection and monitoring system

livestock. Hence, community members set up innocuous predator traps to lure and capture predators [43].

As part of CBNRM, the government of Namibia runs yearly game counts, which are routine wildlife censuses [53], in collaboration with the communities to inform national strategies in regard to ecosystem management decisions. Regular data is collected through paper event books, which the game guards carry and complete to the best of their skills. Community members work alongside with scientists as local para-ecologists, collecting and providing essential ecological data, knowledge and insight, which the scientists would have found difficult to otherwise discover [41]. It has been planned that the para-ecologists will be compensated and recognised for their contributions, consequently creating an alternative source of income. Simultaneously, the para-ecologists will observe, record and preserve the data, and thereafter, pass it down to younger generations.

Furthermore considering that, an integration and automated analysis of all data [56] is not readily available, local community members will do a first-level analysis of the data collected through *Okuwonga*.

4.2   The Lion

Throughout the project, Muashekele et al. [36] co-designed with local game guards the WAR app (Fig. 4). The app went through several iterations, starting with its co-design, development and validation, until its subsequent deployment. The co-design endeavours were based on comprehending the context of the conservancies in the TFCA by establishing the current conservation tools and practices, their advantages and demerits, as well as identifying appropriate alternatives. During a series of co-design workshops, the game guards, together with the authors, outlined designs comprising features and functionality that ensure the WAR app's intuitiveness within its context of use. As reference points for the designs, the game guards expounded their local conservation practices and deliberated on their experiences with different applications such as WhatsApp. The deliberations extended to the specific features and functions that the game guards deem as necessary for a wildlife data collection tool. Thereafter, the features were sketched on paper, offering the game guards a visual representation of the WAR app. Features include custom icons, custom buttons, a camera module and a voice recorder, necessitated by the low literacy rate and overall preference of visual and audio among the game guards. The icons designed represent various wildlife, activities and local practices, thus meaningful and aligned to the local conservation practices and wildlife that the game guards are accustomed to. An automated location tracker and date and time picker were also incorporated, after the game guards detailed the challenges they faced reading conventional maps, and identifying conventional date and time, which are auxiliary tools for the use of the Event Book (Figs. 2 and 3).

Fig. 2. Co-designing WAR app   **Fig. 3.** WAR app in use

The WAR app has been used in different scenarios; HWC incident recording, encroachment, conservancy meetings, game patrols and predator sightings, with specific focus on capturing scarce carnivores - lions, cheetahs, hyenas and leopards. Imperatively, the game guards affirmed the above affordances as essential in eradicating HWC. During use, the game guards affirmed the app's appropriateness. Stating that it is their 'memory', as they store and reference what they have seen through the app. Images taken with the app serve as evidence of transgressions against wildlife, for which if there was no visual evidence would have gone unpunished, which is a common occurrence in conservancies. The app achieves additional pertinence through its instant data sharing and amalgamation abilities. The data is decisive for determining wildlife behaviour and phenology indicators, and fostering wildlife awareness and appreciation amongst community members. In addition, it is used to intensify HWC warning and prevention - for instance, altering the game guards about the presence of lions, giving game guards enough time to enforce conflict preventative measures.

However, there are challenges associated with the synchronisation of the data to the database. The WAR app currently requires an Internet connection for the synchronisation to take place. This is challenging because the areas in which the game guards are based have intermittent network connectivity, thus the data is not frequently and timely synchronised to the database. Ergo, provisions have recently been established in the form of community technology hubs with satellite Internet, a data portal and rugged computers for the transfer and display of WAR app data.

4.3   The Drone

Camera Traps. In the first phase of the project, camera traps, as an established conservation monitoring technology that enables the collection of large amounts of digital wildlife data remotely [68] were used. They capture footage of wildlife in their natural habitat without human interference [41], reducing wildlife inconvenience and exasperation, whilst extending post-human data collection. Ergo, co-design activities with game guards were undertaken, whereby contextual applications of camera traps were devised. The primary application, as stated by the game guards, is the collection of wildlife data in strategic locations within conservancies. Given the limited number of camera traps that were available, the game guards deliberated amongst themselves, extensively, to determine the locations that are appropriate for camera trap placement. Several locations were selected, based on the different experiences and knowledge of the game guards regarding the primary locations of wildlife. Thereafter, camera traps were installed in the selected locations. A set of camera traps were placed at the edge of the main river separating Namibia and Angola, with the intention of continuously recording wildlife and other occurrences at the river. Another set of camera traps were placed at wildlife hot spots. The spots were selected due to the high frequency of animals in those areas for water and feed. Also, the areas had little human movement or interference, thus making them ideal for the placement of camera traps. The game guards further specified where and how the camera traps should be attached, to avoid meddling by wildlife and humans (Fig. 5).

Due to its omnipresence, the game guards view the camera trap as their proxy. According to them, camera traps will conciliatory capture images of sporadic wildlife such as lions, hyenas and leopards, which would otherwise be difficult to do with traditional means. As well, the camera traps will cause caution amongst encroachers, as they will be aware of the constant surveillance in a conservancy. Therefore, reducing wildlife maltreatment and extermination.

Currently, the camera traps installed in the conservancies are not connected to any wireless network, thus requiring game guards to manually retrieve data. This is arduous because the camera traps are located many kilometres away from the villages where game guards reside. Therefore, game guards have to walk for

Fig. 4. Installing camera trap   **Fig. 5.** Camera trap image

prolonged periods, amounting to several days, to collect the data on the camera traps, risking predatory attack. Thus the idea of integrating a drone arose.

Drone Usage Scenarios. Ongoing improvements in unmanned aerial vehicles (drones) have made them ideal tools to support conservation efforts [5]. An automated drone system offers conservationists and scientists a means of automating and enhancing laborious and manual data collection processes [21]. Such systems provide new prospects for the ecocentric study of habitat and behaviour of species [37]. Thus, it can be argued that drones can be used to enable the comprehension of native wildlife and surrounding ecosystems, leading to enhanced conservation and resource management efforts [21].

A series of co-design workshops, during which game guards designed the integration of a drone into the TFCA, proffered a data collection and transfer process as part of *Okuwonga*. First, the game guards and community members flew a drone in order to familiarise themselves with its functionality and possible use. Thereafter, they had focus group discussions, together with the authors, in order to determine the possible use cases of the drone. The primary use cases identified were wildlife monitoring, surveillance and data collection by capturing aerial footage during patrols and game counts. It was advanced that the drone presents an opportunity to create new patrol and game count routes as the drone can carry out surveillance and monitor in areas which are deemed most appropriate but difficult to navigate by foot or vehicle. According to the game guards, drone-enabled monitoring will produce new forms of data that offer an elevated ecocentric viewpoint regarding wildlife movement and possible encroachment activities.

Last, the game guards and the authors outlined a future drone protocol, which prescribes how the drone will be used in relation to other technologies, specifically the camera trap. The protocol encompasses a drone attached with a Raspberry Pi microcomputer that creates an ad-hoc network for the transfer of data from a camera trap to the microcomputer for temporary storage. First, a drone will fly to the location of a specific camera trap. Thereafter, the camera trap will connect to the network broadcast created by the microcomputer. Upon successful connection, a script to commence data transfer and other maintenance tasks will be executed automatically, compensating for the intermittent Internet connection. Second, the drone will fly to a community technology hub, where servers, a data portal and computers for data storage will be hosted for data extraction, processing and transfer. The data will then be assessed by community members and replicated to cloud servers to enable remote access by different stakeholders such as the Ministry of Environment, conservation scientists, NGOs and law enforcement agencies for further action.

Fig. 6. Game guards and community members flying drone

5   Community-based Co-design as an Innovation Enabler

Previous applications of CBCD have demonstrated its methodological strength in creating innovative technologies, such as the secret sign language app with a Penan community in Borneo [67], the augmented reality mementos with a rural San community in Namibia [65], or a crowd sourcing tool with an Ovahimba community in Namibia [8]. CBCD prioritises technology improvements and appropriation activities, ultimately leading to innovative products with higher product quality and enhanced relevance [13,24]. Based on the premises of participatory design, when indigenous rural communities are involved, they infuse their own local practices and values into the design of the technology. It is thus at the intersection of cultures and epistemologies, within a specific design context, that novel and unique ideas and technology concepts are created as enabled through

CBCD. This epitomises the creation of innovation 'through new combinations of knowledge' as accented by Hooli et al. [20].

In the case study presented, *Okuwonga* encompasses indigenous perspectives as much as an ecocentric approach, thereby representing a unique and novel solution. Its use cases are novel and anomalous, as they prescribe and align mainstream technology into a rural context, expanding initial design and use. They conform to the established delineation of innovation, which emphasises new or improved products and processes [17]. Key was the close collaboration and number of co-design sessions held over a period of three years, whereby all stakeholders learned about each others perspectives as well as explored, physically and conceptually, possible usages of technologies. Ubuntu was not only guiding design interactions in terms of emphasising interrelations as design partners but also influenced the design outcome in terms of creating a solution which reconciles positions of humans, animals and technology.

In the pre-design sessions, local communities delineated and reflected on their own CBNRM challenges. In collaboration with the authors possible solutions were co-designed and in a number of cycles prototyped and re-designed until a workable solution was developed [36]. Thereby the local community members acquired technical as well as design skills which amalgamated with their indigenous knowledge and practices resulted in very mature design contributions, incorporating their holistic worldview. The Ovahimba's indigenous inclination to ecosystem interconnectedness, communities advocated for technologies to be used to benefit nonhuman species. Hence, during the CBCD sessions, game guards placed particular emphasis on the consideration of wildlife's essentiality.

6   Conclusion

In this chapter the authors presented a case study demonstrating that CBCD enabled the design of a complex, novel and unique integrated wildlife management system, which reconciled three different perspectives, namely the communities', the wildlife's and the technologies'. Framed in ecocentrism, integrating indigenous perspectives and following the ubuntu philosophy, joint co-design and exploration sessions were carried out emphasizing connectedness. The authors argue that CBCD is an innovation practice which promotes digital transformation of Global South communities in their own terms, embracing local practices and epistemologies.

References

1. Al-Roubaie, A.: Building indigenous knowledge capacity for development. World J. Sci. Technol. Sustain. Dev. (2010)
2. Aspling, F.: Animals, plants, people and digital technology: exploring and understanding multispecies-computer interaction. In: Proceedings of the 12th International Conference on Advances in Computer Entertainment Technology, pp. 1–4 (2015)

3. Aubrecht, M., Bawden, H., Ballengee-Morris, C.: Earthworks rising - exploring, sharing, researching, and building community through teachers, parents, and learners. In: Proceedings of the International Conference on the Foundations of Digital Games - FDG 17 (2017)
4. Blake, E.: Software engineering in developing communities. In: Proceedings of the 2010 ICSE Workshop on Cooperative and Human Aspects of Software Engineering, ACM, pp. 1–4 (2010)
5. Bondi, E., et al.: Airsim-w: a simulation environment for wildlife conservation with UAVs. In: Proceedings of the 1st ACM SIGCAS Conference on Computing and Sustainable Societies (COMPASS) - COMPASS 18 (2018)
6. Brereton, M., Roe, P., Schroeter, R., Lee Hong, A.: Beyond ethnography: engagement and reciprocity as foundations for design research out here. In: Proceedings of the SIGCHI Conference on Human Factors in Computing Systems, pp. 1183–1186 (2014)
7. Choi, C.Y., et al.: Where to draw the line? using movement data to inform protected area design and conserve mobile species. Biol. Conserv. **234**, 64–71 (2019)
8. Colin, S., Heike, W.T., Edwin, B.: Challenges in designing cultural heritage crowdsourcing: tools with indigenous communities. In: Cultural Heritage Communities, Routledge, pp. 96–113 (2017)
9. Crabtree, A., et al.: Doing innovation in the wild. In: Proceedings of the Biannual Conference of the Italian Chapter of SIGCHI, pp. 1–9 (2013)
10. Cumbula, S.D., Sabiescu, A.G., Cantoni, L.: Community design: a collaborative approach for social integration. J. Commun. Inf. **13**(1) (2017)
11. Curtin, B.H., et al.: Designing a raspberry pi sensor network for remote observation of wildlife. In: Proceedings of the 6th Annual Symposium on Hot Topics in the Science of Security, pp. 1–2 (2019)
12. David, S., Sabiescu, A.G., Cantoni, L.: Co-design with communities: a reflection on the literature. In: Steyn, J., Van der Vyver, A.G. (eds.) IDIA2013 Conference: Public and Private Access to ICTs in Developing Regions, pp. 152–166 (2013)
13. David, S., Sabiescu, A.G., Cantoni, L.: Co-design with communities. a reflection on the literature. In: Proceedings of the 7th International Development Informatics Association Conference, IDIA Pretoria, South Africa, pp. 152–166 (2013)
14. Doke, C.M.: The Southern Bantu Languages: Handbook of African Languages, vol. 19. Routledge, Milton Par (2017)
15. Durie, M.: Exploring the interface between science and indigenous knowledge. In: 5th APEC Research and Development Leaders Forum, pp. 2–21. Christchurch, New Zealand (2004)
16. Etieyibo, E.: African philosophy and nonhuman nature. In: Debating African Philosophy, Routledge, Milton Park, pp. 164–181 (2018)
17. Foster, C., Heeks, R.: Drivers of inclusive innovation in developing county markets: a policy perspective. In: Agola, N.O., Hunter, A. (eds.) Inclusive Innovation for Sustainable Development, pp. 57–74. Palgrave Macmillan UK, London (2016). https://doi.org/10.1057/978-1-137-60168-1_4
18. Frauenberger, C.: Entanglement HCI the next wave? ACM Trans. Comput.-Hum. Interact. (TOCHI) **27**(1), 1–27 (2019)
19. Hoffman, J., Pelzer, P., Albert, L., Béneker, T., Hajer, M., Mangnus, A.: A futuring approach to teaching wicked problems. J. Geogr. High. Educ. 1–18 (2021)
20. Hooli, L., Jauhiainen, J.S., Jarvi, A., Nkonoki, E., Taajamaa, V., Käyhkö, N.: Contextualising innovation in Africa: Knowledge modes and actors in local innovation development. In: 2019 IST-Africa Week Conference (IST-Africa), pp 1–9. IEEE (2019)

21. Jiménez López, J., Mulero-Pázmány, M.: Drones for conservation in protected areas: present and future. Drones **3**(1), 10 (2019)
22. Johannesen, A.B., Skonhoft, A.: Tourism, poaching and wildlife conservation: what can integrated conservation and development projects accomplish? Resour. Energy Econ. **27**(3), 208–226 (2005)
23. Kapuire, G.K., Cabrero, D.G., Stanley, C., Winschiers-Theophilus, H.: Framing technology design in ubuntu: Two locales in pastoral Namibia. In: Proceedings of the Annual Meeting of the Australian Special Interest Group for Computer Human Interaction, OzCHI 2015, pp. 212–216. ACM (2015)
24. Karimi, A., Worthy, P., McInnes, P., Bodén, M., Matthews, B., Viller, S.: The community garden hack: Participatory experiments in facilitating primary school teacher's appropriation of technology. In: Proceedings of the 29th Australian Conference on Computer-Human Interaction, pp. 143–151 (2017)
25. Kativu, S.: Local ecological knowledge on climate prediction and adaptation: agriculture-wildlife interface perspectives from Africa. In: Traditional and Indigenous Knowledge for the Modern Era, CRC Press, pp. 227–260 (2019)
26. Kozubaev, S., et al.: Expanding modes of reflection in design futuring. In: Proceedings of the 2020 CHI Conference on Human Factors in Computing Systems, pp. 1–15 (2020)
27. Liu, C., Li, B., Fang, D., Guo, S., Chen, X., Xing, T.: Rhinopithecus roxellana monitoring and identification using wireless sensor networks. In: Proceedings of the 9th ACM Conference on Embedded Networked Sensor Systems - SenSys 11 (2011). https://doi.org/10.1145/2070942.2071022
28. Lynch, A., Fell, D., Mcintyre-Tamwoy, S.: Incorporating indigenous values with 'western' conservation values in sustainable biodiversity management. Australas. J. Environ. Manage. **17**(4), 244–255 (2010)
29. Mabovula, N.N.: The erosion of african communal values: a reappraisal of the African ubuntu philosophy. Inkanyiso: J. Humanit. Soc. Sci. **3**(1), 38–47 (2011)
30. Madden, F.: Creating coexistence between humans and wildlife: global perspectives on local efforts to address human-wildlife conflict. Hum. Dimensions Wildl. **9**(4), 247–257 (2004)
31. Marcia, N.L., Simwela, A.: Ecocentrism for the sustainable conservation and management of elephants in southern Africa. Int. J. Sci. Res. Publ. **9**(5), 614–621 (2019)
32. Marshall-Baker, A.: Design futuring: sustainability, ethics and new practice, by tony fry. Interiors **2**(1), 138–140 (2011)
33. Mbiti, J.S.: African Religions & Philosophy. Heinemann, Portsmouth (1990)
34. Mistry, J., Berardi, A.: Bridging indigenous and scientific knowledge. Science **352**(6291), 1274–1275 (2016)
35. Mkabela, Q.: Using the afrocentric method in researching indigenous African culture. Qual. Rep. **10**(1), 178–190 (2005)
36. Muashekele, C., Winschiers-Theophilus, H., Kapuire, G.K.: Co-design as a means of fostering appropriation of conservation monitoring technology by indigenous communities. In: Proceedings of the 9th International Conference on Communities & Technologies-Transforming Communities, pp. 126–130 (2019)
37. Nguyen, H.V., Chesser, M., Koh, L.P., Rezatofighi, S.H., Ranasinghe, D.C.: Trackerbots: autonomous unmanned aerial vehicle for real-time localization and tracking of multiple radio-tagged animals. J. Field Robot. **36**(3), 617–635 (2019)
38. Nielsen, M.O., Gould, L.A.: Non-native scholars doing research in native American communities: a matter of respect. Soc. Sci. J. **44**(3), 420–433 (2007)

39. Payne, P.G.: The globally great moral challenge: ecocentric democracy, values, morals and meaning. Environ. Educ. Res. **16**(1), 153–171 (2010)
40. Picco, G.P., et al.: Geo-referenced proximity detection of wildlife with wildscope. In: Proceedings of the 14th International Conference on Information Processing in Sensor Networks - IPSN 15 (2015)
41. Pimm, S.L., et al.: Emerging technologies to conserve biodiversity. Trends Ecol. Evol. **30**(11) (2015). https://doi.org/10.1016/j.tree.2015.08.008
42. Pires, S.F.: The Illegal Parrot Trade in the Neo-Tropics: the Relationship between Poaching and Illicit Pet Markets. Rutgers The State University of New Jersey-Newark, New Jersey (2012)
43. Pirie, T.J., Thomas, R.L., Fellowes, M.D.: Limitations to recording larger mammalian predators in savannah using camera traps and spoor. Wild. Biol. **22**(1), 13–21 (2016)
44. Rizzo, A., Caporali, M., Conti, D., Montefoschi, F., Burresi, G., Sinopoli, B.: The design of udoo boards: contributing to the appropriation of digital technology. Front. ICT **6**, 4 (2019)
45. Rülke, J., Rieckmann, M., Nzau, J.M., Teucher, M.: How ecocentrism and anthropocentrism influence human-environment relationships in a Kenyan biodiversity hotspot. Sustainability **12**(19), 8213 (2020)
46. Rust, N.A., Nghikembua, M.T., Kasser, J.J.W., Marker, L.L.: Environmental factors affect swing gates as a barrier to large carnivores entering game farms. Afr. J. Ecol. **53**(3), 339–345 (2014). https://doi.org/10.1111/aje.12188
47. Sadr, K.: A Short History of Early Herding in Southern Africa. Pastoralism in Africa: Past, Present and Future, vol. 171 (2013)
48. Shava, S.: Indigenous/tribal knowledges-definition and relevance in the modern era. In: Traditional and Indigenous Knowledge for the Modern Era, CRC Press, pp. 1–15 (2019)
49. Sibanda, P., Sebata, A., Mufandaedza, E., Mawanza, M.: Effect of short-duration overnight cattle kraaling on grass production in a southern African savanna. Afr. J. Range Forage Sci. **33**(4), 217–223 (2016)
50. Ssozi-Mugarura, F., Blake, E., Rivett, U.: Designing for sustainability: involving communities in developing ICT interventions to support water resource management. 2015 IST-Africa Conference (2015). https://doi.org/10.1109/istafrica.2015.7190565
51. Stanley, C., Winschiers-Theophilus, H., Blake, E., Rodil, K., Kapuire, G.K.: Ovahimba community in Namibia ventures into crowdsourcing design. In: Proceedings of the 13th International Conference on Social Implications of Computers in Developing Countries (2015)
52. Stone, M.T., Nyaupane, G.: Rethinking community in community-based natural resource management. Commun. Dev. **45**(1), 17–31 (2013)
53. Stratford, K., Naholo, S.: Can camera traps count game? Namibian J. Environ. **1**, B-31 (2017)
54. Tavernaro-Haidarian, L.: A Relational Model of Public Discourse: The African Philosophy of Ubuntu. Routledge, Milton Park (2018)
55. Tharakan, J.: Integrating indigenous knowledge into appropriate technology development and implementation. Afr. J. Sci. Technol. Innov. Dev. **7**(5), 364–370 (2015)
56. Trejos, L.M., Kamada, M., Yonekura, T., Reaz, M.B.I.: Wildlife net-gamekeepers using sensor network. In: Proceedings of the 6th ACM SIGCOMM Workshop on Network and System Support for Games - NetGames 07 (2007)
57. Turner, W.: Sensing biodiversity. Science **346**(6207), 301–302 (2014)

58. Wakkary, R.: Nomadic practices: a posthuman theory for knowing design. Int. J. Des. **14**(3), 117 (2020)
59. Weise, F.J., et al.: Lions at the gates: trans-disciplinary design of an early warning system to improve human-lion coexistence. Front. Ecol. Evol. **6**, 242 (2019)
60. Western, D., Waithaka, J., Kamanga, J.: Finding space for wildlife beyond national parks and reducing conflict through community-based conservation: the Kenya experience. Parks **21**(1), 51–62 (2015)
61. Wing, J., Andrew, T., Petkov, D.: Choosing action design research for the process of development, application and evaluation of a framework. In: 1st International Conference on Next Generation Computing Applications (NextComp), pp. 135–140. IEEE (2017)
62. Winschiers-Theophilus, H., Chivuno-Kuria, S., Kapuire, G.K., Bidwell, N.J., Blake, E.: Being participated: a community approach. In: Proceedings of the 11th Biennial Participatory Design Conference, pp. 1–10. ACM (2010)
63. Winschiers-Theophilus, H., Bidwell, N.J., Blake, E.: Altering participation through interactions and reflections in design. CoDesign **8**(2–3), 163–182 (2012)
64. Winschiers-Theophilus, H., Zaman, T., Stanley, C.: A classification of cultural engagements in community technology design: introducing a transcultural approach. AI Soc. **34**(3), 419–435 (2019)
65. Winschiers-Theophilus, H., Virmasalo, V., Samuel, M.M., Stichel, B., Afrikaner, H.: Facilitating design for the unknown: an inclusive innovation design journey with a san community in the kalahari desert. In: Proceedings of the Sixth International Conference on Design Creativity (ICDC 2020), pp. 263–270 (2020)
66. Yang, R., Ford, B.J., Tambe, M., Lemieux, A.: Adaptive resource allocation for wildlife protection against illegal poachers. In: AAMAS, pp. 453–460 (2014)
67. Zaman, T., Winschiers-Theophilus, H.: Penan's Oroo' short message signs (PO-SMS): co-design of a digital jungle sign language application. In: Abascal, J., Barbosa, S., Fetter, M., Gross, T., Palanque, P., Winckler, M. (eds.) INTERACT 2015. LNCS, vol. 9297, pp. 489–504. Springer, Cham (2015). https://doi.org/10.1007/978-3-319-22668-2_38
68. Zhao, Z., Liu, Z., Ye, J., Li, H.: Demo abstract: monitoring wide-area nature reserves based on long-distance wireless mesh networks. In: 2012 IEEE/ACM Third International Conference on Cyber-Physical Systems (2012)
69. Ziegler, M.: Who breathes the smoke. In: Proceedings of the Fifth Workshop on Computing within Limits - LIMITS 19 (2019)

From Staging to Social Protagonism: Digital Transformation Within the Experimental Theater of Cali

Juan Manuel Acuña Guzmán[1], Jose Abdelnour-Nocera[2,4(✉)],
Leonardo Parra-Agudelo[3], and Paula Barriga-Isaza[3,4]

[1] Universidad Autónoma de Occidente, Cali, Colombia
jmacuna@uao.edu.co
[2] University of West London, London, UK
jose.abdelnour-nocera@uwl.ac.uk
[3] Universidad de los Andes, Bogota, Colombia
{leonardo.parra,p.barriga}@uniandes.edu.co
[4] ITI/Larsys, Funchal, Portugal

Abstract. This article shows the process of carrying out an innovation proposal at the Cali Experimental Theatre (TEC) in the context of isolation measures due to the Covid-19 pandemic. Through a process of "infrastructural inversion" inspired on the canonical work work of Star and Bowker, and following Simonsen and Hertzum, we revealed the deep historical connections that not only the TEC but the entire Colombian theatre movement of the 1960s had with the activists of social change such as workers' organizations, trade unions and revolutionary movements. We present the iterative process of how this proposal was co-created with leadership of the TEC exposing infrastructural points of resistance and opportunity in the realisation of digital innovation. Our resulting proposal to the TEC reconnects the theatre group with the equivalent current actants of social change, such as independent journalism, citizen movements and non-governmental organizations, through a digital transformation, positioning it not only as a product of artistic quality but also as a social and historical research group. All this without altering the identity and dramaturgical tradition that the group has maintained intact for 65 years of existence. We conclude the paper by discussing the disciplinary paradoxes and sociotechnical limitations faced by this type of innovation requiring a digital transformation of their performing and delivery infrastructures.

Keywords: Theater · Digital transformation · Infrastructuring

Published by Springer Nature Switzerland AG 2022
J. Abdelnour-Nocera et al. (Eds.): *Innovation Practices for Digital Transformation in the Global South*, IFIP AICT 645, pp. 165–182, 2022.
https://doi.org/10.1007/978-3-031-12825-7_10

1 Introduction

Digital transformation refers to the changes that occur within a sociotechnical ecosystem, when the processes that used to occur in an analogous manner must be adapted or reinvented to fit the digital world. This transformation differs from mere digitization in that it is not only the physical materiality that changes, but it is the meaningful human activity that re-shaped. Digital transformation occurs in as infrastructuring (Star and Ruhleder 1996), which is, not as something on which a system operates, but as the invisible sociotechnical structures that allow the system to work. Digital transformations occur on organized socio-technical practices, which are in continuous evolution and that can grow and articulate with other infrastructures, according to community interests. This transformation can even revitalize political positions that were previously weakened, or even disappeared, due to social, economic, and political changes.

During the year 2020, at the height of the confusion caused by the Covid-19 pandemic, we carried out an innovation process with the Experimental Theater of Cali, seeking to provide a solution, from digital transformation to the problem of the impediment of face-to-face attendance of spectators in theaters and public stages. This infrastructuring process in the specific field of the performing arts, not only evidenced the tensions between the mere change of material support and a true digital transformation, but also led to a deep ontological reflection of the social function of the Experimental Theater of Cali. This resulted in a review of the original postulates of the group that, based on the ideas of Bertolt Brecht, consider the theater as a determining factor of social change, which is fundamentally articulated with other social forces such as political movements, labor unions, theater groups and independent media.

In this article we offer an account about the process that was carried out throughout the semester, between September and December 2020. We seek to investigate the possibilities of digital transformation in an eminently analog medium such as theater, where the infrastructure can vary according to the specific context of operation, in this case the Latin American theater. Our work produced two different proposals, each one aligned to a different concept of infrastructure. The first proposal emphasized the infrastructure as the relationships between spectators and actors through staging, whilst reconsidering the function of the body, space and time of traditional theater. This proposal, based on the digital reconfiguration of the elements of the staging, was rejected by the group for distorting their artistic activity. The second proposal, understands the theater infrastructure as an agent of social change as Bertolt Brecht stated in the 1930, and was based on the articulation of the theater through digital media with the local political ecosystem. It was approved by the group for revitalizing its role as an agent of change.

This article reflects on the possible infrastructure approaches and the ontological conflicts that digital transformation can bring with it, when carried out in contexts with a strong analog tradition.

2 Literature Review

Although the literature that deals specifically with Digital Transformation as a field of action and its application in theater is not extensive (Aebischer and Nicholas 2020;

Boyle 2016), there are numerous theorists who have dealt with the relationship between theater and Information and Communication Technologies. Non face-to-face and the use of digital technologies present ontological conflicts with the theatrical act (Phelan 1993; Auslander 1999), and in turn, enable new aesthetic approaches that relate it to perspectives of the interconnected and networked post-human body (Gianacci 2012). This body unfolds synchronously or asynchronously in virtual or real multidimensional spaces, tipping the balance towards transmedia, over the traditions of the performing arts (Causey 2016). These approaches can be seen more clearly if they are compared to canonical texts such as Anne Ubersfeld's Theatrical Semiotics (1989), which proposes four dimensions for the analysis of theatre: body, object, space and time.

Regarding the subject of the body and its real or animated representation, Furniss (1998) proposed unifying photographic representation and animated representation in the same category. In the same way as Kaplin (1999), who proposed the unification of the human character, puppet and drawing in the same category according to the distance of the controller on the image.

However, it is in the now classic approaches of Bertolt Brecht (1966) regarding innovation, where we can find a possible answer about the relationship between theater and digital transformation, since the play writer redirects the gaze from the pure theatrical form, towards the effect that the theatrical apparatus produces in society. This approach has been carefully observed by Boyle (2016), to propose that theatrical innovation must focus on the impact that it may have on the social system, rather than on the change in the artistic form that might be expected.

On the contrary, the literature on digital transformation applied to other sectors is extensive. The ontological collision in theater and digital transformation can be understood as the fundamental changes that the use of new technologies brings to organizations: changes in the values and characteristics of the end result, changes in the organizational structure that produces them, and changes in the financial structure that supports this new configuration (Hess et al. 2016). A tendency to develop taxonomies of the components of digital transformation can be found right here. Reis et al. (2018) categorize the definitions of digital transformations around the concepts of technology, organization, or society, in similar manner to Henriette et al. (2015), who categorize it around business models, operational processes and user experience. Contrary to these, there are points of view from Hess et al. (2016), that propose four strategic dimensions: technology, product, structure, and finance, Flórez-Aristizábal et al. (2019) focused on four fundamental technological aspects of digital transformation: the internet of things, social media, cloud storage and mobile devices.

Undoubtedly, these sociotechnical approaches could be observed from Bowker's framework (1994), who referred to this type of reinterpretation of sociotechnical systems as infrastructural investments, which can be understood as keen observations about changing contexts that a community took for granted. Star explains it from the point of view of the Gestalt between figure and background, withdrawing the gaze from things or people individually as causes, emphasizing their relational aspect, thus even inverting historical explanations about events that were taken for granted. Similarly, Leigh-Star (Star and Ruhleder 1994; Star and Ruhleder 1996; Star and Bowker 2006) extensively considers the perspectives of the concept of infrastructure.

When referring to sociotechnical relations and rediscoveries of human and non-human actants in information chains, it is inevitable to refer to the canonical texts of the Actor Network theory of Latour (2008) and Law (2004), whose application has been tested in fields as dissimilar as architecture, management, E-learning, finance, etc.

Finally, the equally classic text by Lev Manovich "The Language of New Media" (1998), without losing its validity, continues to propose taxonomic and referential bases to address the converging processes of digital transformation with solid perspectives. Such as?

2.1 The Experimental Theater of Cali

The Experimental Theater of Cali was born in 1955, as a result of the rupture of its founder Enrique Buenaventura with the then financing government entities that opposed his political positions, as expressed on stage. Notoriously influenced by the postulates of Bertolt Brecht, the Experimental Theater of Cali was characterized by a deep interest in fundamentally relating their work to the people, whilst being an agent for the promotion of critical thought and social change. Its growth occurred within the general framework of the New Colombian Theater movement, an artistic and political movement that brought together countless professional, university, and school theater groups. This movement was articulated with labor unions and political movements, characteristic of the hectic Latin American 60s and 70s. In collaboration with other members of the movement, such as La Candelaria theater in Bogotá, the group developed the Method for Collective Creation, which sought horizontal participation of the members of the theater company, opposing the bourgeois vision of the director/omnipotent author that characterized theater from the nineteenth century. During the decades of the 60s and 70s, the Experimental Theater of Cali achieved worldwide notoriety and has since been widely studied by theorists from all over the world. The Experimental Theater of Cali maintains its respect and notoriety intact, even though, stylistically, they remain far from new trends in vogue and from the massive audiences that once filled its room.

2.2 The Method for Collective Creation

For a good understanding of the second digital transformation proposal, it is necessary to specify the method for collective creation published by the founder of the Experimental Theater of Cali, Enrique Buenaventura, and Jacqueline Vidal, who's the current director of the group. By collecting the initiatives and processes that several of the directors and actors had been using since the 1960's, the method for collective creation was published in 1972, and subsequently modified throughout the years. This method, following approaches articulated between semiotics, epic theater, and Marxism, sought the deconstruction of the author's rhetoric in the work, seeking a deeper analysis of the relationship between the work and its context. It aimed at allowing the horizontal participation of the theatrical group and the spectators in the writing of the rhetoric. The former during the staging, and the latter through forums organized after the performance. The group wanted to provide an infrastructure and become a dynamic and living agent of critique and social change, rooted in, and articulated to the context where the work was being produced.

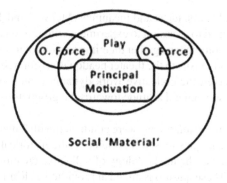

Fig. 1. This is how Experimental Theater of Cali understands how the social forces interact in a play.

As can be seen on Fig. 1, the method was based on the investigation of the social context in which the work was inscribed, using dialectical materialism as a tool (distributed by thematic commissions among the members of the group), with the purpose of identifying the forces in conflict represented in each of the scenes and in the total fable of the text. By using improvisation through analogies and the permanent dialogue of the group, the theater, supported by research methods based on dialectical materialism, explored how to allow themselves to analyze the rhetoric and the context of the work. Key to this, was to remain open to the permanent transformation of the end result through dialogue with viewers after the performances. The method sought, in the words of Enrique Buenaventura, to bring knowledge and a critical stance to the public with the best level of entertainment possible, and became a form of permanent interactive dialogue between society and its conflicts through dramaturgy (Fig. 2).

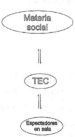

Fig. 2. The Experimental Theater of Cali understands itself as a dialogical vehicle between the social material that's included in their work and the spectators.

3   Methodology

For this research, an ethnographic design strategy based on non-participatory observation was used. The purpose was to understand the ETC as a social system, including their knowledge, practices, beliefs, ideas and meanings (McLeod and Thompson 2009). The group was initially invited to a session to experiment with motion capture, 3D animation and virtual reality technologies and gather their impressions of it. After this, the field work was distributed in weekly visits to the theater headquarters for a period of approximately two months. We observed the collective work dynamics, their personal relationships, hierarchies, methods, and general attitude towards the group itself and the audience that attended their shows.

Then, 8 semi-structured interviews were conducted with 7 members and the director of the theater group. The questions were related to the historical relationship between ETC and the local context, the methodology of collective creation, and the acting technique as applied to it. These questions aimed at providing a clear profile about the vision and identity of the group. All these experiences were systematized according to the three categories - body, space, and time - proposed by Anne Ubersfeld (AÑO?), and and served as the basis for configuring the range of possibilities for the digital transformation of the staging, or the aesthetic and narrative aspects that crystalize on stage during a play.

For the second proposal, which sought to identify the network of actants articulated throughout the history of the Experimental Theater of Cali, it was necessary to review the extensive archive that the theater maintains, which includes costume sketches, character designs, drafts of the plays, news, and abundant reviews and bibliographical references. In the same way, two series of interviews were conducted with six experts not only on the theatrical subject but specifically on the trajectory of the ETC in Colombia and the world. Some of them are active actors, some of them retired actors, two of them were members of the ETC during the 70s and 90s respectively. All of them, without exception, are dedicated to teaching theater research. Using Latour's Actor Network Theory (cita) as a theoretical basis, the interview and archive material were systematized into categories of physical space, cultural institution, social association, or political movement, and served as the basis for the second proposal of digital transformation through the re-articulation of the ETC with current peer actant networks.

4   Proposals

As previously mentioned, the group was approached during the period of August–December 2020, amid the Covid-19 crisis, in order to find a solution that would solve the impediment of face-to-face presence of spectators in theaters of Colombia and the whole world. For both proposals, the definitions of infrastructure by Star and Ruhleder (1996), which they understand as the relationships between organized practices that remain invisible until the moment of rupture. In this case, evidently, the rupture is the impossibility of people presence in the theater. The first proposal considered the infrastructure as a dynamic relationship between the narrative and aesthetic components as displayed in the play. The second proposal, which expanded on the first one, considered the infrastructure as network, including academic, social, institutional, and independent actants, linked by social and political mobilization in relation to theatrical content as research and communication agents.

4.1 First Proposal

Anne Ubersfeld (1989) considers four categories to analyze the elements of theater, and we start from that basis to carry out the first proposal. These elements are character, object, time and space. If we observe these four elements from the perspective of the dimensions of infrastructure proposed by Star (Star and Ruhleder 1996), it can be said that theater is embedded in a series of conventions and practices as old as humanity itself. These conventions are based on ontological approaches as 'natural' as the space-time or body-movement units. Theater is thus assumed as a narrative ritual, which takes place when face-to-face conditions are present. In turn, the absence of any of these elements challenges the theatrical nature of a play.

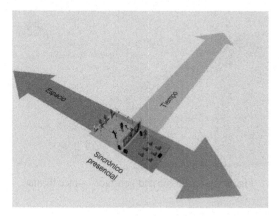

Fig. 3. As understood by ETC, theater has a synchronic and face-to-face nature, as seen in this figure.

As can be seen in Fig. 3, the theater represents a unity of space-time and body that implies the joint function of synchronic action and human presence. The breakdown of this unit, as a consequence of the impossibility of sharing the same space between the

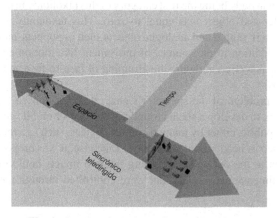

Fig. 4. Synchronic and non-face-to-face theater

public and the actors, implies a series of possible solutions, which keep some aspects of the theatrical nature active while others are permanently lost.

The first solution is based on working on different spaces at the same time (Fig. 4), that is to say, a more non-face-to-face synchronous play, such as a live transmission of the play. The second solution proposes different space, different time, like the projection of a film (Fig. 5). Evidently, the mediation in both cases transforms the free movement of the theatrical spectator's gaze into the characteristic "forced" gaze of the cinematographic frame and assemblage that Vertov promulgated in 1922.

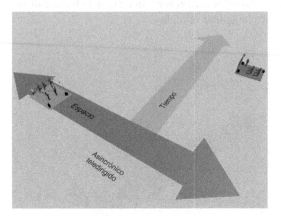

Fig. 5. Asynchronic and non-face-to-face theater

Contrary to what happens with time and space, character and object become a single category. Since 1998, Maureen Furniss anticipated the discussions that are growing day by day with digital transformation and proposed to eliminate the distinction between photographic image and artificial image, proposing a continuum between them that was developed in terms of iconicity according to its similarity with the real referent. Stephen Kaplin (1999) also anticipated the same context by proposing a taxonomy of the characters based on the distance between the puppet controller and the represented object or puppet, the human body being the first category of this taxonomy in the that the distance between controller and object was equal to zero. This taxonomy allows indistinctly including living, inert, digital and analogue objects such as puppets, animated characters and shadows, in addition to the sources of movement like motion capture technology and animatronics, as well as allowing the grouping of face-to-face and non-face-to-face techniques (Fig. 6).

To tackle the problem of the spectator's gaze, it was proposed that 360 recording devices could work to develop a stage around a stationary or mobile center that could be controlled by the public, either by manual control devices, such as a mouse, or by virtual reality devices such as head mounted displays. Likewise, it was proposed that body and space, in addition to the option of recording the real image, could be represented by means of three-dimensional models that were controlled through the motion capture device (Fig. 7).

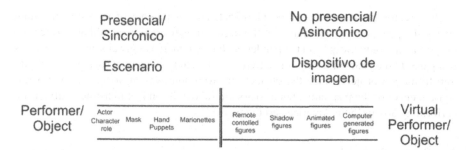

Presencial/ Sincrónico				No presencial/ Asincrónico			
Escenario				Dispositivo de imagen			

| Performer/ Object | Actor Character role | Mask | Hand Puppets | Marionettes | Remote contolled figures | Shadow figures | Animated figures | Computer generated figures | Virtual Performer/ Object |

Fig. 6. Continuum that exists between the actor that works with its body vs. the one that works with virtual objects.

Fig. 7. Capture motion lab at Universidad Autónoma de Occidente, Colombia.

The proposal materialized searching to starting a narrative project of collective creation, which could integrate the group of actors with the group of designers and programmers, based on three possible technological platforms, which sought to dialogue with three essential dimensions of the performing arts: body, space, and time:

- 360 video in animation and motion capture, not synchronous with the viewer.
- 360 video of the actors on stage using HMD devices, which were not synchronous with the viewer.
- Streaming of interaction between real or virtual actors made through motion capture, synchronous with the viewer.

This innovation proposal was rejected by the group, arguing that theater happens only in the physical and shared presence of the actor and the spectator. Theater, as declared by the group, is a single unit that blends body, space and time. Therefore, the proposal wasn't an actual solution, not even temporary, for the problem of the closing of theaters.

Its director, faced with this proposal, reflected on the urgency of accessing the public during the pandemic, concluding that the digital transformation should aim to recover the public, not only away from the pandemic, but also increasingly absent from theaters, compared to the years of maximum activity. This meant a change of route for the digital transformation project, since the obstacle to overcome was no longer the regulatory consequences of the pandemic, but a sociocultural condition that indistinctly affects the performing arts in Latin America and the world.

4.2 Second Proposal

The ETC works through a doubly dialogical way: it establishes the dialogue of the company with the text and the posterior dialogue of the public with the company. This way of working consists of a deep deconstructive investigation of the play and its context, which seeks to highlight the social, political, and economic conflicts that intervene in the formal elaboration of the narrative and visual aspects of the play.

In this second proposal, the theater was considered as a center of thought and agent of social change and, therefore, an infrastructure that articulated dramaturgy with social, academic, and political organizations. Thus, considering the Actor Network Theory (Law 2004) as the monitoring of information along a chain of actants, in addition to interviews with experts in the history of ETC and the extensive bibliography available, mapping was carried out of controversies surrounding the theatrical text that occurred at the moment of greatest impact of the ETC, at the beginning of the 70s. In this way, in addition to the theater audience, a network of mediators was identified who were not only receivers of the theatrical text but also a permanent source of feedback of information and criticism, who formed a rhizome through which the information came and went towards the dramaturgical text, thus forming an ecosystem of critical thought that articulated art with society (Fig. 8).

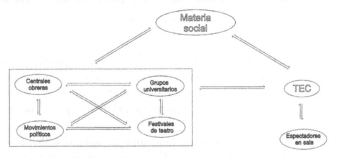

Fig. 8. ETC is an articulated actant that engages unions, political movements, student groups, and theater festivals.

It is not the purpose of this book chapter to give an account of the causes for which this social ecosystem disappeared due to the weakening, mutation or extinction of some of these actants, but nevertheless it is necessary to realize that its reconfiguration left the ETC in a state of isolation (Piedrahita).

There is an intersection between the investigative, social and interactive activities typical of the specific dynamics of the ETC and the new independent digital journalistic media, increasingly strengthened and valued in digital networks. New digital media are characterized by hypertextuality, interactivity, and multimediality (Varela 2005). Some of these, offer a horizontal relationship with citizens capable of communicating, acting, and leading virtual communities to create and promote social movements. All these characteristics have similarities with the mission and vision of the ETC.

It was proposed to strengthen the ETC's network work through a combination of journalistic editorial, graphic design and digital marketing, which makes the investigative material of the works in repertoire available to the user and establishes a critical dialogue between social matter, the theatrical group and the users, in such a way that the play maintains its nature and the investigative and social derivative functions as an independent product with simultaneous artistic and social positioning purposes. This proposal is best explained through the storyboard.

4.3   Storyboard

A user prospect is browsing. The usual websites of this user are opposition journalism and opinion sites.

Whether through advertising or an advertorial, a graphic appears alluding to the premiere of an upcoming ETC play. This graph seeks to reflect similarities between the contents raised in the work and the current events that this type of portal usually deals with.

Upon entering the link we find the transmedia content of the work, organized around the investigative file that took it to the stage (seeking to generate interest in assisting the user physically close to the theater and interest in users in the opposite condition), as well as editorials in charge of the director and its members in which they relate the national news with the content of the work in function. In addition to this, it is found that the page contains a fascinating database of the investigations of her plays, as well as an animated audiovisual with the biography of the master Buenaventura.

In addition to the above, the people who attend the play, whose profile is usually associated with interest in current social and political issues, are told during the dialogue after the show that there is extra material available online, such as talks by the group with experts and researchers, bibliography, images of trials etc. They are also told that there is a digital space for discussion and contributions to the content of the work.

From the digital and direct comments that the play recieves, the group will make reflections, whose discussions and processes will be shown online and will be staged as reworkings.

In the end, the statistical data of the evolution of the work should remain and will become part of the group's repository file.

The digital transformation proposal was reconfigured in expanding the scope of the dialogue between the group and its viewers, opening new channels of opinion through websites, social networks, and digital communication platforms. It also included providing free public access to the research archive, the plays in the teams' repertoire and the historical works that remain archived in the cabinets of ETC's headquarters. Moreover, the proposal sought to position the social media representation of the company at the same level as other independent opinion sites that currently carry out the tasks that face-to-face meetings and the written press did during the political turmoil of the 1960s and 1970s. In other words, the aim was to expand accessibility and dialogue between the public and the company, allowing access to its research and processes, and to position the company as a center for current critical thought expressed through art.

This proposal was presented to the ETC and was received with excitement and approval by the group. The change in attitude was diametric and evident. They felt represented by the idea, which reflects the historical spirit of the group, and understood the intention of recovering political space. The only caveat was to keep the balance between politics and art, since, in the words of the director, they are first and foremost artists.

5 Discussion

5.1 Third Level Problems

The rejection of the first proposal led us to a reflection based on the so-called Third Level Problems. Susan Leigh-Star (Star and Ruhleder 1996), following Bateson's (1972) three levels of communication, distinguishes three levels of problems and discontinuities in information hierarchies. Level one refers to the problems of expertise, and level two refers to procedural clashes, and level three refers to disputes between schools of thought and paradigms that can lead to ontological incompatibility. In this case we face a third level problem, in which the ontological definition of theater for the ETC differs diametrically from the forms proposed by innovation based on information technologies.

Although there are numerous authors who work with new technological forms and there are numerous theatrical companies that experiment with animation, animatronics, streaming and video, Star tells us that although it is possible that the participants of an infrastructure can develop tools that allow communication through these paradigmatic walls, it will be difficult for the participants to identify a clear reward for it. And this is perhaps the case for the ETC: in not finding a clear utility or reward in the development of activities that, from their point of view, have nothing to do with their field, they logically prefer to reject them.

This reflection led us to consider the integration of the specific human needs of the project, in this case the emotions and purposes of the group of artists, their relationship with the dramaturgical tradition, and its relationship with the user experience (Pedersen 2020), seeking to break with conceptual boundaries that could be leading us towards a hasty solution focused on technology and not a mature solution focused on human values (Zinder and Yunatova 2016). That is why we took on the task of understanding the tradition of the ETC, of investigating its value network throughout its 60 years of existence, with the purpose of understanding the circumstances that elevated it and the changes in the context that made it the group lost connection with mass audiences. In other words, the framework of the infrastructure was reconsidered and expanded from a formal relationship between text-staging and audience in the room, to an infrastructure of training, dialogue, distribution and return of knowledge through dramatic form.

Infrastructural investment

It was found that during its beginnings, within the framework of the great movement of the New Theater, the ETC was articulated with a network of professional, university and college theater groups, festivals and labor unions, all in the context of social mobilization and political change, lined up to produce a huge cultural and political impact that was recognized nationally and internationally throughout the 60s and 70s. However, political, artistic and economic changes of globalization weakened and disappeared not only the New Theater movement, that lead to more commercial professional forms of performing arts that nurtured the 1980s and 1990s, but also the entire political movement already mentioned (Piedrahita 1996). The ETC, along with a few small groups, stayed out of this transformation, and has continued for 60 years with the ideology of culture and commitment, facing both artistic and political detractors. In other words, it was found that the infrastructure that supported the theatrical proposal of the ETC gradually vanished throughout the 1980s and 1990s, causing it to lose its validity and artistic and political influence beyond the small local circle.

Bowker et al. (2009) tells us that the past cannot be defined and that we are always looking at it in the light of new developments in the present. Therefore, the definition of the standards, categories and technologies that converge in the infrastructures that govern is an ethical act as much as a political act. Thus, the concept of infrastructural investment, which seeks to make visible the activities that support the existence of an infrastructure, is a doubly political act: it reveals an implicit view of the infrastructure studied, and it will receive a new explicit view from the observer who interprets it.

A condition of all infrastructure is to be embedded in other infrastructures, be it technological or social, and these have a spatial and temporal scope according to their nature. For the Experimental Theater of Cali, the infrastructure encompasses not only the context contained in the theater, but also extends to a network of social and political action that links dialogue with communities, labor unions, and university groups whose common goal is social change, and for which the play represents an effective form of communication, but no less artistic for that, alien to the economic and political hegemonies of the traditional mass media such as television, radio or cinema.

The infrastructural investment made to the ETC's value network revealed to us not only the mistake we were in looking through technology new formal and syntactic aspects to experiment with the group, but also that this technology sought an approach with anonymous mass audiences interested in playful entertainment, leaving aside the political aspects that the ETC has dealt with throughout its history.

Bertolt Brecht, who is among the great influences of the ETC, had already reflected on the value of innovation (1966). Brecht lamented that the artists' efforts to bring the opera genre up to date consisted in renewing its methods of staging, since this type of innovation only succeeded in nurturing institutions that had become obsolete. The German playwright considered that innovation should entail a fundamental change in the theatrical institution's function, and that even if revolutionary works were written, they would have no effect if the theatrical apparatus owned the artists and not the other way around. In other words, exclusively creative innovation of the theatrical apparatus could little do for social change. Brecht called for innovations that would press for changes, that would attack the base of the theatrical apparatus so that it would fulfill its function as a revolutionary catalyst (Boyle 2016). Thus, following Brecht's postulates of innovation, in line with the innovation perspective of the ETC, it became clear that digital transformation had to be related to the impact on the social apparatus that the ETC could have, rather than a massive search of spectators eager for technological novelties and formal dazzle.

5.2 Data Bases and Algorithms

When carefully observing both proposals, it is inevitable to think of the similarities with the approaches of Manovich (1998), who says that although modernity, through the novel, cinema, and theater, privilege the narrative form, the new media privilege the database, the latter understood as the set of total information that enables the user to create the form from their actions carried out through an algorithm. What the second proposal presents can be understood as an exposition of the data base with aesthetic and political ends. Also, according to Manovich, since the theatrical form would remain intact in its analogical and face-to-face aspect, he raises the need to ask about the aesthetics of the database: Is it a list of hyperlinks? Is it a political editorial? Is it an infographical elaboration of the research? Is it all the above in a multimedia piece of content? Whatever the answer, what is proposed from the point of view of digital marketing is to reach the niche of consumers who are looking for artistic content with marked social and political characteristics, and from the historical point of view a repositioning of the ETC against the rhizome of actants of the events of social criticism and formation of the state of opinion.

Thus, the digital transformation at the ETC is configured in a double life of the theater infrastructure: a face-to-face life that happens at the theater headquarters and on company tours, which shows the visible form, the algorithm if you will, of an investigative process that seeks to question social dynamics, and that implies the movement of the spectator to be appreciated. And a virtual life in which the database is given shape, whose infrastructure covers a space-time range superior to the face-to-face form, with its own specific aesthetic dynamics that, paradoxically, implies the configuration of an alternative and completely new group of work that, in permanent contact with the base group, must give shape to this new dimension of the theatrical infrastructure.

5.3 Conclusions

If we compare this proposal with other forms of digital transformation in theater (Kapsala 2018; Aebischer and Nicholas 2020), that impact the stage and the dramaturgy itself, we clearly see how in our proposal we concentrate in keeping intact the ontological nature of the theatrical act, transforming the articulation between the theater group, its political postulates, and the context in which it acts. This, for a group of designers, represents an infrastructural investment, and for the group of playwrights represents a renovation of their fundamental pillars, as are the postulates of Bertolt Brecht. We can consider the insight of similarities between Brecht's concept of "apparatus" and Bowker's "infrastructure" as the innovation that made the proposal possible.

However, following this line, it is also evident that the group must come into contact with the current issues of the independent information networks, just as they did with the issues of interest of university groups and labor unions, their public goal, through-out the 60s and 70s. Thus, it would be possible to recover a public base interested in simultaneously cultural and committed theater, which is currently dispersed and atomized, and which seeks information and political structures that were previously available institutionally through unions and theater organizations.

In addition, practical and procedural concerns arise. The implementation of the proposal requires, following the canon of digital transformation, changes in the organizational and financial structure of the group. Not only is it urgent to obtain computer equipment and audiovisual software, but also the training or permanent hiring of at least one graphic designer who must become a fundamental part of theatrical activities. In the same way, the constant advice of a web manager that enhances the digital articulations between the group and the digital context to permanently position it as an artistic and political protagonist, must be considered among the new budget sections.

Surely it will initially be difficult to convince the direction of the group that the sacrifice of one part of the budget will bring great benefits. But once this happens, this measure will be quickly standardized.

References

Aebischer, P., Nicholas, R.: Digital theatre transformation: a digital toolkit. Final Report. University of Exeter (2020). https://ore.exeter.ac.uk/repository/handle/10871/123464

Auslander, P.: Liveness: performance in a mediatized culture. Routledge, New York (1999)

Bowker, G.C., Baker, K., Millerand, F., Ribes, D.: Toward information infrastructure studies: ways of knowing in a networked environment. In: Hunsinger, J., Klastrup, L., Allen, M. (eds) International Handbook of Internet Research. Springer, Dordrecht (2009). https://doi.org/10.1007/978-1-4020-9789-8_5

Boyle, M.S.: Brecht's gale. Perform. Res. **21**(3), 16–26 (2016). https://doi.org/10.1080/13528165.2016.1176733

Brecht, B.: On Theatre. Bloomsbury, London (1966)

Buenaventura, E.: Esquema General del Método de Trabajo Colectivo del TEC. PubTec. Cali (1975)

Callon, M.: Algunos elementos para una sociología de la traducción: la domesticación de las vieiras y los pescadores de la bahía de St. Brieuc, en Sociología de la Ciencia y La Tecnología (J. Iranzo ed). Consejo Superior de Investigaciones Científicas. Madrid (1995)

Causey, M.: Postdigital performance. Theatre J. **68**(3), 427–441 (2016)

Flórez-Aristizábal, L., Cano, S., Collazos, C.A., Benavides, F., Moreira, F., Fardoun, H.M.: Digital transformation to support literacy teaching to deaf children: from storytelling to digital interactive storytelling. Telemat. Inform. **38**, 87–99 (2019). https://doi.org/10.1016/j.tele.2018.09.002

Furniss, M.: Art in Motion: Animation Aesthetics. John Libbey Publishing, London (1998)

Gianacci, G.: Archaeologies of Presence: Art. Performance and the Persistence of Being. Routledge, New York (2012)

Henriette, E., Feki, M., Boughzala, I.: The shape of digital transformation: a systematic literature review (2015)

Hess, T., Matt, C., Benlian, A., Wiesböck, F.: Options for formulating a digital transformation strategy. MIS Q. Executive **15**(2), 103–119 (2016)

Kaplin, S.: A puppet tree: a model for the field of puppet theatre. TDR/Drama Rev. **43**(3), 28–35 (1999)

Latour, B.: Reensamblar lo social: una introducción a la teoría del actor red. Editorial Manantial, Buenos Aires (2008)

Law, J.: After Method: Mess in Social Science Research. Routledge, London (2004)

Manovich, L.: El Lenguaje de los Nuevos Medios. Paidós, Barcelona (1998)

McLeod, J., Thompson, R.: Researching Social Change: Qualitative Approaches. Sage Publications, London (2009)

Strandgaard Pedersen, J., Slavich, B., Khaire, M.: Technology and Creativity: Production, Mediation and Evaluation in the Digital Age. In: Strandgaard Pedersen, J., Slavich, B., Khaire, M. (eds.) Technology and Creativity, pp. 1–11. Springer, Cham (2020). https://doi.org/10.1007/978-3-030-17566-5_1

Phelan, P.: Unmarked: The Politics of Performance. Routledge, New York (1993)

Reis, J., Amorim, M., Melão, N., Matos, P.: Digital Transformation: A Literature Review and Guidelines for Future Research. In: Rocha, Á., Adeli, H., Reis, L.P., Costanzo, S. (eds.) WorldCIST'18 2018. AISC, vol. 745, pp. 411–421. Springer, Cham (2018). https://doi.org/10.1007/978-3-319-77703-0_41

Star, S.L., Ruhleder, K.: Steps towards an ecology of infrastructure: complex problems in design and access for large-scale collaborative systems. pp. 253–264 (1994). https://doi.org/10.1145/192844.193021

Star, S.L., Ruhleder, K.: Steps toward an ecology of infrastructure: design and access for large information spaces. Inf. Syst. Res. **7**(1), 111–134 (1996). https://doi.org/10.1287/isre.7.1.111

Star, S.L., Bowker, G.C.: How to infrastructure (2006). https://doi.org/10.4135/9781446211304.n11

Ubersfeld, A.: Semiótica Teatral. Ed Cátedra. Madrid (1989)

Varela, J.: Periodismo 3.0, la socialización de la información. Revista TELOS (65), 1–14 (2005). https://telos.fundaciontelefonica.com/archivo/numero065/periodismo-3-0-lasocializacion-de-la-informacion/?output=pdf

Vertov, D.: El Cine-Ojo. Ediorial Fundamentos. Caracas (1973)

Zinder, E., Yunatova, I.: Synergy for Digital Transformation: Person's Multiple Roles and Subject Domains Integration. In: Chugunov, A.V., Bolgov, R., Kabanov, Y., Kampis, G., Wimmer, M. (eds.) DTGS 2016. CCIS, vol. 674, pp. 155–168. Springer, Cham (2016). https://doi.org/10.1007/978-3-319-49700-6_16

Author Index

Printed in the United States
by Baker & Taylor Publisher Services